CW00746994

BALMAIDENS

Joyce, a balmaiden in the Camborne area, early 1900s.

Courtesy of Paddy Bradley

BALMAIDENS

Lynne Mayers

The Hypatia Trust
Penzance
2004

First published in 2004 by
THE HYPATIA TRUST
Trevelyan House
16 Chapel Street
Penzance
Cornwall TR18 8AW

© Lynne Mayers

A catalogue record for this book is available from the British Library

Typeset in Adobe Garamond in-house at the Patten Press
Printed and bound in England by Cromwell Press, Trowbridge, Wiltshire

ISBN 1 872229 48 4

All rights reserved.
No part of this publication may be
reproduced, stored in a retrieval system
or transmitted in any form or by any means,
electronic, mechanical, photocopying,
recording or otherwise,
without the written consent of the publisher.

CONTENTS

ILLUSTRATIONS, TABLES, DIAGRAMS, AND POEMS

Frontispiece   Joyce, a balmaiden in the Camborne area, early 1900s

Page

PREFACE

The Cornwall and West Devon metal mines and smelters of the 18th and 19th century formed a unique and quite separate part of the mining heritage of these islands. It was here that much of our nation's mineral wealth was created, based in no small part on the labour of girls (from the age of eight or nine years old) and young or widowed women. No other metal mining district was so extensive, nor used women and girls in such abundance. Unlike the coalmining districts of Scotland, the North East, Lancashire, and parts of Wales, however, there was no history of women and girls working underground in Cornwall or Devon during this time - they were employed on the dressing floors or smelters only. They continued to be employed in this way even after 1842, when increasing public concern about the 'moral welfare' of women and children brought legislation to limit their employment in the factories and collieries. The last balmaidens were dismissed during the first two decades of the 20th century.

Comparatively little contemporary writing has been found about these women and girls. The only 'first-hand' accounts found so far come from just four sources - five interviews recorded in 1952 by the Women's Institute of women who had worked in the mines and tin streams of Troon some fifty years previously, about eight interviews with women conducted in the 1970s who had worked at the Glass Mine in St. Dennis during World War 2, an interview of the 'last bal-maiden' (Minnie Andrews), made in her ninetieth year in 1967, and a personal recollection from one of the women who worked on the picking belt at Geevor in World War 2. The next 'nearest' first hand accounts are from twenty one interviews conducted for the 1842 Royal Commission researching into the conditions of employment of young people at the mines, and a tiny book entitled 'Patty Tremellin - written by herself'. No journals or diaries of balmaidens appear to have survived, but this story of Martha (Patty) Tremelling, although written after her death, and published in 1841, seems to be based on her journal, and written by someone who had a first hand knowledge of her life. Despite it not being actually written by Patty herself, it gives a startling insight into the world of the balmaiden in the St. Austell area in the 1820s and 30s.

As well as there being so few contemporary documents relating to the life and work of these balmaidens, it has been equally difficult to find surviving relatives who may have archival material or anecdotal stories to tell. About twelve relatives have been kind enough to contribute information about their forebears. But even here, sadly, much of the information is very limited, and with the exception of a few photos, no artefacts or written documents have survived. It is about ninety years now since the last balmaidens went to work at the mines, and these stories are almost lost, as they pass from the communal memory.

Most other writing and observations about these women and girls in the Victorian era comes from middle or upper-class observers. Some were travellers passing through, others artists or writers, together with mine surgeons and adventurers with an interest in the business. Generally, they were far more interested in describing the activities surrounding the underground tasks of mining, or the events at the counthouse, than about what went on at surface on the dressing floors. The best descriptions of the work that the balmaidens did during this period have come from mining engineers writing about the dressing operations for their peer group. The most notable of these are William Pryce (published in 1778), William Henderson (1832), James Henderson (1858), and John Darlington (1878). The amount of space devoted to the dressing tasks, compared with the amount of information given on the other aspects of the mining operation, is also very sparse in much of the 20th century literature. Most has been written from the perspective of the major mining engineering and technological achievements, as an overview of the economic production and management, as a social study of the underground miner, or out of a concern and interest in the surviving industrial archaeology. While all of these are important and worthy subjects, the contribution and work of women and children at the surface at the mines has either received no attention at all, or at best, very limited mention 'in passing'. The place of the balmaiden in the mining economy has only occasionally been seriously discussed, most notably by Gill Burke, Stephany Norwood, and Sharron Schwartz, all during the last decade of the 20th century.

In contrast to the lack of documents written by balmaidens, or of focused studies, there is much brief evidence of the work of these balmaidens scattered about in different places (often only a sentence at a time), in old mining documents, early travelogues, parish and census records, letters, periodicals and newspapers. Because references are hard to find, or in some cases incomplete (leaving many gaps, especially with regard to the finer detail of the dressing processes) it was only by visiting actual mining heritage sites, seeing what is left of the dressing floors, and imagining how they might have been that any really coherent understanding began to emerge of the jobs that these women and children had to do. This involved handling tools, and watching replica or re-installed equipment at work, asking numerous questions of their present day operators in order to try and assess what the everyday problems and challenges were, and beginning to understand the level of skill and strength required for each process.

So, this book is an effort to redress the dearth of record, and to write something from the perspective of the women and children at the mines. The first chapter sets the historical scene of mining quarrying in West Devon and Cornwall, and the place of the women and children in it. It also tries to give a numerical overview of the numbers of balmaidens employed over the years. The next two chapters look at the general life of the balmaidens, at work as well as at home. The subsequent five chapters deal with the tasks allocated to women at the different types of metal mines and smelters, clay pits and quarries. Two more chapters look at the costs of working at the mine, in terms of health, education and accidents, and what happened to the balmaidens when the mines closed. The final chapters look at some of the myths and ideas about balmaidens that have built up over the years, and compare that with the real people. This includes cameos of fifteen women and girls whose stories have survived and who, together, illustrate many different aspects of their lives.

It has been almost impossible to separate the history of the mines in Cornwall from those in West Devon, especially those on the east bank of the River Tamar. A few records for this area have found their way into the wrong county, and others appear to be in the wrong county due to changes in the county boundary over the years. Mine management and personnel did not necessarily observe county boundaries in their work, and certainly the policies for employment of females was the same, so it seems appropriate to include both geographical areas in the book.

Many of the areas in west Devon and Cornwall also show a complex array of mining and extractive activities (for instance, in the St. Austell area) where women and girls may be involved in a range of employments. They moved between one and another, and members of the same family sometimes worked in different industries, such as the copper mines and clay works. The scope of this book, therefore, goes beyond just the metalliferous mines (copper, tin, lead, etc.) and includes those women and girls who also worked at the manganese mines, clay works and slate quarries.

Neither is the book restricted just to balmaidens (ore or stone dressers), but it also extends to other women and children who were involved at the mines. For instance, there were the counthouse women who were employed doing domestic duties. Girls sometimes were responsible for the ponies or horses which operated machinery at surface, and others were waggoners. Some operated pumps, and some made or repaired dressing equipment. Occasionally, there were women who were mine or clay pit managers. During the world wars some women were employed to carry out tasks which the men had previously done, such as hosing out clay from the clay pits. There is also emerging evidence that women and girls worked at the tin and lead smelters. This book includes any females who received economic benefit directly from working at or for the mine. It does not, however, include women adventurers who had bought 'shares' in a mine, or inherited their husband's interest in a mine at their death, unless they were actively involved in the management. For instance, nineteen women held shares in Wheal Agar in 1893 but so far there is no evidence that they were active in the managing decisions of the mine, or that they attended any of the business meetings. Also, this book does not include the very small number of women who may have worked at the surviving tin mines in Cornwall, since the introduction of Equal Opportunities Legislation in the 20th century.

If this book has moved us to feel for the women and children who worked at the mines of Cornwall and Devon, sometimes under appalling conditions. I hope we will also be moved to consider the plight of today's child miners (or indeed, any women and men who continue to labour in mines where there is no adequate provision for their health and safety). Despite international agreements abhorring and outlawing child labour at the mines, there are still hundreds, and possibly thousands, of children working underground or in health-threatening working conditions at surface. Work is continuing among communities in the Philippines and in Burkina Faso to relieve the abject poverty which drives families to send their children into the mines. Authorities in Vietnam are yet to find out how many children are still working in illegally-operated gold mines in the remote Bac Kan Province. In May 2003, seventy two children were discovered working under terrible conditions, carrying baskets of earth and rocks through water up to their waists, for up to 14 hours a day. The youngest was ten years old. In some cases, their parents had sold them in desperation to the mine owners, whilst others had been abandoned. Some had run away to the mines, lured by the tales of wealth and regular wages. Looking at the history of women in mining in Cornwall, it has always been the poorest of this world who have been the most vulnerable to exploitation and danger, with little redress should things go wrong. We still have much to do to wipe out inhuman and life-threatening forms of labour, especially for children.

Finally, I have envisaged this book as only a first tentative step in unravelling the history of the many thousands of women and girls who laboured at the mines in the south west. I hope it will spark discussion and stimulate memories so that more accurate information will come to light. I am conscious that there will be many errors in this text, either from mistaken transcription or from inaccurate assumption. I would be very grateful for any comments, corrections or additional information which will continue to carry the subject forward.

ACKNOWLEDGEMENTS

I wish to thank all those who have helped and encouraged me in the writing of this book. When I first mentioned the possibility of writing a book on the subject of balmaidens I was warned, from several quarters, that there was not enough documentation and that it would not be possible. Thankfully there are many other people who have proved this assumption wrong, and have been very willing to share whatever information they have, so that this book could be created. Without them this book would not exist.

Very special thanks go to Jan Gendall, John Tonkin, and John Symons, who have given unstintingly of their time, both in sharing ideas, knowledge, and resources, and who have also been kind enough to comment on the texts relating to their particular expertise. I must also thank Justin Brooke for his transcript of an interview with Minnie Andrews in 1967 (reputedly the last surviving 'old style' balmaiden), and allowing me to quote freely from it. Also, my grateful thanks to Mrs. Phyllis Lockett for her first hand account of working on the picking belt at Geevor Mine during the second World War.

A very big thank you must also go to those descendants and relatives of women who worked at the mines and clay pits who were kind enough to respond to my various public requests for information, and have shared their family research or oral history with me, allowing me to publish what has sometimes been very personal detail. These include Adele Casbolt, Edna Collins, Jenny Elliston, Val Flint-Johnson, Frank Houghton, Arthur Jacob, Isabel Jamson, Gillian Johns, Sharon Kay Jones, Lesley Morton, John Saunders, Alison Shaw, Norma Smitian, and Harry Trembath.

I am indebted to the many institutions, heritage sites and voluntary organisations who have allowed me access to their archives, and to their willing and helpful staff, many of whom have gone out of their way to find elusive and rare material. Among these, I mention the Blue Hills Tin Streams (Collin Wills), Bodmin Museum (Maureen Tooze), British Geological Survey (Tim Colman), Carnglaze Slate Caverns (Caroline Richards), Cornish Family History Society (Pat Fawcett and volunteers), Cornish Studies Library (Kim Cooper and Neil Williams), Cornwall Record Office, the Courtney Library and the Royal Institution of Cornwall (Angela Broom and Rob Cook), Delabole Local History Society (Brenda Burnard and Wesley Mills), Delabole Slate Co. (Pamela Free), Exeter Local Studies Library (Ian Maxted), Family Records Centre in Central London, Geevor Tin Mine Heritage Centre (Ben Beckwith), Helston Museum (Mrs. Spargo), Institute of Mining and Metallurgy Library, Morwellham Quay Museum (Antony Power), Morab Library, National Trust (Cornwall), Northern Mines Research Society (Sally Bassam), PRO at Kew, St. Ives Archive Study Centre (Janet Axten), Wayside Folk Museum, Zennor (Sara and Bob Priddle), Wheal Martyn Museum (Brian Strathen), The Wellcome Library, and The Women's Library, London. Also I thank the many members of the on-line Mining History mailing list for their patience with a continual stream of abstruse questions, and especially to those who have been able to answer them, including Tony Brooks, Peter Claughton, Bryan Earl, Martin Roe, and Jan Wegner. There have also been a network of people around the world who have helped with information on aspects of migration, including Roger Bradford, Kelly Dixon, Richard Francaviglia, Heather Hobbis, Ron James, Vivian Martin, Sylvia Pettem, Daryl Povey, Dieter Retz, Sally Sanjani, Christine Teale, and Mark and Karen Vendl.

Various other authors and researchers have also offered help and encouragement - Tony Brooks, Caroline Cudmore, Bryan Earl, Alan Kent, David Langsworthy, Catherine Lorigan, and Sharron Schwartz.

The sources of poems, photographs and illustrations are acknowledged in the text, but special thanks go to Paddy Bradley for his help and encouragement, and for allowing us to use photos from his extensive collection.

There are many who have made it physically possible to visit the various archives and heritage sites in Cornwall. David and Juliet Jenkin offered hospitality, encouragement, access to their archive resources, and helpful comments on the script, and a very special thank you goes to them. My husband, Peter Boorman has acted as chauffeur for many hundreds of miles and over some unforgiving terrain, has had to endure hours of 'mining' conversations. He has transcribed pages of hardly legible records, been dragged down mines, through hedgerows, and to just about every mining heritage site in the UK. He has been the IT specialist, invaluably retrieving lost information in moments of computer crisis, and has also acted as proof reader. He, and my sons Kieren and Marcus, have been unstinting in their encouragement and patient in the extreme, while our lives have been taken over by this project. I am greatly in their debt.

Finally, my thanks also go to Philip Budden for his skilful editing and constructive suggestions, and to Melissa Hardie of Patten Press and The Hypatia Trust, for her encouragement, sharing an excitement about the subject, and enabling me to publish this research.

ABBREVIATIONS USED IN TEXT

CEC   Children's Employment Commission: report by Charles Barham on the Employment of Children And Young people in the Mines of Cornwall and Devonshire, and on the State, Condition and Treatment of such Children and Young Persons 1842 (in this case using the pages numbers of the transcript by Ian Winstanley, PICs Publishing 1999 for easier reference)

CMHRS   Coal Mining Resource Centre - www.cmhrc.pwp.blueyonder.co.uk

CSL   Cornish Studies Library, Cornish Studies Centre, Redruth

CRO   Cornish Records Office, Truro

CT   *Cornish Telegraph*

RCG   *Royal Cornwall Gazette*

RIC   Royal Institution of Cornwall, Truro

WB   *West Briton*

WM   Wheal Martyn Museum Archives

Chapter 1

BALMAIDENS - THEIR HISTORY

Introduction

The majority of women and girls employed at the mines and clay works of Cornwall and West Devon were involved in the various stages of ore or clay dressing, and were colloquially known as 'balmaidens'. The term 'balmaiden' can be found in accounts of Victorian travel writers and various governmental reports from the middle of the 19th century onwards. In the 18th century, Pryce does not seem to have heard of the term (1778), and females working at the mines tend to be referred to as maidens (maid'ns) in the 18th century cost books. The earliest references to 'Ball Maidens' come from the *West Briton* in 1819 and 1823 respectively.[1] 'Bal' is Cornish for 'mine', but was widely replaced, from the 18th century, with the word 'Huel' and then 'Wheal'. The word 'bal' was sometimes incorporated into the name of a mine, such as Balmynheer, and has occasionally been retained as the name of a hamlet or village, as at Higher Bal (St. Agnes) and Baldhu. Balmaiden, or variably written bal maiden and bal-maiden, then, was a term often used to describe young women who worked at the Cornish mines, or sometimes, more loosely, to describe all females working 'at surface' at the bal. By the end of the 19th century it seems it was a general term used for all females working on the dressing floors, regardless of age or status, as Muriel Sara remembers from her childhood in the 1890s:

'Women of all ages, married or mere girls, they were all known by that name.' [2]

Other terms have been used for female ore dressers, over the centuries, some of the titles being applied to both male and females performing the same tasks. William Pryce, in his description of tin streaming in Cornwall, published in 1778, describes ore dressers as lappiors:

'Leavings from the stamping mills which are carried by the rivers to lower grounds; and after some years of lying and collecting there, yield some money to the laborious dressers, who they distinguish by the name of Lappiors, I suppose from the Cornish word Lappior, which signifying a Dancer, is applied to them, in this from the boys and girls employed work, and moving up and down in the buddles, to separate the Tin from the refuse, with naked feet like to the ancient Dancers.' [3]

However, 'Lappior' is not a word that frequently appears in the literature. The women and girls were also often referred to by the specific task assigned to them, such as 'cobbing girls', 'bucking women' or 'spalling maidens', or more generally, 'mine girls'. The term 'balmaiden' does not appear in the census returns, as the enumerators are instructed not to use local terminology. For instance, Inch found eight different terms used as an alternative to balmaidens in the 1881 census for Gwennap, all of which were rather functional: tin miner, tin mine girl, tin miner's girl, labourer in a tin mine, tin mine labourer, copper mine labourer, worker in a copper ore, and mundic miner.[4] Other terms sometimes used in the census include mine maid, copper dresser, tin dresser or lead dresser, 'working at mine', or 'dressing ore'. The occasional 'working at bal' also can be found. There are the same restrictions on the use of words placed on district registrars, so similar phraseology appears on marriage and baptismal certificates. For instance, Lavinia Terrill, an ore dresser, was described as a 'miner' at her marriage at Camborne Parish Church in 1845. The women and girls who worked at the slate quarries were referred to in the census records as 'quarry girls' or 'quarry women'.

There were small numbers of women and girls who were employed at the mines and clay works who were not involved in the dressing operations, but undertook various other tasks. Probably the largest of these other groups were the counthouse women who were employed to do housekeeping duties at the mine office, as most of the larger mines would employ one such person and, in some cases, as many as three. Sometimes young girls were employed to look after animals at the mine; for example, Grace Briney who was a whim horse driver. Older women were sometimes involved in transport of ore or slate, as donkey drivers, as at Delabole, or waggoners, as at Wheal Prosper and New Trelawny. In 1828, a child whose gender is not indicated was paid to collect moss from the moors, for sealing the cracks in the clay pans at Ninestones Clay Works. This job would be done immediately prior to filling the pans with the liquid clay slurry. Grace Morcom was paid 9s 0d for 'holing 2 copper bottoms' at Poldice Mine in March 1789. This was probably punching out the very fine holes in the copper base of the jigging sieves.[5] Emily Richards, of Camborne, was described as a 'sample refiner' at a tin mine in the 1891 census, and was probably involved in preparing and mixing samples at the sampling house, for the assayer.[6]

There are also records of women carrying out what would normally be deemed as 'men's jobs', such as kibble (bucket) landing and working the pumps. During the World Wars it was not unusual for women and older girls to be drafted in to undertake some of the processes which had previously been the preserve of men, such as the women who worked hosing out clay in some of the clay works bottoms in WW1, and those who worked on the tin picking belts in WW2. There are also a few accounts of women who actually became managers of clay works or mines.

History

Women and children were probably involved in mining activities in Cornwall from the days of antiquity, but earliest written records of females working at the tin mines and lead smelters date from the 14th century, and for copper from the beginning of the 18th century. In all of these records, the work done by the women and girls was at the surface. In Cornwall there seems to have been a long standing tradition that it was unlucky for women to go below ground, and so there is no record of them having been employed as hauliers below surface, as they were at the collieries in Wales and the north.[7]

Mining in the days of antiquity

Copper was mined in Cornwall from the Bronze age. Unfortunately, women and female children do not usually leave identifiable archaeological evidence for their presence in the workforce, so it is not proven that they worked underground. It is assumed that these copper mines were developed by small communities of extended family units, with distributions of tasks probably by age and gender. The Bronze Age copper mines, recently uncovered on Great Orme in North Wales, for instance, have such small underground tunnels and caverns, that only children could have worked them. Of course, the gender of the children is unknown. However, mining has traditionally been a woman's task in areas of America and Africa, before colonial settlement. In Wisconsin, some of the mine leases of the 19th century, when first issued, were given to native American women. Their method, known as fire-setting, involved drift mining, and kindling fires at the rock face then applying cold water to fracture the ore. These women then smelted the ore in make-shift furnaces, and apparently extracted a greater concentration of lead than the early settlers.[8] So although evidence and documentation is lacking, it is possible that women were involved in copper mining processes in Cornwall at a very early stage and, as in other cultures, may even have had prime responsibility for this part of the family economy. However, it seems that after the Bronze Age very little copper mining took place in Cornwall until the 16th century.

Tin mining, like copper, has an ancient history in Cornwall, probably dating from at least 3000 years ago. For many centuries ore was retrieved from where it was washed out into streams or outcropped at the surface. Unlike copper, tin extraction seems to have been more or less continuous, from ancient times. Archaeological evidence suggests continued low level production through the Roman period and beyond, to supply both the British and European market.[9] As with the early copper mining in Cornwall, we can only speculate as to the involvement of women and girls in this process.

The first surviving written documents that confirm that tin was being mined in Cornwall are from the 12th century, and relate to the transfer of administrative power from the King to the Stannaries. Suggestions of early mining activity in Cornwall come from Thomas Beare, the Bailiff for the Blackmore Stannary, when he writes in the latter half of the 16th Century:

'It appeereth by working of our Tinners in Cornwall that the Saxons being heathen people were skillful workers of and serces (searchers) for black tyn, which in thos ancient dayes wrought not with spades and working tooles made of Iron as we have now in our tyme, but all of the hart of oake ... for prooff where of diverse workers of our ttyme have fownd their shovells spades and mattox made all of oke and holm.' [10]

Mining from 1200 to 1690

It is during this period that there are enough surviving documents to give a fairly clear picture of mining in Cornwall and West Devon, especially with regard to tin mining. At this time, all the mines in England were owned by the Crown, and most of our information comes from the court records relating to the setting up and workings of the four Stannaries. These documents do not generally mention women in the workforce. Certainly when Thomas Beare wrote about tin mining in his own century (around 1550) he does not mention women or girls, whereas he does mention the employment of boys in the ore dressing process. Similarly, other 17th century accounts describe tin being dressed by boys, but not women or girls.[11]

There is an exception. In the *White Book of Cornwall*[12] we read of one 'Abraham the Tinner' who was involved in a court case for non-payment of his workers in 1357. It seems he owned two mine workings and four stream workings at Crukbargis Moor, and had failed to pay the wages of his workers. He employed 'over 300 men, women and children'. This is the earliest written record of females employed at the mines or tin stream works in Cornwall that has yet been found.

Tin extraction at this time was generally from stream works, the sea, drift mining (following lodes into the hillside), or at its most complex, sinking shallow shafts. Generally, we imagine the men and older boys would be involved in the heavy work of digging, constructing water leats, and heaving and barrowing the heaviest loads of rock and ore. The women, girls, if employed, and younger boys would presumably be involved in washing, panning, sorting ore from rubble and breaking down rock-bearing ore. Initially this was done with mortar and pestle, or the equivalent of small hand corn mill. By the 16th century water stamps were being used to break down the larger pieces of tin bearing rock, prior to manually breaking the smaller pieces.

Although day to day management of the tin mines had long since been handed over to the Vice Wardens of the Stannaries, other mines remained under control of the Crown up until the end of the 16th century. Another very early reference to females working in the mining industry comes from surviving accounts for the silver-lead mines at Calstock and Bere Ferrers which had been opened up by the Crown at the end of the 13th century. These exchequer rolls indicate that about seven hundred people may have been employed at this time, including women washing ore at the lead smelters.[13] It is in these records that we find the earliest named balmaidens. Later, in 1480, some of the men employed at Bere Alston were paid for dressing ore as well as mining, possibly suggesting that they had brought a team of people to carry out both processes. These teams would almost certainly include women and children. Mining at this time was a very well paid activity compared with other artisan trades or unskilled labouring.[14]

Similarly, copper mines were still under the control of the Mines Royal in Elizabethan times. When the value of copper was realised, in the production of brass for armaments, German mining experts were encouraged to come to England with their skills. They brought many workers with them, including ore dressers, smelters and smiths, who then lived in barracks or lofts on site. At the Cumbrian copper mines, this certainly included their own male ore dressers.

Eventually, from about 1568-1605 the Company of Mines Royal started to release control of the mines by giving leases out to individuals to set up mining operations. It was at this time that Customer Thomas Smythe was given a lease by the Crown to mine copper in the Illogan, St. Just, St. Ives, St. Agnes, and Perranzabuloe areas of Cornwall. Letters survive relating to some of these ventures. It seems that only a handful of men were employed at each mine and from the itemised pay lists they appear to be mostly German. Again, there is no mention of women or girls. These small mines closed when the main shareholders died, and no more copper was worked in Cornwall for about a hundred years.[15]

Contemporary descriptions, by Georgius Agricola, of mining operations on the continent in the 16th century indicate that it was quite normal for women and boys, but not girls, to be involved in the copper dressing processes. Here are descriptions of some of the processes in southern Germany:

'The work of sorting the crude metal or the best ore is done not only by men, but also by boys and women. They throw the mixed material upon a long table, beside which they sit for almost the whole day, and they sort out the ore; when it has been sorted out, they collect it in trays, and

when collected they throw it into tubs, which are carried to the works in which they are to be smelted.' [16]

'Into this sieve a boy throughs the material to be washed, and a woman shakes it up and down, turning it alternately to the right and to the left.' [17]

There is also evidence of women being involved in the silver dressing operations at Kutna Hora, about 70 km east of Prague, in the late 15th century. A wonderful colour illustration of the working silver mine survives, showing several women at work on the dressing floors. One is washing ore in a large vat, others carrying ore between the different processes on platters or in baskets, and one who looks as if she is being subjected to a mouth search! [18] The discovery of drawings of an early 16th century window at St. Neot's Church (sadly replaced in the mid 19th century) has led to a discussion as to whether the depiction in one of them was of a tinner and his balmaiden wife, which would give a very early date for documented evidence of women in the workforce. [19] However, the case is not proven, as the woman depicted looks to be in a costume that could have been worn by most women of the time. The elegant gloves in her hands perhaps indicate a woman of some standing, rather than a balmaiden.

In 1660, the anonymous writer in *Britannia Baconia* says that the ore-dressing tin in Cornwall was 'chiefly done by boys' [20] implying that sometimes other people (such as women or girls?) were also involved. As the lone reference to women working at Crukbargis in 1357 indicates, the absence of records does not necessarily mean absence of women and girls in the workforce during this period. It may just be that they were not recorded. Even in the 19th and 20th century women workers are not always mentioned in the ledgers and cost books, even when present in large numbers in the workforce. They sometimes remained invisible, either recorded as an ore dressing cost, or as a total amount of money paid to the surface captain or tributor responsible for dressing.

Mining from 1690-1860

A major development in the dressing and smelting of ores, at the beginning of the 18th century, was the introduction of the reverbatory furnace. When ore had been traditionally smelted at a 'bole' or ore hearth, the very finest particles were usually lost, so there was no point in trying to extract this portion from the parent material. In the reverbatory furnace a gentler draft was used for reaching the high temperatures required for smelting. It was found that very fine ore particles were not destroyed but could be smelted and recovered for the first time. This resulted in far more attention being paid to the 'slimes' – the fine-grained residues from the washing sieves and buddles. [21] Consequently, from about 1710, more complex dressing operations were introduced. In these more extensive dressing operations, with the slimes being collected and rewashed countless times, there was a significant increase in the numbers employed on the dressing floors. This was especially true for tin dressing.

Descriptions of mining in Cornwall at this time come mostly from several generations of well-to-do travellers who recorded their journeys, historians, or professional miners. When Celia Fiennes travelled into Cornwall in 1695, she described passing close to twenty tin mines in the St. Austell area, and about another hundred (probably meaning the number of shafts rather than mines) between Truro and Redruth. Her attention was caught by the great number of men and boys working at the pumps on a continuous rota, in order to keep the mines clear of water, but she did not mention the activities on the dressing floors, nor any women or girls at work:

'There was at least 20 mines all in sight which employs a great many people at work, almost day and night, but constantly all and every day includeing the Lords day which they are forced to, to prevent their mines being overflowed with water; more than 1000 men are taken up about them; few mines but had then almost 20 men and boys attending it.' [22]

By 1700, the Mines Royal had ceased to operate as such, and had allowed private landowners to lease out all the mining rights to private adventurers. In these early days (before about 1720) all the mining concerns in Cornwall were relatively simple, due to lack of technological development. Once free of the Mines Royal, stream or sea tinning, or mining for tin where the lodes outcropped near the surface, could be done by the extended family unit, or small companies. One of the early records of women involved in tin extraction in Cornwall comes from the pen of William Pryce, who reported that in about 1720 families were retrieving stream tin from the salt marsh and sea at Perranarworthal:

'I have been told, that about seventy years back, the low lands and sands under Perran Arworthall, which are covered almost every tide with the sea, have on its going off, employed some hundreds of poor men, women, and children, incapable of earning their bread by any other means.' [23]

An early record found of named women working at the mines or smelters was in cost and receipt books for Calenick Smelter. With the introduction of the first coal fired reverbatory furnaces in Cornwall, women were paid to barrow coal from ships on the shoreline to the smelters. They were also employed to sieve the coal, culm and cinders. Between three and twelve women were employed at Calenick from 1704 to 1707, of whom nine were named. [24] [25]

From 1718, with the introduction of mechanical pumps, ore could be more easily won from below the water table. Installation of horse whims and, later, winding engines also meant that ore could be raised more efficiently and safely. At the same time, the new techniques were developed for ore dressing. These improvements required far more investment and a greater labour force, so these larger and deeper mines were financed by groups of adventurers, and increasingly, from 1750 onwards, by mining companies. It was at this time, too, that the real value of copper was recognised, and there was a rush into investment in copper mines, in preference to tin.

It is not known how many women and girls were working at the mines prior to the introduction of these new technologies, but with the improved capability of bringing ore 'to grass' came the need for a cheap workforce to process the ore as quickly as it was raised. So from about 1720 it seems that women and children were drafted in numbers not seen before, as they had the necessary skill and dexterity to process the ores, and were cheaper to hire than men. One of the earliest records of women and girls working at the copper mines comes from the *Pool Adit Cost Book*, where there were about twenty five named female dressers recorded between 1729 and 1731. [26] In 1736, the vicar of Ludgvan laments the difficulty in obtaining house servants, as so many of the young women were 'employed about copper'. [27] In March 1742, twenty seven balmaidens were employed at Wheal Dudnance. [28]

By 1750, when Dr. Pococke (Bishop of Neath) was travelling through central Cornwall, women and girls seem to be a well established part of the commercial mining workforce. This is his description of a mine in Chacewater:

Engraving of Dolcoath Mine, Camborne, c. 1831, showing women and girls spalling, cobbing, and bucking.
Courtesy of the Royal Institution of Cornwall

'A succession of men are always at the mine, except on Sundays. They work eight hours, from six until two, and from two until ten, and then again from ten until six. When they come up, they call it 'coming to grass'. When the ore is brought up, women and children are employed in breaking it, and separating the 'country' (waste) from the ore, and the tin from the copper.' [29]

Similarly, the implication from the travel writings of Swedish 'industrial spy' R. R. Angerstein, in 1754, is of widespread employment of females in Cornish mining:

'In Cornwall, most men are miners, and children and young women are occupied in the stream-works and on the dressing-floors.' [30]

The new technologies transformed Cornish tin and copper mining at an amazing rate during the 18th century. A manuscript from the second half of the 17th century indicates just how extensive some mines and tin streams were at that time, with about 1,000 people employed at St. Agnes Bal and Trevaunance Valley:

'Continuously great numbers of Boyes and humane youths are employed about washing, vanning or cleansing tin.' [31]

It is from the second half of the 18th century that we begin to find accounts of women and girls at the mines in considerable numbers for the first time. By the time William Pryce wrote about mining in Cornwall in the 1770s he took the presence of women and girls on the dressing floor for granted:

'Copper ... being placed in the more interior strata of the earth and requires greater skill in hydraulics and mechanicks. The expense of coal, candles, timber, leather, ropes, gunpowder,

and various other materials, added to the labour of men, women, children and horses, occasion such a vast monthly charge, as will not easily be credited by those who are unacquainted with Mining.' [32]

He gives one of the earliest detailed accounts of the work of women or girls at the copper mines in sorting, cobbing and bucking the ore. He goes on to compare this with the tasks performed by women and girls at the tin and lead mines. He is one of the first writers to give a clear account of these different processes.

A Cornish tin mine in 1858, showing women and girls working at the racking frames, barrowing, and carrying baskets.

Courtesy of the Cornwall Centre Collection

The first statistics of the number of women and children working in or at the mines in Cornwall were published during the 19th century, as a public concern developed about their working conditions and moral welfare. This concern became expressed in a Government decision to establish a Royal Commission to investigate the conditions under which children and young people worked in the mines in England, Scotland and Wales. The Commission gathered evidence during 1841, and their report was before parliament in 1842. Despite this growing concern about the effects of the balmaidens' work on their well-being, the legislation which was enacted as a result was only applied to coal mines. No change was made to employment practice at surface or underground in the metalliferous mines at this stage.

Post industrial revolution: women or technology? (1860-1920)

There was always an intimate connection between the market value of the minerals mined, and the amount of dressing that made extraction economic. Thus in times of high prices, it was worth extracting from poor grade ore, which required more extensive labour. Conversely, when prices were low, only the best grade ores would be worth processing, with the low-grade ore being cast aside, and so surface workers would be laid off. As early as 1826, W. J. Henwood succinctly describes this relationship, with regards to tin:

'We reject portions that will not repay the cost of dressing.' [33]

With increased technology, machinery could be used to extract ore at less cost, and this was particularly true when applied to the extraction of the poorer ores. Hunt summarised this in 1887:

'Every time the tin stuff is handled, be it by boy or girl, the cost of the dressing of the ore is increased. By automatic machinery this might be avoided, and considerable saving secured. All that has been said in reference to the dressing of tin applies equally to copper and lead ores.' [34]

So by about 1850 technology and public opinion had already begun to spell out the last days of young women and girls working at the mines in Cornwall. At Condurrow, for instance, in 1858, new equipment was installed when there was a so called 'shortage of available labour' to dress a backlog of tin:

'At Condurrow Mine, having a large quantity of tin remaining in the stamps leavings, and being unable to get hands to dress it, and which with manual labour would be attended with heavy expense, they are preparing to erect 10 or 12 self-acting frames, to be set in motion by a water wheel on the mill floor. Those at work in the north east floor (10 of them) and attended by one girl, are effecting more work than 12 girls in the ordinary way.' [35]

At Condurrow one girl and self-acting frames, replaced twelve girls at the manual frames. Schwartz makes the point that when mechanical crushers were installed for breaking down copper ore-stuff, to replace the arduous and costly task done by the female buckers, not only did many girls lose their jobs, but that the new machinery was invariably operated by boys or men. So throughout Cornwall and West Devon nearly all female buckers had been replaced by 1858, except for a few small mines which still employed girls to do this task, and generally the new crushers were now overseen by boys.[36] In the same way, when mechanised frames were installed at St. Day United Mines in 1858, one boy replaced twenty or thirty girls. Similarly, with each step of technological development, tasks previously done by women were generally handed over to men and their machinery.

The world supply of minerals, and the copper and tin economy, had always affected the amount of employment available at the mines in the south west. Concurrent with the technological changes there was a dramatic fall in the price of copper from about 1866, so that many Cornish copper mines began to close. Some mines discovered rich tin lodes at depth, and changed from copper to tin production, which sometimes required less labour on the ore dressing floors, again affecting the number of females employed. This change from copper to tin, however, needed considerable investment so some mines chose to continue with a cheaper labour-intensive system, rather than paying for expensive new machinery.

By 1870, due to the 'improved' technology and the slump in copper prices, the number of women and girls employed, officially, at the mines had fallen by about 50% to 4,450. Another blow to the industry came in 1873 when tin prices also plummeted, having been very high in 1871 and 1872, due to new discoveries in Australia. More mines closed, leaving only 307 remaining open. During the 1870s lead production also began to drop in the south west, as mines were exhausted, throwing more out of work, especially in the Perranzabuloe and Newlyn East area.

Meanwhile, significant changes were taking place with regards to employment practice. In 1872, legislation was introduced for the first time to restrict employment of women and children at the metalliferous mines. Employment of any child under the age of twelve, either above ground, or below, became illegal. Regulations were also brought in about the safe use of machinery.[37]

By 1876, the various *Elementary Education Acts* were also in place, providing a network of schools throughout the country, and legislating for compulsory education for children up to the age of 10 years old. This was followed in 1878 by the *Factory and Workshop Act* forbidding employment of any children under 10 years of age, and restricting children between the ages of ten and fourteen to working no more than thirty hours per week. These Acts effectively removed many young balmaidens from the workforce, and placed them, for the first time, in full-time education. Many others would only be employed part time, if at all, totally changing the age structure of the women and girls engaged on the dressing floors. Even so, in 1890 the Chief Inspector of Factories complained that Cornish Mines still 'Swarmed with children of insufficient age'.[38]

Whereas there had been a considerable migration of miners from Cornwall, from the 1840s onwards, both to other parts of the UK and overseas, the combined events of the mid 1870s led to mass migration, on a scale not seen before, of able bodied men and women from the south west. Those mines that stayed open restructured from the cost book system, which discouraged sensible investment, to limited liability companies, and continued to become increasingly mechanised. It is suggested that more men were sacked than women or children at this stage, as they were the more expensive to employ. An example of this was the proposed replacement of the 'burning house man'[39] by a woman or child, at Penhalls Mine in 1879.[40]

Although records of women and girls working at the mines in the census material only indicate the minimum possible totals, due to probable under-recording, the trend over several decades for the parish of St. Agnes, which also includes part of the mining area of Perranzabuloe, indicates these dramatic changes. For 1841, 1851, and 1861, the numbers of females employed were 332, 357, and 363, respectively, whereas, by 1891, only 22 were described. However, it seems that considerable work was still available in the Camborne and Illogan area, where 236, and 443, females were recorded respectively. Even for Camborne though, this represented about one quarter of the number employed in 1861, whereas for Illogan the figures had remained much the same.

Of 307 mines open in 1873, only 23 were still open in 1895, and all had become limited companies. In the 1890s there was an attempt by the government to ban all female labour at the mines throughout Britain. A sizeable delegation of pit brow lasses travelled to London from the Lancashire collieries to lobby MPs, and the move was also opposed vigorously by the mining companies in Cornwall:

'To prevent the employment of 'bal girls', under present conditions in most of our Cornish mines would be to render the struggle which is being so gallantly fought against adverse circumstances in many cases practically hopeless. From the other point of view it would mean an enormous amount of suffering and distress by reducing the already low family wage fund. It can, we believe, be said with truth that at the present day there is nothing necessarily demoralising or degrading, or injurious to health in the surface work of women and girls at any well regulated mine in the West of England.' [41]

The bill was defeated, and females continued to work at surface in the various collieries and mines in Britain.

In Cornwall, with new equipment designed for crushing and separating, there was redesigning or rebuilding of most the remaining dressing floors, with subsequent job losses for the ore dressers. The introduction of frue vanners and shaking tables (that separated the ore) meant that nearly all job losses between 1896 and 1900 in Cornwall were women surface workers, mostly those at the racking frames. Subsequently, during the early part of the 20th century, many of the processes on the dressing floors became transformed with the advent of electricity. For instance, spallers at Dolcoath were no longer needed when electrical powered stone breakers were installed in about 1907. The last women at Tincroft were dismissed in 1914, when stone crushers were installed there. A correspondent in the *Mining Journal* made this final lament:

'The latest innovation is the doing away with the spalling maidens and their attendant knights, with a consequent lessened cost of some £400 per annum, the work previously so done being more efficiently executed by the existing stone breakers and an ingeniously arranged system of sliding shoot, hoppers, sampling tables and drop doors, by means of which the ore from tributers and sampling is despatched to the stamps with no handling whatever.' [42]

This gradual but incessant replacement of female labour with machinery run my male overseers is well illustrated by employment figures from Devon Great Consols. In 1849 almost 50% of the 275 surface workers were female. This figure steadily declined until, in 1900, when the number of surface workers had been almost halved, only 1% were female. A few women continued to work at the tin streams during the beginning of World War One, but seem to have finished altogether by 1918. Only a handful of mines remained open in Cornwall and West Devon beyond 1918. Dolcoath was probably one of the last to continue to employ females, with a few spalling women still working until it closed in 1922.[43] This was the end of an era.

Wartime jobs for women

During both World Wars mining was a reserved occupation, so miners and clay workers were not normally called up into the armed forces; but inevitably some men volunteered for active service and left their jobs. In the clay industry in the First World War, with no available men to replace them, young women were sometimes called on to do their very heavy manual work in the clay pits, extracting clay. Other women took over administrative posts. A Miss Lidgey, from Lanner, managed the Magdalen Mine near Ponsanooth during WW1.[44]

With trade blockades in operation and new requirements for minerals, a potash felspar mine was re-opened in the St. Austell area during the First World War, in order to meet an increased demand in the glassmaking process. Young women were called to work there to dress the mineral. Similarly, women were employed at Wheal Mary Ann in Menheniot, to re-dress the waste heaps for wolfram.

During the Second World War, some mines re-opened in the South West to meet a desperate requirement for home produced ores. Government inspectors looked at tin mines in Cornwall, with a view to re-opening for war work, but very few were thought viable. Generally those mines which were already working were encouraged to increase production. Geevor was one of these, and women were employed to sort ore on the picking belts, also replacing men who had left for war service.

Balmaidens – the statistics

Studying the statistics of the number of women and girls working at the mines in Cornwall and the South West is fraught with difficulty. Only occasional regional collations of numbers were made of those at the tin, copper and lead mines, and those that exist use different criteria. Some totals included the West Devon Mines, some were for Cornwall only; some counted all surface labourers together, some separated out the numbers of male and female workers. Some recorded the numbers of women and children, and others just the total number of employees above and below ground. Some totals distinguished the number of employees at the copper, tin and lead mines, others were overall totals for workers at all the mines, others were totals for just copper or tin. No overall figures are available for employees at the clay works or the slate quarries, independent of the census material.

Some of the most detailed statistical information comes from the *1842 Royal Commission of the Employment of Women and Children at the Non-Metalliferous Mines*, but even here the author reports that a proportion of mines never sent in their returns. Even for those received there were occasional discrepancies and contradictions in the figures, or parts missing. The author believed that there was an under-reporting of the number of boys at the mines, for fear of the information being used for conscripting them for military service, but he makes no comments on the accuracy of the number of women and girls.

Another detailed source of employment figures at the mines comes from Sir Charles Lemon's tables for 1836-7, giving information about the main tin, copper and lead mines in Cornwall.[45] Here again, the information is not presented in a consistent form. Of the 160 mines recorded, only 108 gave separated numbers of women and children employed. In 1864 Spargo published an overview of Cornish mines which also gave numbers of female employment in 1861, but, again, the information is not consistent in format, and is sometimes missing altogether.[46] Even statistics based on official reports and inspections, such as these, need to be treated with caution. There were many reasons why mine managers may not have given accurate figures, especially after 1872, when under-reporting may have been quite common if managers had been employing under-aged children.

A further source of statistics for women and girls working at the mine is the general population census. As employment details were only collected from the 1841 census onwards, this source gives us no insight into the first century of 'industrial' employment of women and girls at the mines. From the years available there seems to be considerable variation as to how much information was given, both in different censuses, and between different enumerators in any one year. However, an even greater problem with the census material seems to be the probable, and considerable, under-reporting of female employment in general. This may be illustrated by the case of Martha Buckingham, one of the balmaidens interviewed by the 1842 Commission. The Commission records her working at Consolidated Mines on 15th May 1841 and for the previous four years. However she was not recorded as working at the mines, just three weeks later, in the census of 5th June. There was no occupation recorded at all. This was also true of her sister Mary who, according to the same evidence, was also working at the mine. In contrast, Martha's two brothers were recorded as tin miners, indicating a probable gender bias in the census recording of that parish.[47] Similarly, less than 5,500 women and girls were described in the 1861 census as working at the mines, which is considerably less than the other recorded estimates of the time.

Parish Registers are not very useful in indicating over-all figures. They give very limited information about employment; only giving the occupation in marriages registered from 1837, and at burial, if the death is work-related.

Following the employment history of any one mine is just as difficult. Many mine records are missing, or were never made. Those that survive are rarely consistent in their presentation. Cost Books are usually the best sources of information about female employees, and some pay lists give names of the individual balmaidens working each month. In others only a total sum for the women's and girls' pay appears, or as a total for all the surface labourers, especially where the dressing floor operations were contracted out, and so may include the boys and men as well.

The proportion of females at the mines

Very few total or comparative statistics of balmaidens are yet available across the parishes. The greatest concentration of women and girls at work at the copper and tin mines from about 1851 to 1861 appeared to be working in the Camborne-Redruth area and in the parishes of St. Agnes and Perranzabuloe.

Richard Lanyon collated the number of women and girls working at the mines in Camborne, using the 1841 census information. He found 222 female mine workers recorded as living in Camborne, and 527 in the rural parts, totalling 749 for the parish. This constituted 9% of the female population in Camborne itself, and 18% of those living outside, and 14% on average. This is interesting as it implies that most of the mining communities were based outside of Camborne itself, rather than in the town.[48] In the parishes of St. Agnes and Perranzabuloe in 1841, 297 and 31 mine women and girls are recorded in 1841, being 56% and 34% of the females employed respectively and 8.5% and 3% of the female population.[49]

The proportion of women and girls in the mine workforce in Camborne in 1841 was 27%.[48] In the parish of Lanner, in 1851, as many as 31% of women employed were employed in mining (although this had been reduced to 10.7% by 1891).[44] Deacon found that the percentages of females working at the clay works from the 'clay parishes' of Roche, St. Stephens, and St. Dennis, were 1.5% in 1871, and 0.1% in 1881.[50] This percentage was very much lower than in the mining areas.

The *1861 Census* for Cornwall shows that the parish with the highest total number of females employed at the mines was Camborne, with 875. Of these, 365 were dressing tin, 319 dressing copper, with 231 unspecified. The parishes of St. Agnes, Gwennap, Redruth, Illogan, and St. Just, reported the next highest totals, each with between 350 and 450 balmaidens recorded.

In 1836, the proportions of women and children out of the total mine workforce at the tin mines in Cornwall, compared with the copper mines, did not seem to be significantly different, being 38% and 41% respectively, and 43% in those mines extracting both tin and copper.[45]

When comparing the proportion of females in the mine labour force in the St. Ives area in 1836 with 1864, four mines showed an increase and two a decrease. There was an overall increase from 26% in 1836 to 34.5% in 1864. However, these workforce percentages were very variable, and presumably depended on local employment policy and available labour. At thirty mines in the St. Just area, for instance, in 1864, only 15.5% of the mine workforce was female, a total of 805 out of 5191 employees.[46] This was possibly because many girls went into service in Penzance.

The main employers

With such incomplete documentation there are many mines for which no records have survived, and probably just as many who never recorded detailed employment figures to start with. However, the largest mines were the ones for which records or descriptions are still available. Dolcoath Copper Mine was one of the largest employers, if not the largest, in the early 19th century, with the number of females engaged certainly being in the hundreds and was possibly more than 400. But, in 1836, with 290 women and children employed, it no longer featured at the top of the list of large copper mines. The largest employers, then, were Consols and United Mines, a consortium of several mines in Gwennap, who employed 869 women and 597 children, Fowey Consols and Lanescot with 308 women and 144 children, Charlestown Mines with 120 women and 263 children, and North Roskear with 190 women and 150 children.[45] In 1841 the major employers were still Consolidated Mines (300-400 females), and Fowey Consols (341 females) but with East Wheal Crofty employing 243 females. By 1864 the picture had changed radically, with many of these large copper mines having closed, or having changed over to mining tin. The days of the Cornish copper mines with huge pay rolls were gone, with no mines employing more than about 50 women and children still operating. Only those which were mining both copper and tin had a larger pay roll - Wheal Seton, for instance, still employed 260 children.[46]

The tin mines generally seemed to have had smaller numbers of employees than the copper mines. The largest recorded employers of women and children in 1836 were Wheal Vor with 327 women and 255 children, Great Works Consol with 46 women and 74 children, and Wheal Reeth with 18 women and 66 children. By 1841 the largest employer was probably still Wheal Vor with 164 girls employed under the age of 18 years. The next largest employer appears be North Roskear, but with a much smaller workforce of 128 females in total. By 1856 Great Wheal Vor had diversified and was building copper dressing floors in addition to its large tin dressing areas. They employed a total of 236 females in 1856 [51] and 374 surface workers, with probably slightly fewer females, in 1863.[52] By 1864, the largest tin mine was Dolcoath with 383 children, but very few tin mines employed more than 100 women and children at the time.

Although the major mines employed a significant proportion of the female workers between them, the experience of many women and girls would have been of small operations. In 1836, 42% of the mines employed less that 20 women and children, and a further 15% employed between 20 and 49.[45] Only six mines employed more than 250. By 1864, the percentage of mines employing less than fifty women and children had risen to 86%, with only one mine employing more than 250.[46]

Total numbers of balmaidens

Owing to the scarcity of statistical material, and because it is almost impossible to compare like with like, it very difficult to assess the total number of girls and women who may have worked at the mines in Cornwall and West Devon. Only informed guesses may be made. The starting point must be the overall figures available, from various sources, inconsistent and sketchy though they are.

Although it seems that women and girls were first employed on a more commercial scale at the tin and copper mines from about 1720, the first available estimate of the total number of balmaidens at work comes from 1787, with between 1,200 and 1,800 females working at the mines in Cornwall.[53] By 1799 Vivian considered that between four and five thousand women and children were employed (probably a least 2,500 females).[54] Spackman recorded a total of 2,276 females working in all the mines in Cornwall in 1827. Of these 2,098 were at the copper mines (constituting 15% of the workforce) and 130 at the tin mines (constituting only 2% of the workforce) and 21 at the lead mines.[55] Lemon, quoting statistics for 1836, records totals of 4,413 women and 4,428 children at one hundred and nine mines in Cornwall. He observed that about 40% of the workforce at this time were women and children.[56] Some of the largest mines had only submitted total workforce figures, and so, using his percentage estimate, we can project an approximate total for all one hundred and sixty mines of about 10,000 (approximately 5,000 women and 5,000 children).

By the time of the 1842 Royal Commission, 4,136 females were reported to be employed by the mines which returned questionnaires. Of these, 2,700 were over the age of 18, 1,740 between the ages of 13 and 18 years old, and 696 under the age of 13. Barham estimated that there was an under-reportage of about one third, thus bringing these projected figures to approximately 5,550 (3,600, 2,320 and 930 respectively), for Cornwall and West Devon.[57] However, Watson, not stating his sources, estimates that as many as 60,000 people were employed at 112 copper mines, and another 12,000 at the tin mines in 1842,[58] this being over twice the number reported in the 1842 Commission. Based on his figures, even allowing for only 20% of the workforce being female, this would indicate a total of 14,400 females - greatly in excess of the Commission's estimate.

When Leifchild was writing in 1855, he quoted Mr. Henwood as estimating 5,764 women and 5,764 children working in Cornwall, and a 'Cornish friend' suggesting 7,000 females were working in 1854.[55] It seems a great coincidence that these first numbers are the same for women and children, suggesting a typographical error in one of the figures. Even allowing for this, a figure of about 5,000 women and 2,500 girls seems to emerge for the employment figures for the 1850s.

In the following decade Barton quotes total figures of the mining workforce for Cornwall and Devon, as being 40,000 in 1861,[59] with an estimate that one third were probably women and children, giving a figure of over 13,000. Williams described 50,000 people being employed at 340 mines in Cornwall and West Devon in 1862[60] indicating a minimum of 10,000 females in the workforce, assuming, again, that they make up as little of 20% of the total.

None of these figures are supported by the 1861 census, which gives a total of about 5,400 women and girls. Of those ascribed, 49% worked with tin, 40% with copper, 5% lead and 4% clay. This probably confirms the suspected under-reporting of balmaidens in the census

Mine	Parish	7 yrs	8 yrs	9 yrs	10 yrs	11 yrs	12 yrs	13 yrs	14 yrs	15 yrs	16 yrs	17 yrs	Total under 13 yrs	Total 13 to 18 yrs	Total over 18 yrs	Total all ages
Levant	St. Just					1	3	2	3	2	4	10	4	21	34	59
Botallack	St. Just							1			1	1	1	1	16	17
St. Ives	St. Ives								3	2	1	1	1	0	12	20
Providence	St. Ives						1	2	1	1	2	1	1	8	8	16
Marazion	Marazion									2	7	4	2	13	Nil return	15*
Wheal Darlington	Marazion					2	2	1	5	10	4	3	4	23	Nil return	27*
Wheal Friendship	St. Hilary			3		1			2	5	6	1	4	14	40	58
North Roskear	Camborne	1	1		4	1	7	10	3	6	5	8	14	33	100	147
South Roskear	Camborne		1			2	1	2	2	2	1	3	4	10	31	47
Dolcoath	Camborne	2	2	3	9	8	12	18	10	24	11	11	34	74	20	128
Tincroft	Illogan						1	3	3	2	2	11	1	10	Nil return	11*
Wheal Uny	Redruth									4	1	6		11	3	14
Wheal Unity Wood	Gwennap	1		1	3	4	6	2	8	8	3	2	15	23	Nil return	38*
United Mines	Gwennap			7	5	9	4	7	7	10	8	12	25	44	182	251
Polberro Consols	St. Agnes				1	2	3	2	3	8	4	4	6	29	14	39
Wheal Kitty	St. Agnes				1	1		6	5	6		5	2	24	12	38
Charlestown Mines	St. Austell			2		7	11	15	11	19	11	18	20	74	75	149
Wheal Friendship	Mary Tavy			1	2	6	5	7	8	14	7	6	13	40	30	83

* incomplete totals

CEC 1842 tables 11 - 15

Table 1. Number of females, by age, employed at mines producing tin and copper, in 1841.

material. By 1866, as mines began to close, Rowe reports 18,000 miners in the Cornish mines, one sixth (3,000) of whom were estimated to be female.[61]

By the time of the 1871 census 1,544 children between the ages of thirteen and eighteen were recorded as working at the mines, and 4,450 women, giving a probable total for the female workforce of just over 5,000.[62] Reiding, visiting from America, quotes a total of 2,000 females working in Cornwall in 1881, but does not give his sources.[63] By 1891, the next available figures, there were 5,893 surface workers recorded in the tin mines in Cornwall, a proportion of whom would be male. Seven years later, in 1898 there were only 2,444, less than half.[59] No other total figures for females at the mines in Cornwall have been discovered after these dates, and certainly from about 1900 onwards the number of balmaidens working at the mines was only in the hundreds. In 1906 it was reported that the total number of people employed in Cornwall and Devon had dropped to 6,380, of whom only 600 were boys and 'only a few girls'. Most of these, of course, were in Devon.[59] The last record of women being employed was in 1920, other than war work in World War Two.

The main period of commercial employment of women at the mines in Cornwall and West Devon seems to be for a period of approximately two hundred years from 1720-1920. The statistics indicate something under 2,000 being employed by the end of the 18th century, rising to at least 5,000 to 7,000 by the mid 19th century, and possibly as high as 14,000 (depending on the sources). The proportion of women and girls in the workforce seems to be generally higher in the first half of the 19th century, possibly as high as 40%. With improved technology, and men or boys being employed to supervise machinery the proportion of females in the workforce decreased rapidly in the second half of the 19th century. It is generally considered that the number of women and girls working at these mines in West Devon and Cornwall peaked around 1860.

There are no clear figures available for women and girls working at the lead or manganese mines, slate quarries or clay pits. It seems that their commercial employment in these enterprises extended for a much shorter period of time than at the tin and copper mines. It probably did not exceed one hundred years, and, in the case of manganese, not more than twenty or thirty years. Estimating the numbers of women and girls who worked in these quarries, mines, and pits, is very difficult. Maximum numbers employed at each place seem rarely to exceed twenty or thirty, so the indications are that they would total only a few hundred at the peak of their employment, probably prior to about 1850.

So how many balmaidens were there? It is impossible to even hazard a guess at how many worked at the mines, stream works, and quarries, prior to about 1720. For the period of commercial employment of women and girls, which lasted for approximately two hundred years (between 1720 and 1920), the total number can only be vaguely estimated, based loosely on the available statistics.

Taking the metalliferous mines only, we could assume a minimum of between 1,000 and 2,000 females were employed in the first eighty years up to 1800. This may be greatly understated, bearing in mind Angerstein's observation that 'most men are miners, and children and young women are occupied in the stream-works and on the dressing-floors'.[30] With a rapid increase in mining technology, and the concurrent development of the extensive dressing floors, there appears to have been a massive increase in the number of balmaidens over the next sixty years, peaking in the early 1860s, probably at a minimum of 7,000. This was followed by a decline to about 5,000 by 1870, and 500 by 1900.

Taking an average 'working life-span' of a balmaiden of ten years before 1870, and five years after 1870, a very rough total number of balmaidens can be projected at 55,000 individuals. This figure does not include the non-metalliferous mines, works and quarries for which we might add another 500 per decade of their economic life, using a figure of about 100 years, totalling another 5,000. This brings us to a very rough estimated total of 60,000 women and girls employed at the mines, quarries and clay works in Cornwall and Devon during the 200 years of commercial production between 1720 and 1920. As each of the component figures of the calculation is based on the more conservative figures available, it is almost certain that the real figure would be in excess of this amount, and perhaps considerably so. In addition, these figures do not take into account those who were employed before 1720.

Year	Total	Category	Counties	Mines	Ref.
1787	1,200	Females	Cornwall	All	53
1799	4,000 - 5,000	Women + boys	Cornwall	Copper	54
1827	2,276	Females	Cornwall	All	55
1837	10,000	Women + children	Cornwall	All	56
1841	5,500	Females	Cornwall + W. Devon	All	58
1854	7,000	Females	Cornwall	All	55
1861	13,000	Women + children	Cornwall + Devon	All	59
1866	3,000	Females	Cornwall	Tin	61
1871	5,994	Women + children	Cornwall	All	61
1881	2,000	Females	Cornwall	All	59
1891	5,893	Females + males	Cornwall	Tin	59
1898	2,444	Females + males	Cornwall	Tin	59

Table 2. Various totals of surface workers at mines between 1787 and 1898.

Chapter 2

BALMAIDENS AT WORK

Employment practices

In the early days of small mining concerns, women and girls would have constituted part of the extended family or community working unit, and would probably not have had any negotiated employment rights or wages as such. It was only as the mines became larger that they would have received wages in their own right.

In Cornwall, however, there was an intermediate stage, where the women and girls were part of a 'tribute' team, who were contracted out to extract and dress ore from an agreed part of the mine. The 'tribute' system is thought to originate, in part, from the need for flexibility in working patterns. Miners often needed to supplement their income with other seasonal occupations such as cultivating smallholdings or fishing. A tribute team was not employed by the mine adventurers as such, but agreed a kind of sub-contract for the task in hand. On 'setting day' each tribute team would bid for a given area to be mined during the subsequent two months, at a pre-set rate for dressed ore extracted. Fines could be imposed if the team did not work their pitch, and the risk factor was transferred (very largely) to the tribute teams. Deducted from their earnings were various costs for candles, explosives, work done by the blacksmith, carpenter, etc. In the early days, the tribute team included the ore dressers, and, as ore was landed from the shaft (by their own landers) it would be brought to their own dressers and kept quite separate from ore dressed by any other tribute teams. Depending on the relationships within the tribute team, the women and girls may have received a direct wage from the chief tributer, be given 'pocket money', or nothing other than their 'board and lodging' if the money went into the communal family purse. At most larger mines there were also two types of miners - tutworkers and tribute workers. The tutworkers were paid at a flat rate for sinking shafts, and driving levels. They did not need to employ surface dressers, as their task was primarily to open up new areas in the mine for ore extraction.

Tribute teams often could not afford the labour or the time to dress the poorer grades of ore, especially when the price of tin or copper was low. This ore was often cast aside into waste heaps. As a result, at some mines, other groups of tributers or ore dressers were paid to dress this waste, quite separately from the tribute teams because they:

'… cannot often afford to dress the coarser parts of what they raise, they reject it. It is let to others who stamp and clean it, having a proportional price likewise.' [1]

As mines began to extract greater quantities of ore, and in some cases, more than one type, the organisation of separate teams of ore dressers at surface became more and more complicated. It became the norm by about 1820, certainly by 1840, that a combined workforce of ore dressers was employed and paid for by the mine managers, and each tribute team charged a sum for dressing depending on the amount raised. For instance, William Cullum & Co., a tribute team at Fowey Consols, was charged 5s for dressing ores in December 1841.[2]

In some mines, the whole dressing floor operation was taken over by one enterprising tributer, who would agree to prepare so many tons of ore ready for smelting in a given time, in return for a percentage of the market value. In 1841, between 50 and 60 boys and girls were employed independently in this way at Charlestown Mines[3], as were all the dressers at Balleswidden.[4] A similar arrangement operated where tin was taken to be dressed at independently owned stamps. The women and girls would then be employed by those who held the agreement or lease. William Sincock employed between 34 and 36 females at the 'stamps and burning house' at Wheal Agar in 1893-4, and was paid accordingly. (These women were accounted for quite separately in the cost book from the spalling women, who carried out the initial preparation of the ore for the stamps, and who were paid directly by the mine manager).[5] A similar practice of paying a subcontractor for organising female workers sometimes occurred at the clay works, where small groups were involved in carrying the clay blocks out to dry on the hillsides.

Recruitment

In the larger mines, responsibility for the surface workers, including recruitment, was with the surface captain. In smaller mines it was with the purser or mine agent.

When mines first opened, it would be many months before material was brought to the surface ready for dressing. Even then the numbers of females required on the dressing floor would be small. Gradually as operations were rationalised and got under way, then the numbers employed in dressing would increase.

Although there is little information, it has been implied that in the eighteenth century girls may have started work at the mines around the age of 8 years old. The main sources of later information about the ages of girls and women at the mines, quarries or clay pits in the mid 19th century are the 1842 Commission on Employment, and the population censuses. From the 1841 census, this average age of commencing work seems to have risen to about 9 or 10 years old. The various employment returns received by Barham for the various mines in Cornwall and West Devon recorded no girls of 7 years old, and only twelve 8 year olds.[6] When Richard Lanyon was asked in 1841 about the age at which children begin work at the mine, however, he suggested a lower age than the records suggest, and also that there had been a recent decrease in this average age:

'About seven years very commonly. Girls begin at the same age. They are put to work earlier than formerly.' [7]

In 1841, Barham estimated that there were about 700 girls (13% of the total females employed) under the age of 13 (mostly from 9 years old upwards) working at the mines. There were 1,740 (53%) between the ages of 13 and 18, and 2,700 (34%) over the age of 18.[8] In 1841 in Kenwyn, one of the major copper mining parishes, 17% were under 13, 39% between 13 and 18, and 44% over 18 years of age. In a study of the manganese dressers of Coryton and Marystowe (Devon) in 1851, a slightly higher percentage of very young girls were employed: 18% were under 13 years old, 39% between 13 and 18 years, and 43% over 18 years old. Also from the 1851 census, for all parishes in Cornwall, it seems that 36% of the female labour force in the copper mines was under 15 years old, 22% between 15 and 20 years old, 17% between 21 and 24 years old, and 25% over 25 years.[9] By 1861 the overall percentage of girls employed at the mines under the age of 15 years had dropped to 22.4%. From the 1841 figures of employment for the commission, and from census material, indications are that girls were not taken to the mines until slightly older in the St. Just peninsula, and that the girls seem to have gone to work at the copper mines at a slightly younger age than at the tin mines.

The age at which girls were being brought to work on the dressing floors in the late 1850s and 1860s seems to have risen slightly compared with the 1830s and 1840s, with the youngest being about 9 or 10 years old, but the average being from 11 to 13 years old. By 1861, only 8% of the women and girls recorded as employed at the mines in Cornwall were under 13 years old. The parishes which seemed to employ the highest percentages of young girls in this age group were Camborne, Illogan and Kenwyn, with 12.1%, 10.4% and 10% respectively. With the *Metalliferous Mines Regulation Act 1872*, making employment of children under ten years old illegal, and the *Factory and Workshops Act 1878*, few children were 'officially' employed beyond the mid 1870s. After that date, girls do not seem to have been openly recruited until about the age of 14.

From about 1780 to 1870 there was almost continuous poverty and under-employment in Cornwall, so that recruitment of ore dressers was rarely a problem. Parents would present their children to the surface captain for work, as they reached the appropriate age. In 1841, the mine captains often complained that undue pressure was placed on them by desperate families to take children 'too young', at between 5 and 7 years of age. The mine agent at Tresavean remarked that children were being brought earlier because of:

'difficulty in obtaining relief under the new Poor Law' and children 'are brought by their mothers who complain they cannot get bread for them'.[10]

Among the very youngest balmaidens recorded in the 1841 census were 5 year-old Elizabeth Sims of Kenwyn[11] and 6 year-old Ann Johns, who were probably tin dressing at Wheal Vrea.[12] Similarly, the youngest recorded in the 1861 census were two 5 year-olds: Matilda Michell of Connor Downs[13] and Mary Roberts of St. Just.[14] It is impossible to tell whether these are recording errors, or whether these children were truly working at the mines at this age.

A good proportion of the girls sent to the mine came from families where there was no father. In 1841, the Poor Rate Collector for Redruth observed the following: 'Girls seldom go to the mine whilst their father is alive.'[15] In the Marystowe area in 1851, of twenty five girls and women who were recorded as working at the manganese mines, over half (thirteen) were either supporting widowed mothers or were widowed themselves. A similar pattern was observed among the women and children working at Delabole Quarry in 1851. In 1861, 13 year-old Mary Hannah Reynolds and her two brothers, of Polwheveral near Constantine, were working at the mine, probably Wheal Vivian, in order to support themselves, their grandmother and mother.[16] Similarly, girls were often working at the mine because their father was abroad, as were Eliza, Hannah and Jane Jeffery of Illogan, and Ann and Grace Richards of Camborne in 1861.[17]

Young people had to support not only widowed mothers or young siblings, but sometimes disabled members of the family as well. For example, Jane, Fanny, and Henry Remfry, who were 25, 20, and 21 years old respectively, and lived in Blackwater in 1841, were all working at the mine and supporting their mother, an 'infirmed' 15 year-old sister Christiana, as well as a baby sister.[18]

It was not unheard of for women or girls with some sort of disability themselves to be employed at the mine. Mary Hendon, 22 years old, who had been deaf from birth, worked at a tin mine in the Gwinear area in 1861.[19] Similarly, 16 year-old Catherine Peeps, who was also deaf, was working as a mine girl in the Liskeard area.[20] In contrast, a blind woman was employed as an ore dresser in the Columb Major area. She was 62 year-old Betsy Miner.[21]

Girls were also sent to the mines from the workhouse. Mary Ann Roscorla had been sent in this way to Tresavean Mine by 1841, and at 12 years old was in lodgings.[22] Similarly, Gracey Brinney was taken from the workhouse at a very young age to look after the horse at the horse whim at a mine in Redruth, in the 1780s.

On occasion it seems that groups of women presented themselves for work, and that one would receive payment for the whole group on pay day. This certainly seemed to have been the case of the barrow women at Calenick Smelter in the first few years of operation in the early 18th century, and possibly with women laying out the clay at the clay works in the early 19th century.

Sometimes whole families offered themselves for work, and it was not uncommon for all the girls of eligible age of one family to be working together, as with Elizabeth, Mary Ann, Jane, Grace, and Susan Hill, aged from 10 to 25 years, working at Sparnon in 1861.[23]

Although married women were generally discouraged from working at the mine, it was not uncommon for widows of all ages to ask for work, on the death of their husbands. This must have been the case with Harriet Knuckey, whose husband, Philip, died on 23rd December 1849 at Wheal Trehane. She was left with an infant son, and gave birth to a second child six months after his death. By March 1851 she was lodging in a house in Menheniot with her children, and working at the mine.[24] Similarly, Mary Webster, who was killed in a boiler explosion at the unfortunately named Boiling Well Mine in 1858, appears to have gone to the mine to work to support herself after her husband, too, had been killed in a mining accident.[25]

Women who had never married often continued to work at the mines, sometimes into their old age. Among the oldest balmaidens, in 1841, were Blanch Coombe (80 yrs) and Mary Ivey (85 yrs).[26] In 1861 there were eighteen women working in Cornwall over the age of sixty, and seven over the age of seventy-five. By 1871, these figures had increased to an incredible twenty-seven and ten, respectively.[27] Even in 1881 elderly women were still being employed, including 64 year-old Mary Abbott working at the Delabole Slate Quarries.[28] In 1891, the very oldest appears to be 93 year-old Mary Thomas (b. 1798 in St. Agnes), who was recorded as a tin miner. At the time she was living with a 63 year-old widowed daughter and two granddaughters, in Illogan.[29] The story of the elderly unmarried woman working at Carn Brea in about 1880[30] graphically illustrates the great fear people had of the workhouse, being perceived, by many, as the only alternative to toiling at the mine. Some mines seem to have had a policy of giving preferential employment to older single or widowed women, and this appears to have been the case in the Crowan area in 1861, when

36 of the 95 females employed were all over the age of 50. Some women were still working at the mine, into considerable age, in order to support aged parents, such as Mary Bastin, working at 59 years of age, to support her widowed mother who was 86.[31]

The length of time which girls and women remained employed at the mine depended very much on personal circumstances, as well as on the local mining economy. If the average age of starting work was between 9 and 11 years old, and the average age of marriage about 19 or 20, then many girls would have worked for about ten years, right through their teenage years. For instance, Ruth Snell of Calstock was recorded as working as a 'copper dresser' and as 'work at mine' in the 1851 and 1861 census respectively.[32] Assuming her employment had been continuous in that time, it indicates that she was working from at least the age of 13 years old until she was 23 years old. The longest known period of continuous employment was the elderly woman at Carn Brea, who stated that she had been working at the mine for forty years.[30] Working for twenty or more years was by no means uncommon; for instance, census entries for Sophia Waters of Blackwater[33] and Elizabeth Blight of St. Agnes[34] suggest that they both may have worked as balmaidens from at least 1841 to 1861.

Very often the girls were no strangers to the mine and, well before they were due to start work, would be sent with dinner for other members of their family. Minnie Andrews was one:

'I was five years old when I first took father's crowst across to Carn Camborne.' [35]

This meant they became familiar with the layout, the different processes, and the language of the dressing floors from an early age. Their lack of awareness of the dangers however sometimes led to tragic accidents, such as with 9 year-old Mary Dale, in October 1893, and 8 year-old Ada Harris, in December 1896, both of whom died after falling through arsenic flues at Botallack and East Pool, respectively.[36] [37]

The girls would usually continue to work at the mine until they were married, on average at about 19 years old, and only a very small proportion left to seek alternative employment as long as there was work to be found at the mines. Some were still working there in their mid twenties or later, especially if they remained unmarried. Some women returned to the mines if widowed or abandoned, leaving young children with family or an older child, or sometimes even having to leave them on their own, as with a suicidal mother at Wheal Basset.[38]

Surface workers and labourers were expected to give two weeks' to one month's notice, and this was probably enforced by the threat of withholding wages for that period. This was quite possible with the workforce being paid either one or two months in arrears. However, it seems that there were no written agreements, and arrangements could be very fluid on both sides. There was no job security as workers could be, and often were, laid off with no notice. When mines ran into difficulty, wages were frequently reduced, and sometimes no payment was made at all. When bad weather made it impossible for the dressing floors to operate there was no system of retainment pay. In 1872, when mine workers held out for the abolition of the 'five week month', and an impassioned plea was made for fairness by a Mr. Bassett on this issue of notice and dismissal:

'Surface hands should be entitled to receive the same notice which they give; they were often discharged at a moment's notice, whilst if about to leave of their own accord, they are obliged to give a fortnight's notice.' [39]

On the other hand, non-attendance at work, without adequate reason, was a frequent complaint heard from the mine agents. It seems that sometimes women and girls were poached away from one mine or clay works to another when more attractive pay or working conditions were offered. Minnie Andrews, the 'last balmaiden', worked in a number of different mines, and commented:

'We go the places where we gather most money, see?' [40]

In order to encourage loyalty of the workforce, some mines offered monthly bonuses for continuous attendance. At Wheal Vor, in 1841, the older women and girls were given an additional 1s, and the younger girls 6d if they had attended the dressing floors all month.[41]

Different mines, or, more accurately, different mine captains, sometimes had different views on employing girls and women. For example, at South Caradon (and probably Wheal Mary and Wheal Trelawny as well) in Menheniot, Captain Peter Clymo Jnr. would willingly employ women, as well as very young children from 7 or 8 years old. Similarly, at Carn Entral in 1861, of 20 females recorded as working at the mines, 14 were 16 years old or under, one being 7 years old.[42] In contrast, Captain Thomas Trevillion, of Herodsfoot Mine, preferred to employ only males for surface dressing, as he believed they 'worked better'.[43] [44]

Employment on the dressing floors was not necessarily continuous, even when mines were in full production. Although ore stuff could continue to be raised from underground independently of weather conditions (with the exception of severe flooding), the processes on the dressing floor could be adversely affected. Although the women and children normally continued to work through appalling weather conditions, only taking shelter in extremes, there were occasions when work had to stop completely. Cost Books for the late 18th century indicate fewer balmaidens working in the winter months than in the summer. When George Skerry wrote about the Chiverton Mines in 1799 he described female surface workers only being employed in the summer.[45] At Wheal Cock, during 1822 and 1823, twice as many women were employed between April and November as from December to March.[46] In February 1841, work had to stop at many mines when the dressing floors and apparatus was covered in snow. Again in February 1855, which was described as the worst weather for fifty years, the only tin stamps still working in the parish of St. Just were at Wheal Owles and Boscean. All the other surface workers in the parish were thrown out of work.[47]

Conversely, those women and girls working at water-powered stamps could not work when the water supply was insufficient, often from May to September. At Levant, the dressing floors were short of water in June 1892, and the balmaidens sent home until the dressing floors were operating again. Some mines were able to make use of a temporary solution to water shortages, as at Spearn Consols in 1870:

'Messrs Holman and Son of St. Just have just come to the rescue of the idle 'heads' (stamps) and unoccupied boys and girls. They have a travelling steam engine which rolls alongside the disused stamps, buckles itself to the axles.' [48]

Hours of work and holidays

In the late 18th century and most of the 19th century the balmaidens' working day at the metalliferous mines started at 7 a.m. in summer, and at dawn in winter, except at 'sampling', for about two weeks in every eight, when they started at 6 a.m. They normally finished at 5 p.m. in summer and dusk in winter. Some tasks, such as bucking, sometimes continued for a short while in candlelight during winter, but in general it was not efficient or effective to try to separate ore in poor light. Breaks were allowed during the day with half an hour or an hour for dinner, and sometimes a short break mid-morning called 'crowst'. No time allowances were made for age, so even the youngest girls, of 8 or 9 years old, would be expected to work these hours from the outset.

The hours worked by the women and girls at the clay works, however, were slightly different. Up until 1853, the normal hours of work were eight hours per day, but with many working 'days and quarter' or 'days and half', making ten or twelve hours, and for which they were paid accordingly. In 1853, however, when workers asked for an increase in pay, it was only given in return for extending the standard working day to ten hours. A confusingly persuasive broadsheet was published by the 'clay masters' to counter the complaints of the workers, and the longer working day was adopted.[49]

'A movement seems to have taken place amongst you for an advance of wages, this advance will be given almost to the full extent you ask ... to extend the time if the present days work from 8 to 10 hours; that those less able, or less willing to work than others, may still get, by working three quarters of a day, the same amount of wages as at present - with half an hours less work; and those who are more able, or more willing, may make, if they choose, the full wages of 2s per day.'

Some girls or women were employed by the 'task', at an agreed price, and their working day would finish when the task was completed. At 'sampling' the surface workers, having started an hour early, still might not finish work until 8 p.m. The normal working week was from Monday to Saturday lunchtime, with a half day on the monthly pay-day. This meant that in an average week, the number of hours worked by the women and girls were at least fifty in summer, and forty-five hours in winter. At sampling this could rise to between fifty-five and sixty-five hours.

By 1841, generally, no work was undertaken on Sundays. The exception to this would be where water-powered tin stamps were in operation in areas where water supply was at a premium. In these cases, stamping continued around the clock, seven days a week. Women and girls were then sometimes required to take their turn at the stamps on Sundays. In 1867 there was an attempt to introduce Sunday working on the dressing floors at Condurrow. The surface workers threatened to strike, and the managers withdrew the suggestion.[50]

The women and girls did not usually do shift work as dressing at surface normally only took place during daylight hours. However, girls and women were employed on day and night shifts during the peak of copper production in 1845 at Devon Great Consols, to keep a constant supply of dressed ore ready for shipping from Morwellham Quay.[51] Continual shifts were also worked at the manganese mills there, at this time.[52] Also there were some tin steam operations on the Red River which had continual shifts working day and night.

In the 18th and early to mid 19th century Christmas Day and Good Friday were the only regular holidays during the year, but at some mines Whit Monday or the Parish Feast Day were celebrated as a holiday as well. If these were not official holidays, the women and girls very often used to take unpaid leave, or work in lieu, in order to take part in the celebrations. In some parishes the feast day was an extended holiday, as at St. Just. Here, in the 1840s, three days, Monday to Wednesday, were taken for the carnival, and attendance at the mine was very low on the subsequent Thursday and Friday. [53]

Midsummer's Day was a special day at the mines, when normal work was suspended and there was a general clean up and repair, both below ground and above. One of the tasks was to deck headgear or one of the engine houses with a new flag, or greenery. When all was completed, the workers were given a bonus, and allowed to go early to the local Midsummer Fair. The women and girls received six pence, the men received one shilling. [54]

There were also other less regular celebrations at the mines. The occasion of the christening of a new engine, or the opening of a new mine, was, in effect, another feast day. A grand parade would be arranged through the nearby neighbourhoods, with local bands playing music, and local inhabitants joining the procession to the mine. Mine workers in the procession took their customary order of precedence, with the managers and clerks first, followed by the underground workers, the male surface labourers, and then the women and children. [55] Local dignitaries would also be invited. After the engine was 'christened' and started up, the special guests were entertained to a feast at the counthouse, and the workers provided with a roast ox, and plenty of beer and cider. The rest of the day would be spent celebrating, with games and competitions.

The china clay parishes held an additional annual holiday, usually in the summer months, as described in this report of 1859:

'It is the practice on some day of this season of the year for those employed in the clay works to enjoy a holiday to commemorate the first discovery of clay in the locality; and on Saturday last the persons employed under Mr. John Lovering, working on the lands of Mr. Thomas Gill, walked into the town of St. Austell in procession, headed by a band of music, and after paying a visit to the residence of their employer, they halted outside the Globe Hotel, where the lord of the manor is staying, and gave three hearty cheers for him, when Mr. Gill, with his usual liberality, presented them with a donation, to add to their day's enjoyment.' [56]

Major national events were also celebrated. During national peace celebrations in June 1798, William Jenkin gave a mug of ale to each of his three hundred plus employees at Tincroft. [57] At the end of the long protracted war with the French, celebrations were held at many mines in July of 1814. For instance, at Dolcoath:

'Tables and benches were prepared for 1,500 under the windows of the counting house, where some of the principal adventurers and their friends met to celebrate together with their men, the return of peace. Flags of all nations were displayed throughout the mine, which with innumerable triumphal arches, added much to the gaiety of the scene, and the whole was rendered under a completely cloudless sky. On a signal given by a cannon, the captains marched their companies of men, women and children, preceded by a band of music to their appointed tables: half a loaf, two pounds of beef, and three pints of porter were allotted to each individual.' [58]

Similarly, in June 1856, the end of the Crimean War was celebrated at Wheal Owles with a parade, followed by a huge dinner of beef served outside the Counting House, for all the boys and girls under the age of 15, all 'provided by the purser'. [59]

Rates of pay and methods of payment

The rates of pay for the women and girls at the mines did not change significantly over many years. Levels of pay were never high, compared to the cost of living, and mining families nearly always had to supplement their earnings with other income. If the earnings of the men were low, the balmaidens were consistently paid less, not unusually half of the amount paid to their male counterparts on the dressing floor.

As mentioned before, in the early 'family' mining operations, or where the females were part of the tribute team, it is probable that the majority never received wages, as such. But once employed by the mine management they were paid an agreed rate. Most commonly they were paid for the number of barrows dressed. Alternatively, women and girls were paid at a set rate per day, or for a particular task.

The earliest recorded pay found for females in the mining industry in Cornwall was for women and children washing ore or slag at the silver-lead smelters in Calstock in the early 14th century. The adults were paid between 4d and 6d per week, and their 'assistants' 2d or 3d per week.[60] The next earliest entries were for the barrow women employed at the Calenick Smelter between 1704 and 1707. They were paid about 2d per ton for carrying coal from the shore to the yard, or 6d per day for barrowing and sifting at the smelter. The frequency of payment varies, but they were usually paid every one or two weeks.[61 62]

In the early part of the 18th century it seems that most female workers at the mines, despite their age or task, were paid at a standard rate of 4d per day. This was true at Pool Adit in 1731, where all twenty-one girls or women on the payroll were paid the same.[63] This is consistent with reports of girl and boy pickers at the copper mines being paid 4d per day in 1759.[64] Prior to the keeping of regular cost books (accounts) it is quite possible that mine workers would work for many months without being paid, but sometimes being given loans against their earnings until the mine came into profit. Certainly, the early 18th century cost books do not necessarily record wages being paid every month. Sometimes there is a gap of a month or more. Even after proper accounting records began to be made, mine employees may not have been paid regularly. A cost book for Wheal Comfort, St. Ives, from 1832-34 shows a woman being paid 6s for a total of eleven months work of washing and mending an agent's clothes.[65] This was a long time to wait to be paid.

Subsequently, it appears that the women and girls began to be paid different rates for different tasks, as at Cook's Kitchen in 1766.[66] Girls working there in October were earning either 4d or 5d per day, averaging 7s 4d per month. Similarly, at Wheal Towan in 1772 they were paid between 4d and 6d per day[67], whereas women breaking ore at Wheal Uny in 1773 were all being paid 5d per day.[68]

Increasingly the rates at which the women and girls were paid depended on their age, and the task they were carrying out. At Consolidated Mines in 1836, for instance, girls under 12 years old were paid 8s per month, 12 and 13 year-olds 12s, 14 to 17 year-olds 15s, and those 18 years and over 18s.[69] At Fowey Consols, the average wage of over three hundred females during 1837 was 16s per month, ranging from 8s 8d to £1 3s 10d.[70] Minnie Andrews describes being paid according to her age - 16s at 16, 18s at 18 etc. but up to a maximum of 22s.

Some women and girls were paid by the number of barrows dressed, or were set a daily task of dressing so many barrows in a day. Some form of tally system must have been used to record their payments. Up until about 1870 so few of the women and girls were able to write, or perhaps even add up, that a system of notching tally sticks was probably used, as described by a traveller in 1824:

'The ore ... when raised form the mine, is divided into ... shares; these shares are measured by barrows, an account of which is kept by a person who notches a stick for that purpose.' [71]

The system used was probably the same as that used in the coal mines, where each person delivering a wagon or barrow would carry a stick which was notched for each full wagon or barrow delivered. At the end of a shift the tally stick would be split lengthways, the barrower and the tally clerk both keeping similarly marked portions as their 'tally' for the day. [72]

Conditions of payment could vary even between pay-days. At Wheal Cock, in 1822, bucking maidens received two different rates for bucking - 12d for either 4.5 or 7 barrows - presumably depending on the quality of the ore to be dressed. Some of the same women were also paid at a daily rate, in the same month, as well as by the barrow. [73]

The wages paid reflected the prices that could be obtained at market for the dressed ore, and, in the course of the late 18th century and throughout the 19th century, there were great fluctuations in the prices of copper, tin, and lead. It was not unusual, therefore for employees to have their rates of pay reduced. For instance, at Tresavean in 1841, the amount that the bucking girls were paid went down from 1s for six barrows dressed, to 1s for eight barrows. [74]

Overtime was sometimes available for the girls and women, depending on the backlog of ore waiting to be dressed. It was not normally compulsory, but it was commonly feared that a balmaiden 'might lose her place' if she were to turn it down out of hand. It was not unusual for the older girls to stay on after 5 p.m. for another two hours or so, to buck or cob an extra one or two barrows. For those women who were paid by the day, extra time was paid for by the day. For instance, at Wheal Agar in 1893, the spallers regularly worked up to a total twenty five days per month. [5] In August 1833, Elizabeth Grose, who worked at Ninestones Clay Pit, was paid for a total of thirty one days. [75]

There was overtime available at Consolidated Mines during 1841. [76] Extra work at sampling was not considered overtime, and it was not usual for extra wages to be paid for this. Where overtime was paid, the girls were sometimes allowed to keep it by the family, as pocket money. [77]

Wage levels for the women and girls also varied according to the region, and the overall availability of labour. In 1837, the average wage for surface workers in the Penzance area was 42s per month, and in the Camborne-Redruth area it was 41s, compared with the St. Austell area at 45s. [78] In the 1840s, the wages had increased slightly across the board, but the same pattern could be observed, with the lowest wages paid in the Camborne, Redruth, and St. Agnes area, at 12s per week, compared with 13s in the St. Just area and 14s in East Cornwall/Devon. The most well paid women and girls in 1842 were in the Wendron and Kea areas where the average weekly wage was 18s. It was estimated that 6d per day, or 15s per month, was the amount needed to feed and clothe a young person at this time. [79]

By the 1850s, the youngest girls coming to the mines were being paid 2d or 3d per day while they learnt their trade. It was then increased to 3d or 4d per day (7s per month). This was no more than the women and girls had been earning one century before. [80] Even in 1864, when the Kinnaird Commission was investigating conditions at the mines in Cornwall, they discovered that the women were paid between 8d and 1s per day, and the girls were still receiving between 4d and 6d. [81] The rates paid at the lead and silver mines were very similar, with the women and girls being paid between 6d and 1s per day at New Trelawney Mine in 1867.[82]

Wages at the clay works tended to be kept at roughly the same level as at the tin and copper mines in the same area, in order to prevent losing employees to the mines. There is evidence from the clay works that different groups of women were paid in different ways and at different rates. At any one time, there could be women being paid a daily rate, usually 6d to 8d per day in 1830s, whilst other women were being paid a price per ton that they have cleaned varying between 4d and 5d per ton. Those who were involved in carrying clay out to dry on the hillsides seem to be paid indirectly by a sub-contractor who in turn received 1d per yard of bricks laid out.[83]

In 1873 there was a sudden drop in the price of tin, and by October of that year wages had declined by 20%. In 1880, when tin prices had recovered, it was only after the mine employees in the Camborne area vociferously demanded an increase, that wages were raised again.[84]

In 1893 balmaidens at Dolcoath were being paid 1s to 1s 2d per day for spalling or 4d or 6d per ton.[85] Minnie Andrews remembers being paid between 18s and £1 per month when she was working in the 1890s. In 1893, at Dolcoath, the spalling girls were paid between 3d and 5d per ton, depending on the hardness of the rock, and could break 3 to 5 tons per day, which would earn them 25s to 40s per month, a maximum of under 2s per day. It was observed that they often broke more ore than the men who worked alongside them, who were paid 2s 6d per day. At Wheal Agar in 1893, the spalling women earned 1s 3d per day - half the pay of the men.[5]

From as early as 1720, full-time male employees of a mine were encouraged to pay into the 'sick club', and possibly for a surgeon as well, from their wages. For female employees, paying into the 'sick club' or for a surgeon was either optional or just not on offer. It was considered by the management, and often by the women and girls themselves, as not viable due to their employment not being 'long term', and that the benefits derived would be limited. Although the funds paid into the 'sick club' were used, in part, to pay a mine surgeon, the conditions under which the doctors could treat injured or sick employees, whether at the mine or at home, were often appalling. As early as the 1770s Pryce was recommending that all employees, including the women and children, should contribute 3d per week into a county-wide fund. This would provide £4,500 per annum for specially designated doctors based at a miners' hospital, probably to be based in Redruth.[86] This suggestion was not taken up. From 1794, however, local mine adventurers had been subscribing to the Truro Infirmary, where most of the patients were either injured or sick miners. There was no particular provision for balmaidens but it is possible that some balmaidens were treated there, but on the basis of being 'deserving poor', rather than employees of the mine who had paid into a sick club.

Although it was not the norm, women and girls did pay into a sick club at Dolcoath in the early 1840s, but the managers reported 'it had failed'.[87] However at Fowey Consols, at about the same time, the balmaidens paid 1d from every 5s earned, up to a maximum of 5d. From this subscription they could claim 12s per month if they were ill.[88] In 1864 balmaidens at South Caradon Mine were paying 2d per month 'for the doctor'.[89] At Wheal Agar, in 1893, all the spalling women were paying 6d per month into the 'club',[5] and this had possibly become the norm by this time. A hospital for miners was eventually set up in Redruth in 1863, but there were no facilities for women or girls until 1890. Perhaps those women spallers at Wheal Agar who were paying 6d per week for the sick club, may have been entitled to go there.

In the earliest accounts, for Calstock from 1702-9, surprisingly, the women and their assistants who were washing black slag were paid very regularly. They were paid weekly in arrears, either on a Saturday or a Sunday.[61][62] This was not to be the subsequent pattern in the South West.

General payment of wages was always at least one month in arrears. In some mines employees were required to work for two complete months before payment, and were then paid two months in arrears. An experiment was tried at West Wheal Basset in 1872 to pay the surface workers weekly, but the outcome of that is not known. The first Saturday in the month was traditionally thought of as payday, and the subsequent Monday described as 'Mad' or 'Maze' Monday because of the perceived over-indulgence. However, the *Cornwall and Devon Mining Directory* for 1862 shows that the only consistent thing about payday was that it was monthly. In the parish of Perranzabuloe for instance, at East Wheal Golden, payday was 'the Saturday after the first Friday', at Great Retallack 'the Friday before the first Saturday', and at Wheal Hope 'the Friday before the second Saturday'. It seems pay day could be Friday or Saturday, and fall at any time of the month. In some mines, such as Wheal Vor, the women and children were paid on the Friday evening and the men were paid on the following Saturday morning.[31]

Two penny mining tokens. The one on the left was issued by Scorrier House in 1812 and the one on the right by Devonshire Copper Mines in 1811.

Payment was usually made by the mine purser (bookkeeper) at the counthouse. There was a prescribed hierarchy in the order of payment. It was usual for the tutworkers and tributers to be paid first, followed by the male labourers, then the older women and girls, followed by the children. In the case of the children, they would not normally receive their own pay if there was an older relative working at the same mine. The names of the employees would be recorded in a ledger, and the recipient asked to sign for it, if capable, or to mark with a cross. Most pay ledgers are now lost, but sometimes the names and marks of individual employees appear in the mine cost books. Interestingly, the cost book ledger for Wheal Agar from 1893 to 1898 doesn't just record the names of the employees, but has printed columns for an accumulative total of the numbers of 'girls', boys and men employed in each month.[5]

Various dubious practices took place in the methods of pay. These were often extended to the women and children, and, in some cases, purposely directed at them. Some mines paid in credit notes or tokens that could only be cashed at the mine shop or the counthouse, removing the option of buying cheaper goods elsewhere. Tokens were in use, in particular, between 1811 and 1818. Due to the high price of copper, many of the general currency cartwheel pennies had been taken out of circulation and melted down, leading to a severe shortage of coinage. Some mines began to mint their own pennies, the most notable were those owned by John Williams in the Gwennap area, Dolcoath Mine, West Wheal Fortune in Ludgvan, the Rose Copper Company Mines, and the Great Devon Consols. With rumour that the issuing houses were not redeeming the value of their own coins because of claims that some were forged, all coins of this type were taken out of circulation from 1818.[90] What financial difficulties these tokens may have caused in households dependent on their meagre value is hard to imagine. Particularly vulnerable would have been the lowest paid, i.e. the girls and boys.

At some mines early on, workers were paid, or given 'subsist', by credit at the mine shop, which again meant they were they were having to pay over the odds for their goods. Once in debt at the mine shop, it made it increasingly difficult for them to leave the employment of the mine, and many families were never free of this debt.

Another example of sharp practice was the payment of groups of children together using a large currency note, so that they needed to go to the shop to buy something, in order to obtain change to separate out each child's wages. At Levant, in 1841, groups of 5 or 6 children were paid together with a five pound note plus change, necessitating the note to be exchanged at the shop in this way.[91] In contrast, however, at East Wheal Crofty and at Consolidated Mines it was reported that 'each child was paid the exact sum due to them'.[92]

Most mines recognised that their employees could be in strained financial circumstances, and operated the system of 'subsist' or 'sist'. This was an advance made on the wages, in cases of severe need. The women and girls were allowed to apply for subsist, as well as the men and the boys, and could apply for up to half their wages. This, of course, was deducted from the subsequent wages, and could be applied for from about half way through the month. In 1893, all the spallers at Wheal Agar were applying for their 10s subsist on a regular basis, and seemed to have become a way of being paid fortnightly rather than monthly.[5]

Sometimes workers were not paid at all. The earliest record of this was in 1357, when 'Abraham the Tinner' failed to pay his three hundred men, women and children working at his four enterprises at Crukbargis. Much later, when two men from Illogan took over a lease for water stamps near South Condurrow in 1878, they employed several children to help with the tin dressing. However, once the ore was dressed the men took it to be sold, and were never seen again. Needless to say the children remained unpaid.[93]

When mines were failing, it was not uncommon for the wages not to arrive from the bank. This often happened with no warning to the workers, or sometimes even the purser. This left mine employees being owed one month's wages, or sometimes two, with no means of redress. Sometimes, the mine captains or pursers found a token amount of money from their own pockets for those most in need. When work at Boscaswell Downs suddenly stopped in 1874, three hundred employees including 'men and women, girls and boys drawn from every strata of the hierarchy from the chief ore dresser … to the counthouse cleaners were left with two months wages due.'[94]

As the mine was probably already mortgaged, little hope was held out that any of the workers would gain any compensation. Although under Stannary Law, the mine employees had first priority for payment, in practice mortgages and loans were usually honoured first. These employees were all severely affected by the loss of two months' wages.

'From what has now transpired it would seem that the mine must have been for some time getting into difficulties and it is stated that the plant has been heavily mortgaged … when Saturday week came, which was pay day, the unfortunate employees found there was no money forthcoming to pay them. According to the usual system of paying monthly and holding a months wages in hand, they were minus each two months pay.' [95]

A similar situation arose with the closure of Pednandrea and Wheal Prussia a few months later:

'Distress in the Redruth Area: The fact that the men and girls not having been paid on the regular pay day, has also added to the evil, there being two months kept in hand at the mines.' [96]

In desperation, when it became obvious that a mine was in difficulties, some mine employees filed petitions to the Vice-Warden of the Stannaries for the winding up of the mines for which they worked, in the hope, presumably of gaining some recompense. This was the course of action taken by the men and women of Boscaswell Downs:

'And so on Monday, the resumption of work under such circumstances being out of the question, something like 200 of them - men and women, girls and boys - came into Penzance, a distance of six miles, in a body, and applied for summonses. Meantime the case is one of extreme hardship. The loss of two months wages will leave nearly the whole of those who sort aid of the law on Thursday practically penniless.' [97]

In a similar case in April 1874, involving Budnick Mining Consols at Perranzabuloe, of the fifteen petitioners to the Stannary Court, four were women employed at the mine: Catherine Warne, Grace Penna, Ellen Higgins and Frances Trebilicock.[98] It is unlikely that any of these cases received any recompense.

Industrial relations

With the advent of mining unions elsewhere in the UK during the mid and late 1860s Cornwall was to remain steadfastly 'un-unionised' until the mid 1870s. The tribute system, which was competitive between groups of miners, as to who would take work for the lowest price, tended to mitigate against corporate action. This meant that the Cornish workforce were entirely dependent on the goodwill of the managers and adventurers in terms of working conditions and pay. They rarely had any realistic power to influence decisions, with others always being ready to take their places should they be dismissed.

Relationships between the mine owners and employees were particularly fragile at Devon Great Consols, Devon's largest copper mine. Disputes had arisen between the women and children working on the dressing floors and management on several occasions in the late 1840s, with regards to wage levels. Wages paid to the pickers had remained at 10d per day during 1847, despite desperate food shortages, due to failure of the potato and turnip crop, and massive increases in the price of wheat, from 10s to 30s per cwt. Eventually the mine owners agreed to increase the pay by 2d, to 1s per day. However, as wheat prices dropped in 1849, they reduced the pay to the original 10d, and then in January 1850 threatened to reduce the wages again to 9d. John Henry Murchison described the response of the surface workers:

'I had scarcely arrived at my first visit (January 1850) than 200 of these youngsters of both sexes came clamouring to the counting house complaining that their wages had been 'cut' and that they could not live on 10s 6d a week.' [99]

The 200 pickers working on the dressing floor walked out and went home in protest. When they arrived at the mine the following morning, the gates were locked and they were told they were no longer needed. Murchison describes the scene the following morning:

'On the second day they presented themselves and offered to resume work on any terms. They were, in fact, engaged at 1d/day less than was given to the strangers and those who had not misconducted themselves.' [99]

So despite their efforts, the women and children ended up worse off rather than better as a result of their actions.

As the Cornish miners became more politicised there was an increasing number of strikes recorded from the 1870s. Even after the establishment of unions in the county in the mid 1870s, it seems that the membership lay with the men, and little was done by way of protecting the employment rights of the women workers. Particular causes of dissatisfaction among the female workers were the ore prices rising without subsequent increase in wages, or male surface workers being paid significantly more for similar work. The women and girls working at Dolcoath went on strike for higher wages in September 1871.[100] The girls at surface at Wheal Basset Mines also went on strike in January 1872 for an increase in pay from 9d to 11d per day, as tin prices rose to unprecedented heights.[101] In the following June surface workers at Ding Dong Mine went out on strike over working hours.[102]

In 1877, there was also trouble at West Seton when management wanted to increase working hours for the same pay:

'The executive at West Seton resolved that the girls employed in dressing copper should work half an hour longer per day, and not leave off until half-past five, instead of five o'clock as before. The management say that the girls cannot work a full day in winter and therefore, they should be willing to work a little longer in summer. The new rule was to begin on Monday last, but the girls left precisely at five o'clock as before. On Friday morning two or three were turned off for leaving before time on Thursday, and because of this all the rest, numbering nearly a hundred, struck and walked to Camborne, singing Sankey's hymns, and otherwise amusing themselves.

On Saturday most of the pickers (the younger girls) went to work again, but the older ones, numbering about fifty, remain out on strike. The girls employed in the tin-yard have always worked until half-past five.' [103]

This situation was not resolved in the balmaidens favour in this case either. Married women returned to their original hours, but for reduced pay. The single women had to work the extra half-hour for the same pay.

When tin ore prices were again improved in 1880, there was a series of strikes in the Camborne Mines by the surface workers, asking for their share in the increased profit. Mr. M. G. Penrose, one of the adventurers at Dolcoath, tried to persuade the management to increase the wages of the women and girls. As an act of goodwill, he actually gave the balmaidens, over one hundred of them, an extra 1s out of his private purse. [104] The strike had started at Dolcoath, and spread to Cook's Kitchen, Tincroft, and some of the other mines, resulting in a march through Camborne. A subsequent increase in pay was granted by the adventurers, and this was one of the few occasions when striking workers were able to negotiate better working conditions. [105]

The working environment

Both from the descriptions of earlier years, and the photos of later years, it is clear that the working environment on the dressing floors was noisy, dirty, dangerous and chaotic. A visit to a present day quarry or workings may give us some idea of the noise, mud, and dust. Dressing floors were never tidy or clean places, and, in the days of the balmaiden, rarely purpose-built. They would have developed in a haphazard fashion, according to requirements, water supply and general topography in a very 'Heath Robinson' sort of way, but with some degree of logic and intuitive ergonomics.

All of the surviving photographs of balmaidens at work show the very crude working environment, but none more so than the one of the dressing floor of St. Ives Consols taken in the mid 1860s. From the picture, it can be seen that all the surface workers have to pick their way through mud and slippery surfaces, with only narrow walkways, between hazardous pools, tanks and piles of ore and waste. The balmaidens themselves seem to perch precariously on the narrow planks between their racking frames, some three to six feet above the ground. This following 'word picture', probably penned in 1853, gives us a flavour of the environment:

'Looking around we may see vast heaps of rubbish, interspersed with clusters of wooden sheds, among which streams of water are flowing in nearly all directions. Men and boys may also be dressing ores; but the most conspicuous of the persons there engaged are young women and girls'. [106]

For the best part of a century, from 1720 onwards, most of the work was done in the open air, exposed to all weathers. The engraving of Dolcoath Mine by Allom, dated about 1831, shows picking, spalling, cobbing and bucking all being done outside, with a few women possibly working under cover.

Pictures and photos of the 1850s and 1860s show racking being carried out under open fronted sheds. Whereas the photos of women and girls taken from the 1870s onwards show them in charge of groups of racking frames in the open air. It tended to be the larger mines which provided shelters for cobbing and bucking, and sometimes for the pickers as well. In

St. Ives Consols dressing floors in 1863, showing girls working at the racking frames, and clearly illustrating the hazardous and dirty working conditions.

Courtesy of Paddy Bradley

the smaller mines there was usually less provision. Even as late as 1864, however, many large mines were not providing even the basic necessities in terms of shelter for work.

'Where the comforts of those employed are attended to, the women and children work under cover of wooden sheds with glass let into the roof, but with many, even in the large mines, they are needlessly exposed to the inclemency of the weather'.[107]

The spalling women always seem to have worked in the open air, from the earliest days until in the early 20th century. Muriel Sara describes how balmaidens working at the tin streams in the late 1890s would be allowed to take shelter in the dinner shed only if it rained heavily, implying that they continued work in the open in light or moderate rain:

'If there was an extremely heavy shower or it was croust time, then the maidens gathered in a big long shed to sit around the fire in a corner, drinking strong tea out of terrible old cracked mugs, almost as brown as their tea.' [108]

At least one 20th century writer noticed that the machinery and engines were afforded more shelter and protection than the workers:

'There may have been something picturesque and romantic about quaintly dressed balmaidens, accompanied by the lusty youths who did the more laborious part of the work in the dressing floors, scattered about the moors and valleys of Cornwall, but the life was hard, the pay small, and in winter exposure to the storms in the open air meant, all too often, suffering and hardship. The engines and boilers were housed, the stamps and buddles were in the open; the burning house and tin house were the only other parts covered in. What would be expected in the way of efficiency when working under conditions of such exposure?' [109]

Balmaidens were not issued with any uniform or clothes for work and would be expected to provide their own. However they were provided with tools and equipment. The initial cost of these would be charged to the tributers, including any repairs or sharpening of the tools. The girls would be expected to report to the tool house on arrival at the mine, to be issued with the tools they might need - bucking or cobbing hammer, barrow, rake, fork, shovel or sieve. They would then have to return them at the end of the working day.

Noon was the traditional time for dinner at the mines. It was usually half an hour, and at some mines this was extended to one hour in the summer. Most surface workers ate their mid day meal (crib) at the mine; it was not usual for employees to go home, even if they lived close by. An exception to this was Wheal Friendship in Devon where the mine agent reported 'the principle part of the girls reside very near the mine, and generally go home for their meals'.[110] Food was not provided at the mines for the many who stayed; the workers would bring their own. In the early days the mines did not even provide a place of shelter (crib house) for the surface workers to eat, or provide any drinking water. In cold or wet weather they would find what warmth and shelter they could around the dressing floors, in the engine house, the dry (where underground workers' clothes were dried) or the smithy.

By 1841, some mines were allowing the women and children to warm their food in the dry, and providing a small barrel of water, as at Consolidated Mines.[111] At Carnon Mines, there were two small sheds where the workers could eat. Pasties could be warmed in an oven attached to the furnace, and they could also heat water to make tea.[112] At Dolcoath, dinner sheds had been provided for all the surface workers by 1864:

'We have four establishments with a large enough oven in each of them to contain 200 pasties or hoggins. Then we have benches around a long room where they can sit down, and hot water is always prepared by dinner time'. [113]

It was reported that some mines made a charge for the use of these ovens, as at Fowey Consols, where 1d per week was deducted from the surface workers' pay. [114]   Later in 1864 the Kinnaird Commission was particularly impressed with arrangements for eating at North Roskear Mine:

'There are six dining houses on the floors. This prevents a large number congregating together. These houses have in them an open fire, and also an oven with shelves in it for warming the dinners. Half an hour before the bell rings for the hands to leave work, one of the girls for each house goes in, prepares the fire, boils the kettle, makes the tea, puts the pasties in the oven etc, so that when the bell rings and the dressers go in, they can sit down to a warm meal at once'. [114]

Interestingly, at East Caradon no provision for dinner sheds was made 'on purpose' - implying that this would encourage time-wasting.[115]   It was also reported that there was no special provision for warming dinners at the lead mines in Menheniot where the surface workers used the engine house. The discomfort of eating cold food in the open air on a cold or wet day was noted:

'At some of the larger mines sheds are provided for young people to dine in, also small ovens in which to warm the pasties. Otherwise they dine in the open air, and when the weather is chilly and their dinners consist of cold fish or vegetable pasties, their lot is anything but enviable.' [116]

Although the Commissioners of 1864 strongly recommended the provision of dinner sheds, concern for the conditions under which the mine workers laboured was still being expressed two decades later. This letter appeared in the *West Briton* in 1887:

'Sir, It has occurred to me that if some hot refreshment were served out on the mines at suitable times to the miners and also to the women and girls, who now work so cheerfully and uncomplainingly at the drudgery (and in all kinds of weather), that it will do more good to them than one can first imagine, and no doubt prolong their lives very considerably indeed. The miners, who have to leave their homes in the early hours of the morning, and then walk some of them four or five miles to work, should be able to obtain their cups of coffee, cocoa, milk or soup on the mine, at a very small charge when they desire it, before they go to or return from their work.' [117]

It is not known that any mine made this provision other than Dolcoath 1836-1841, when soup was provided for the underground workers only.[118]

A senior girl or woman was responsible for going to the sheds to prepare the tea and warm food which the others had brought. Mixing of the women and girls with the boys and men at crowst or lunch time was not encouraged, so different dinner sheds were built for the different groups. Minnie Andrews was one of the women who was given the task of making preparations for the dinner.[40] Similarly, when the women were brought in to work on the picking belt at Geevor during World War Two, they could make their own tea in the tea shed, but had to make their own arrangements for a mid-day meal.[119]

No reference has yet been found to the provision of appropriate private toilet facilities for the women and girls. It was accepted that the men and boys below ground just used any abandoned corner. In later days, a latrine, colloquially referred to as 'the parson's house', was erected for the male surface workers. For the most part, presumably, the women and girls had to 'make do' as best they could.

In general, although self-interest was a major motivation for the mine adventurers, there were also occasions where philanthropic concerns surfaced. For instance, the mine managers sometimes provided emergency supplies in times of desperate need, and widowed women and their children often seem to have been priority for employment. During the food shortages of the 'hungry' 1840s, and later in 1867, some mine captains obtained wheat flour or bread in bulk, which they sold on to their employees at reduced prices. Some required repayment by the miners when times improved, others absorbed the shortfall in cost themselves.[120] However, despite some charitable actions on behalf of the mine owners and managers, the provision for the comfort and well-being of the mine employees was usually minimal.

'A mine spreads out its vast machinery.
Here engines, with their huts and smokey stacks,
Cranks, wheels, and rods, boilers and hissing steam,
Pressed up the water from the depths below.
Here fire-whims ran till almost out of breath,
And chains cried sharply, strained with fiery force.
Here blacksmiths hammered by the sooty forge,
And there a crusher crashed the copper ore.
Here girls were cobbing under roofs of straw,
And there were giggers at the oaken hutch.
Here a man-engine glided up and down,
A blessing and a boon to mining men:
And near the spot where, many years before,
Turned round and round the rude old water-wheel,
A huge fire-stamps was working evermore,
And slimey boys were swarming at the trunks.
The noisy lander by the trap-door bawled
With pincers in his hand; and troops of maids
With heavy hammers brake the mineral stones.
The cart-man cried, and shook his broken whip;
And on the steps of the account-house stood
The active agent, with his eye on all'.

From 'Labyrinths' by John Harris, Cornish Miner 1820-84

Chapter 3

BALMAIDENS AT HOME

Balmaidens' lives were set within the context of the mining communities, where the daily routine, outlook and attitudes revolved almost entirely around the mine. This description from the early 19th century gives the feel of one such village:

'Early in the morning the scene becomes animated. From the scattered cottages, as far as the eye can reach, men, women and children of all ages, begin to creep out; and it is curious to observe them all converging like bees towards the small hole at which they are to enter the mine. On their arrival, the women and children, whose duty it is to dress, or clean the ore, repair to the rough sheds under which they work. (In the evening)... as soon as the men come to grass they repair to the engine house to wash ... and put on their clothes. By this time the maidens and little boys have also washed their faces, and the whole party migrates across the fields in groups, and in different directions to their respective homes'. [1]

The way in which the mine impinged on their daily consciousness is also captured in these words about Gunnislake, in the Tamar Valley:

'The bell from the count house on the mine opposite (the Devon bank), provided a timepiece for the workers in the field, for those men waiting to go on core. For all of these the counthouse bell spaced out the day and the night.' [2]

Housing conditions and family economy

The majority of balmaidens lived at home with their families. The very youngest, of course, were still dependent on the support of their parents, and even for older girls it was not the custom to live independently before marriage. Balmaidens who did not marry, and continued to work at the mine, also usually continued to live at home. Only the married or widowed balmaidens might be living independently in their own homes. There were also a small number of balmaidens, such as Mary Ann Roscorla at Tresavean Mine, who had no supporting family and who lived in lodgings. [3]

In Cornwall and West Devon it was not usually the practice for mining companies to provide housing or communal lodging houses for their employees, as it was in other parts of the country. This was probably due, in part, to the short term contractual nature of the tribute system, which meant that individual miners were only tied to a particular mine for two months at a time. It may also be because the miners often needed to supplement their income through other seasonal employments, which at certain times of the year took them away from mine employment. As miners' wages were so low and unpredictable, many families cultivated a smallholding, or took part in the local fishing industry. In 1842, one in ten of the miners in the St. Just area, for instance, had a part-interest in a seining team. Both fishing and agriculture required seasonal input of labour, and Cornish miners were well known for arranging their mine work around their land and sea harvests. This pattern of work was not conducive to mining companies providing housing for their workforce. An exception to this was when the Duke of Bedford built two hundred and fifty cottages at Tavistock, Gulworthy and Morwhellham for his workers at Devon Great Consols, between 1850 and 1860. This was after public protests at the terrible overcrowding and squalor in these communities. The rent for these cottages was 1s 3d per week, plus 1d for a stove.[4]

Generally, however, mining families had to build their own homes where they could. In the early days, when mining concerns were small, the head of a mining household would usually build some simple dwelling within the confines of the tin or copper bound that had been leased. As the mines grew larger and required more hands, local families came to work from their existing homes, or new workers migrated from the rural parishes. Before the *Enclosure Acts* of the end of 18th century and beginning of 19th century, new families moving into an area had the right to build a home on common land if they could build it overnight. In practice this meant erecting a temporary shack, and having a fire burning in its chimney before dawn. The cottage could then be built properly with time. These were called 'sun-rising houses'. After the *Enclosure Acts*, families would negotiate a lease of a non-productive corner of land from a landowner, in order to build. These early cottages were usually cob built with thatched roofs, and often only had one room, with a 'talfat', a platform reached by a ladder for beds or storage. Later, from about 1840, miners began to build more substantial and larger stone houses, some with two rooms downstairs, and two rooms upstairs. However, these often accommodated more than one family. The lease with the landowner was generally for 'three lives', sometimes with the option to buy additional 'lives' at the time of signing the agreement. Three named persons would be recorded on the lease, and it was valid for their lifetime. It was not until about the 1880s, along with other working class families, that the mining families in Cornwall began to have the luxury of more than about four rooms for their accommodation.

The plots of land on which the early miners' cottages were built were usually of one acre or more, with the intention that it could be brought into cultivation. Clearing these rocky and often steep corners was a mammoth task in itself. The whole family would be involved in maximising the production from this smallholding, each with his or her own particular tasks. The main crops were potatoes for human consumption and for feeding livestock, wheat or barley, and turnips. Land left uncultivated was sometimes used to keep a cow or a pony, the latter to be rented to the mine for transporting ore, and most families planted a few apple or plum trees. Normally a family would hope to raise a pig to supply ham and bacon at Christmas time, with some salted down in a bussa (a large earthenware pot for salting fish or meat) for the rest of the year. Some of the meat would usually be sold to buy a replacement pig for the following year. It was said that the Cornish found a use for every part of the pig except its squeal! Many villages had a pig club so that miners could buy and sell pigs co-operatively. If a family was able to raise two pigs in a year, the extra income made a great difference to the economy of that family:

'The miner was thus always secure of a good supply of potatoes and other vegetables. The quantity of potatoes which he produced was frequently not only sufficient for the consumption of his family but also for the feeding of one or two pigs. When he killed his pig generally at Christmas, he would sell enough of it to enable him to buy another young pig or two. If he killed two pigs he would sell enough to enable him to pay the rent for his plot of ground for the year. The chief

advantage was that in many cases it enabled the parents to send the children for some part of the day to school.' [5]

Where these miners' plots were situated on very poor land cultivation would be extremely difficult. The families might resort to growing pillas, a small grained naked oat which would grow in very poor soils, and perhaps keep goats or sheep. Throughout Cornwall pillas was commonly grown, on small patches of land which were too poor to grow wheat or barley, up until the 20th century.

Seining for pilchards, would also have a significant effect on the economy of the household. In a good year, a share in a seining team would provide high protein winter food, cheap 'train' (pilchard) oil for rush lights, and, hopefully, extra income from the surplus.

Unlike other mining communities, where housing was offered along with work, once a Cornish miner had invested money and effort in building a home and clearing a plot for cultivation it was unlikely that a family would want to leave. This meant that the whole family was dependent on the availability of local employment, and, if the local mines failed, mine employees would usually choose to travel considerable distances for work, rather than move. It was not uncommon for balmaidens to walk up to six miles to work and back, although most walked about three or four miles each day.

Not all mining families, however, lived in a rural situation. From the mid 18th century, mining towns began to develop around the chief mining centres, with more limited opportunities for food production, and with all the attendant health hazards of industrial areas. These are words from an anonymous traveller, in June 1795:

'Redruth is a long town, near a mile long, in a Vale in the center of the mines, so that it is in a Cloud of Smoak, which is the reason we did not breakfast ... Camborne to Penzance: The country is filled with smoke from the number of steam engines. The whole country in these parts consists of Tin, Lead and Copper Mines, with few trees, no fruit trees nor vines, and very little corn, but a great number of goats'. [6]

With six to twelve children per family being normal during the 19th century, mining households must have been very crowded and busy. These households often had lodgers, in-laws, or married children, living with them as well. Where possible a 'linney' or lean-to was added to the house to give extra accommodation. Even so, how these tiny cottages and houses accommodated so many is hard to imagine. The situation would have been eased slightly where the men and underground boys were working different 'cores' (shifts), so that they would not all be home at the same time. There were three cores in a day, starting at 6 a.m., 2 p.m., and 10 p.m., and for those working in the same tribute team, there would be family members taking over from each other at each shift. Those on early shift would be sleeping overnight, and home for the main family meal in the evening. Those on the afternoon shift would also be sleeping overnight, but those on night shift would be taking over the vacated beds of the early shift workers when they came home in the morning. So there was a saying in Cornwall that 'in mining parishes beds were never cold'. As one group of men and boys left for work, another would be returning. Balmaidens, however, did not normally work shift patterns in this way, so the female ore dressers in one household would almost certainly be working the same hours, 7 a.m. until 5 p.m., unless at sampling.

In these crowded and busy households, privacy for these young girls and women must have been at a premium. It would be a very exceptional home for a balmaiden to have a bed of her own, let alone a bedroom of her own. At best, most would be sharing beds with their sisters, or other female members of the household, in a room set aside for them. At worst, they may have been sharing the same sleeping space as parents or members of the opposite sex, including lodgers, as reported by the 1842 Employment Commission:

'The houses are too small to admit proper separation of sleeping rooms and it often happens ... that men come from a distance and lodge with families, in which case they frequently sleep in the same room with the females'. [7]

There was no internal sanitation or water supply to these miners' cottages. Once the water supplies of the area were being drawn off and paid for by the mines, it seems that water supply for domestic use was often a problem. Sometimes the younger members of the household had to walk many miles to obtain water, as one of their evening tasks. The lamentable lack of water supply to each household was noted even as late as 1864:

'The absence in most instances of a good supply of water owing to its being drawn off at the low levels by the pumping engines at the mines is a drawback to sanitary improvements.' [8]

All the members of the household would have to wash at the stone sink in the kitchen, or outside near the well or pump, if there was one. Hot water was a luxury, usually just for bath time once a week if they were lucky. Prior to about 1780 there was probably no privy at all, with the family having to make do with a system of buckets to be emptied in a piece of the land set aside for such purposes. Subsequently, there might be a shed down the garden somewhere. Clothes were washed by hand in the linney or outside, or at the warm water outlet from the engines at the mine. They would then be laid out on the ground or on bushes to bleach and dry. A water supply to the house, and a flushing outside toilet, were probably luxuries not experienced by most balmaidens until late in the 19th century, if then.

The balmaiden, however old or young, would contribute a vital part of the household economy. Her earnings were a crucial element in the survival of the family. Her role of worker was important, and would take her away from the home from early in the morning until mid-evening, and yet she would also have domestic duties at home, as a female member of the household. In 1841, some of the balmaidens described having such duties at home as needlework, preparing food, and collecting water. Patty Tremellin told how she, as a young girl, had to prepare food and clean the house, as well as carry out nursing duties, on her return from the mine. Balmaidens' tasks would also include childcare, and assisting with cultivation of crops or tending animals on the family smallholding.

Just as the boys were 'groomed' for a life at the mines from an early age, being given toy mining tools and encouraged to play mining games or solve mining puzzles with their elders, it is very likely that girls were prepared in the same way too.

The daily routine

Balmaidens, regardless of age, usually started work at 7 a.m. Most would have to get up by 6 a.m., and those who lived three or four miles or more from the mine would have to get up even earlier, some as early as 4 a.m. During sampling, the women and girls started work an hour earlier still, which would require a 3 a.m. start for some. Because of the long walk and the strenuous working day ahead of them, the girls would try to have breakfast before leaving. In reality, however, it was usually a very basic affair, consisting of some barley bread or pillas with water, or, if they were lucky, some milk. Pillas would be set to sprout and was toasted and then ground to make a porridge. In times of real hardship they would leave home without having had anything to eat at all. One widowed woman, left with small children to support, who took up work at Wheal Bassett, spoke of sometimes leaving the house and children with no food at all in the morning, only buying food after a day's work and having claimed 'subsist'. [9]

The balmaidens would also need to prepare the food that they would take to the mine, unless they lived sufficiently nearby that food could be brought by younger brothers or sisters later in the day. If taking their own food, it would invariably be either a pasty or a hoggan. The hoggan was probably a good poverty indicator over the years, reappearing when wheat prices were high, to be replaced by the more favoured pasty when times were not so hard. The hoggan was made of unleavened barley bread, with a little green pork or potato set in it. The sweet version of this was the fuggan, made with dried fruit (figs). It was generally very indigestible and very poor fare. In 1841, one mine agent described hoggans as 'hard as street tiles'! [10] The pasty, which was much more nutritious and easier to eat, had

Cornish balmaidens according to Simonin in *La Vie Souterraine* (1867) showing contrasting apparel.

its outer pastry made from wheat flour, would certainly contain potato and turnip, and, with luck, a little pork, ham, or even mutton. Grace Bowden and Martha Williams both took pasties with them for their dinner at Trethellan Mine.[11] The balmaidens would pack their pasty or hoggan in a white linen 'flour bag' tied with a piece of string, known as a 'crib-bag'[12] or 'frail'.[13]   Inside their crib-bag they would usually slip a smaller one containing some dried mugwort or pennyroyal for their tea, then they would tie the bag around their waist or under their skirts. At some mines, the tea making was done communally, so that each balmaiden would need to provide her own cup, make a contribution towards the cost of a kettle, and take it in turns to provide 'tea' for the group. Those that could not afford this, drank hot water.[14]

Going to work in summer, the women and girls would wear a light calf-length dress, covered with their best apron, plus a gook or bonnet, and what was, usually, their only pair of shoes. In winter they would wear a heavier, warmer dress covered with a shawl, a felt bonnet, and possibly boots if they had any. They would also carry with them their food for the day, their change of apron if they had one, and protective gloves or leg bands to put on at the mine. They probably had a handkerchief and some knitting or crochet tucked into a pocket.

They would have to walk up to six miles to the mine, in all weathers, normally walking in family groups, and collecting friends on the way. Many of the mines in Cornwall were in wild, exposed places - either on remote moors, or out on headlands or cliffs. This made spectacular walking in good weather, and atrocious, sometimes dangerous, conditions in bad weather. These groups of balmaidens were renowned for their singing, as they made their way to and from the mine.

Once at the mine, the balmaiden's working hours were regulated by the mine bell, which marked the beginning and ends of shifts, crowst and dinner time. Some mines allowed a short break during the morning around ten o'clock, but their main dinner break was at mid-day. For those who lived close to the mine this was the time for meeting up with the sisters or brothers who had brought their food. They may well have been brought a hot meal of fish or potato stew and were probably the envy of those who had to eat cold hoggans or pasties. Where more than one member of a family was working at a mine, it was usual for them to gather together for their meal. Otherwise, the surface workers were strictly segregated by gender at this time.

After eating, there was usually time for recreation. The youngest girls would play various games together if they had the energy. This was the time when some of the most serious accidents occurred on the dressing floor, with young people 'off their guard' and forgetting the dangers of moving machinery. The older girls and women would bring their needlework, and chat. It was also a good opportunity to try and talk to the men and the boys, although this was generally discouraged by the management.

In a few mines, balmaidens who lived close to 'the bal' went home for dinner. This was particularly the case at Wheal Friendship, Devon, when in 1864 it was reported that so many went home that no special provision was made for people to stay.[15]

There was no afternoon break, and most of the balmaidens finished work around 5 p.m. unless it was sampling time. Working at surface was always a very dirty job, with dust in dry weather and mud in winter. The tin ore, especially, left its unique red-orange stain on clothes and skin alike. The girls and women would do their best to clean up before leaving the mine, finding some source of relatively clean water in which to wash their hands and faces. They would change from their working 'towsers' into their best aprons, before leaving, and then carry their working aprons home, over their arm.

On arrival home, usually their mother or an older sister would have prepared the main meal for the day. Seated around the family table in the evening would be the men, women, boys and girls who had just come home from the mine, plus those boys and men about to go out for the night shift. The meal would be basic, based on the few home-grown vegetables and fruit, and meat or fish as available. Potatoes, boiled or roasted, were the mainstay, with parsnips or turnips, served with 'tea' made from mugwort. In season, there might be apples or plums from their own small orchard. In the coastal areas, especially if the family had an interest in a seining team, there would be salted pilchards to see them through the winter. Alternatively, dried Newfoundland cod was sometimes bought for the main meal, and served as niflin or towrag. In season there might also be fresh fish, usually conger, pilchards or mackerel.

After this simple communal supper, the balmaidens would then have their own domestic duties to complete before bedtime. Depending on their age, they would go to bed between 7 p.m. and 10 p.m. Working clothes were not washed during the week, as the women and girls normally only had one set. If wet, they would be hung up around the fire to dry overnight, as best they may. Often they were still damp when the girls came to wear them the following morning.

The balmaiden and her earnings

Some balmaidens never saw their earnings, either because they were not paid individually, their wages forming part of the total earning of the tribute team, or because their wages were collected by the adults in their family. In these cases, they may have been given pocket money to spend. Other balmaidens collected their wages for themselves, but would usually hand the total amount over to their parents or parent, out of which, again, they may have been given some money to spend. In some families, depending on their economic circumstances, girls were allowed to keep their overtime pay.

However, around the age of 18 or 19, they would usually come to an agreement with their parents over an amount to pay for board and lodging, and then be allowed to keep the rest. The average amount for board and lodging in 1841 was about 14s per month from earnings of about 18s.[16] Some balmaidens, of course, were independent of their families. When Grace Bowden was working at Trethellan in 1841, she was paying 6d per day for her board and lodgings in Lanner when her earnings were 9d per day.[17] These older girls and women, who were able to keep more than just 'pocket money', usually started saving for their marriage.

On pay day, the girls often treated themselves to some small luxury out of their pocket money, if they had any. Sometimes the pursers at the mine did not pay the girls separately but as a group, so they had to go to the mine shop to buy something, before they could share out their wages. If they were wise, however they would resist buying at the mine shop as items could be up to 25% more expensive than at the market or village shop. Pay day was usually market day, and at some mines the market was set up in the immediate vicinity, with stalls selling food, clothes, household items and trinkets. Invariably, the packman, 'Johnny Fortnight' or Johnny-go-Fortnight', would also turn up on pay day, and regularly in between. This travelling salesman would not ask for cash payment for an expensive item, but entice the girls to buy, allowing them to pay by fortnightly or monthly instalments.

Some balmaidens, of course, were lured into agreements that they could not fulfil, ending up in court, not having understood the nature of the debt they had taken on. However, the girls and women would mostly buy small items such as handkerchiefs, ribbons, brooches, or earrings. Balmaidens also treated themselves in other ways. Minnie Andrews described how on pay day, she and her friends would 'call at Brea Inn for a penny glass of porter'.[18] As an alternative to getting into debt with Johnny Packman, the young girls sometimes took the initiative and formed a 'Dress Club' enabling them to buy special clothes, which they then took turns in wearing, much to the disapproval of the local clergy.[19]

Dressed for the occasion

It seems that balmaidens made little additions to their working clothes as a mark of their individuality, but when eventually released from their working environment at the week-end, liked to make rather bolder fashion statements. Victorian commentators certainly had much to say about the way in which balmaidens spent their earnings on clothes. Simonin, visiting from France, and writing in 1867, makes the following rather strange observations and, as the text is accompanied by an illustration of Cornish ore dressers one assumes he is referring to the balmaidens, but some of his meaning appears to have been lost in the translation:

'In England, the women and girls either do not sing, or if they do, they often sing out of tune. To make up for this however, they are dressed coquettishly like regular ladies, wearing on their hair the cornette, or the net, and elegant and well fitting boots on their feet'.[20]

Many Victorian commentators remarked on how well dressed the miners, and especially the mining women were on Sundays or holidays, with the inevitable insinuation that they were dressed 'above their station', and beyond their means. This description comes from the pen of R.M. Ballantyne in his novel *Deep Down* and is more neutral in its attitude:

Cartoon sketches from the 1870s, contrasting the balmaidens' dress for work and for Sunday best, by George Seymour Jnr.

Courtesy of the Mining Journal

'No one who entered the Wesleyan Chapel of St. Just that morning for the first time could have imagined that a large proportion of the well-dressed people who filled the pews were miners and balmaidens. Some of the latter were elegantly - we might say - gorgeously attired, insomuch that, but for their hands and speech, they might almost have passed for ladies of fashion. The very latest thing in bonnets, and the newest mantles, were to be seen on their pretty heads and shapely shoulders'. [21]

Seymour has left us with a wonderful glimpse of this transformation, from working days and weekend, in his cartoons of 1877 entitled "Balmaiden Friday" and "Balmaiden Saturday". These should possibly read "Balmaiden Saturday" and "Balmaiden Sunday", as are the L. Adams watercolours of the same drawings held by the RIC. Apart from owning a 'best' dress for Saturdays or Sundays, and their working clothes, in the 'good times' balmaidens might also have a second best for wearing to church meetings and other activities during the week. Money was always at a premium, but the women and girls made sure that the pennies spent on jewellery, ribbons or lace were creatively invested.

Dressed for work

Although many Victorian commentators remark on the neatness and cleanliness of the women and girls working at the mines, their tasks could not possibly have kept them clean. Working with ores, wet or dry, is a messy business. Workers with tin ore, for example, became covered with a russet dust or deposit, which stained badly. In most of the earliest photographs the balmaidens all look very clean, but are posing in their clean 'walking out' aprons, without their protective leg, arm or hand coverings. Only in post-1890 photographs do we begin to see them as they really were, in their grubby hessian 'towsers'. [22]

We may conclude that clothing worn to the mine would be long past first or even second-best, and were probably hand-me-downs. It was considered lucky for boys going underground for the first time to have a new duck suit to wear, but it is unlikely that new clothes were made in the same way for the boys or girls working at surface. They would presumably wear old everyday clothes, modified for wearing at the mine. A visitor to Dolcoath mine in 1893 describes the balmaidens' clothes in this way:

'The balmaidens had not the white sunbonnets and almost spotless apron which they sometimes wear at their work; for here they work in the open and had to cope with the drenching rain. But their faded dresses, of varied hues, which at one time were smart 'Sunday best close' and their coarser sack aprons and padded home made cloth gloves (to prevent their hands from being galled by the hammers with which they spalled the stone) were an admirable match for our white 'cappen's [23] *suits'.'* [24]

An early Victorian traveller and writer, describing women at the Cornish mines in 1835, suggests that the balmaidens were not always adequately dressed for the prevailing weather conditions, and then makes a quite extraordinary observation:

'The large pieces or blocks are broken with hammers by women, called balmaidens, many of whom are very good-looking; but they seem to require warmer clothing, and must find their occupation painful and tiresome; they were all without stays.' [25]

Unfortunately there are no records of what the younger girls wore. The only picture is from Henderson, who drew a group of girls at the picking table. It is difficult to see exactly what they are wearing, but presumably relatively short frocks. The older girls and women

Studio portrait of two Dolcoath balmaidens, wearing their best aprons, and showing unusual starched
headwear. One has her work apron over her arm.

Courtesy of the Cornwall Centre Collection

all seem to have worn either mid-calf, rather than ankle-length dresses or skirts as their
one concession to the working conditions. Scandal seems to have been averted, as the
potentially exposed legs and ankles were covered with protective bands or coverings. The
dresses, or cotton blouses and cotton or linsey skirts, worn over numerous petticoats as was
the style, served basically as an outer coat. In addition, in cold weather a long-sleeved bodice
(Garribaldi, or in dialect a 'gollibolder') or shawl was worn. By the 1880s fashions began to
change and the women wore coats instead of the garboldi and layers of petticoats. Muriel
Sara remembers the costume of balmaidens towards the end of the 19th century:

*'In the summer they wore cotton or print dresses and big coloured print bonnets. In the winter
they needed old coats and shawls, with perhaps their heads wrapped in flannel beneath their
bonnets, as it was very cold work'.* [26]

Protection of the arms and legs from the weather, and from cuts and bruises, was very important. Some women or girls wore removable over-sleeves, usually of hessian, to protect the dress or blouse. The legs were wrapped in cotton bands, in summer, and wool or flannel bands in winter. These were a vital protection from flying shards, and from the cold and wet ore and waste that often accumulated around the feet and lower legs, and this was especially important for those women and girls who were cobbing or bucking. In 1858, Henderson describes bucking girls as putting on 'kitty bags' when they reached the mine. These were waterproofed leg protectors probably made from a mixture of resin, tallow and pitch (kit) and applied to canvas. Similar protectors may also have been made from hand-made ropes of straw, which were worn more generally and were called 'thumblebinds' or 'thumblebeans'.[27] By the turn of the 19th century, when cobbing and bucking was rarely done by hand, it seems that bands and kitty bags had been replaced by thick woollen stockings.

The balmaiden's apron appears to be almost a badge of office. For those who could afford it, ideally two aprons were required: a best white apron, and a coarser hessian one for work. The best one was usually made from herden, flour bag material of coarse hemp and flax, which could wash very white, and would be worn to and from the mine as well as for photographs and special occasions at the mine itself. In the novel *Norah Lang - the Mine Girl*,[28] Norah refers to this apron as her 'Ulster'. Once at the mine, the girls would change into the hessian one, called a towser, for work. These were usually waist length, and occasionally had a bib. As well as ties at the waistband, they might also have ties around the hips in order to give better protection. There is no evidence of this custom in Cornwall, but in some European countries an apron tied at the hip indicated a married woman, loose hip ties indicated a single woman.[27] Minnie Andrews described how it was a great matter of honour to have a clean apron, at least at the beginning of the week, and described how much time and effort she put into washing hers white again.[29]

Suitable shoes were a problem for the balmaidens, as so many families could not afford

A pair of balmaiden's shoes with metal tipped toes.

Courtesy of Bodmin Museum

more than one pair per person, and sometimes not even that. In the *1842 Employment Commission Report* it seems that some wore ankle-high boots or stout shoes giving good protection, but others had flimsy or unsuitable shoes for the work. A pair of undated balmaiden's shoes may be seen in Bodmin Museum. They have wooden soles and irons, leather uppers and ankle straps, and iron toecaps. Towards the end of the 19th century it seems some women and girls wore clogs. Others wore hobnailed boots. Phyllis Lockett, who worked at Geevor in World War Two, described how the women working there often preferred to wear clogs, as they lasted longer.

By the very nature of their work, balmaidens' hands were particularly vulnerable to damp and cold, as well as to bruises and cuts. Sharron Schwartz describes the cobbing and bucking girls as wearing short pieces of India rubber piping on the fingers of their left hand to protect themselves from the blows of the hammer. (Women working on the dressing floors in Anglesey protected their fingers with iron rings, but it is not known whether Cornish women did the same).[30] As the girls and women were continually handling wet and dirty ore stuff, in winter they protected their hands with old warm stockings made into a sort of padded mitten or cloth bands. Frances Richards, a balmaiden at Devon Consols in the 1860s, described to her daughter how they used to bind the palms of their hands with these dry rags. When they became wet they hung them up to dry on the hot water pipe in the miners' dry.[31] By about 1880, these cut-up stockings or bandages appear to have been replaced with proper gloves.

The head-covering was a crucial part of the protective clothing, for those working outside in particular. Their heads and necks needed protection from cold, wind and wet in winter, and sunburn in summer. In addition they needed protection from excessive noise levels, and from flying splinters.

The most common headgear appears to have been the gook, the traditional loose bonnet with a wide brim over the eyes and ears, gathered at the neck and under the chin, but falling loose again over the shoulders. This form of headwear was not unique to the balmaidens in Cornwall, but was worn generally by other women in the South West, as well. Simple white cotton versions were commonly worn in the summer, and some had a loop under the chin so that the ends of the gook could be drawn through to give extra protection to the face and throat. Some women pinned the gook right across the face, leaving only the eyes uncovered, to protect themselves from the effects of the sun. Sometimes bright prints were used in summer, instead of the more traditional white cotton. In winter, variations of felt or padded cotton gooks or bonnets were worn. It has been suggested that the styles of the gook worn by the balmaidens varied from area to area, some unique to specific parishes or areas. Although sketches drawn by Mary Mills indicate variation, there is no surviving corroborative evidence.[32]

A rather elaborate style was the 'yard of cardboard'. A diminutive form of this seems to be worn by the balmaidens photographed in a studio. Seymour, in his charming sketches of balmaidens, caricatures the style. Descriptions of headwear worn by balmaidens at Botallack, in 1865, and tin streamers at Consols seem to describe this type:

'A pasteboard foundation covered with a piece of gaudy calico fastened on the head by means of ribbons, while large wings fall and float around the face. Such an apparatus serves at once as bonnet, cap and veil - it admirably protects the face from the sun; and the mining girls are very anxious to retain their ruddy complexion.'

'They used to wear a picturesque headdress, something like a sun bonnet. The top part was flat, stiffened with cardboard and covered with print, and from this a frill hung over the ears and back of the head. It was tied firmly under the chin, and effectively protected the wearer from the sun'. [33]

The alternative summer headwear was the straw bonnet, again making its appearance in a variety of colours and styles. These bonnets were made from bent grass (bents) or sea grass (finny grass).[27] By the turn of the 20th century, it seems that they had largely replaced the gook. A Miss Carvolth working at Tobias Uren's Tin Streams in Gilbert's Coombe, Redruth, was probably one of the last balmaidens to wear the traditional gook in about 1920, and still changed from her work towser to her white apron to go home.[34] A later description of women working at tin streams in Redruth after 1900 indicates the gook going out of fashion:

'They wore a towser in work and a white apron going to and for. They didn't wear the gooks then, just a bonnet with a hat pin stuck in it.' [35]

It seems that the work dress of the balmaiden remained very similar for over a century. However, by the start of the 20th century there were significant changes in clothing in general, and also a comparative improvement in the financial condition of most mining families. By the time women were being employed at the mines and clay works during World War One, the typical full skirts with layers of petticoats, and gook or straw bonnet had been replaced by more practical shorter and slimmer lined dresses and skirts. These were worn with knee boots, belted coats, and fur or woollen hats in winter, and cotton pinafores in summer. The balmaiden's image had been given a make over!

Social activities

The main social life in these mining communities, of course, happened informally amongst neighbours; chatting together on doorsteps in fine weather, popping into each others' houses for a chat in cold weather, and by 'walking out' with friends to the market or fair. The more organised activities revolved around the chapels and pubs. As it was not acceptable for women or children to go to the taverns, their formal socialising took place at the church or chapel. Although the women and girls would be precluded from the business meetings there, and neither could they usually hold any significant office, there were plenty of activities in which they were involved. Apart from Sunday worship, in the morning and evening, they were encouraged to attend class meetings, Bible studies, or belong to the choir. They were also encouraged to teach in the Sunday School if they could read and write, or attend, if they could not, as well as to visit the sick and needy. There were also social groups, such as the sewing circles. On most nights of the week there would be some chapel-related activities, if the balmaidens had the time or energy, after their long working day. Most of Sunday would be taken up with attending various services, Bible studies and Sunday Schools. For instance, 17 year-old Fanny Francis, working at United Consols in 1841, was helping as a Sunday School teacher at the local Bryanite Chapel.[36]

However, it was more usual that balmaidens were the pupils, rather than the teachers, at Sunday School, often attending Sunday School until they were 17 or 18 years old. Unfortunately, balmaidens from the poorest families often felt excluded from these activities, as they only had their working clothes to wear. In most mining communities, from about 1840, there were evening classes, set up for young people from the mines, in reading and writing, and in some cases to teach basic mining skills, but girls seem to have

Nanpean Wesleyan Church Choir, 1906. At least one of the young women (front row left) became a felspar ore dresser during World War 1.

Courtesy of the Cornwall Centre Collection

been largely excluded from these.

Most balmaidens were working at the mine on a Saturday morning, and sometimes into the afternoon, but it was common practice, when they had finished, to go to the local market, sometimes known as 'Giglet Fairs'.[37]   Most major towns had a Saturday market, and the one at Redruth was among the largest. Even in 1778, four or five thousand people would attend each week, and apparently the most available commodities for sale were shoes and boots. These Saturday markets were, apparently, the time for 'miners to treat their balmaiden sweethearts to a bowl of soup'.[38]   For those without a 'sweetheart', this was a time to band together with their friends from the mine, to have a good time. Contemporary writers describe how these groups of mine girls were readily identifiable on market day. A change in style of dress worn by the balmaidens, between the earlier years and the middle years of the nineteenth century is rather patronisingly described in this newspaper account of a Whitsuntide Fair, in 1844:

'Formerly it was a rich sight of itself to see the mine girls in their ill-assorted dresses, in which every variety of gaudy colour - the stronger the contrast the better - was called into active service. If the day was wet, the treat was much the greater, for then the white muslin frocks, the green boots, the yellow bonnets and the red and glowing cheeks of the distressed maidens, were seen to greater advantage. But the times are changed, and those who come to a Cornish fair must expect to see the country girls clad in the same attire as their sex of the towns - the only difference being perhaps the want of a nice discrimination in the choice of colours that harmonise and blend, and in the love, if that be possible, of greater finery.'[39]

It seems that there were other social opportunities for balmaidens which were not so openly accepted. Patty Tremelling describes attending 'dance floors' in Truro in the late 1820s or early 1830s, with other girls from the mines.[40] These 'floors' were, apparently, sometimes built in or over the tops of oak trees, such as the Meavy Oak, and the Trebursey Oak at Launceston. [41] Such dance floors were associated with 'loose morals' and were definitely frowned upon by the chapel communities.

Cornwall has been well known for its choirs, especially those based in the mining communities, and the balmaidens grew up in this tradition of music. The men and boys sang as they made their way down into the mine at the beginning of the day, and also at the end if they had breath. It was a way of 'not being alone' in the dark, and a way to keep up the rhythm of climbing, while making the long journey up the ladders to the surface. Commentators described the wonderful harmonies resounding around the caverns of the mine, when the men sang. The balmaidens seem to have formed spontaneous singing groups too, either travelling to and from the mine, or at work. It certainly seems they were told to sing hymns when visitors were around on the dressing floor in order to create a good impression. One visitor in 1855 commented 'How well the girls take their parts.' [42] This comment, by E. L. T. Bickford-Harris appeared in a newspaper article in 1887:

'It is the custom for the female employees at the various mines in Cornwall to sing on returning from their daily labours. Some of these 'lasses' have wonderous voices'. [43]

The admirer then went on to publish a long poem entitled 'The Cornish Mine Girls' Song' which begins:

Eve minstrels! Oft I've heard ye sing,
Have marvelled much how ye could fling
Such liquid notes that richly ring,
And thrill us ere they die:

Apart from singing at work, balmaidens would be part of the 'family' chorus and probably also the chapel choir. In the novel *Norah Lang - the Mine Girl* the heroine is described as going twice a week to choir practice at the chapel, and being selected as one of their soloists for church services and concerts.

There is no clear evidence as to whether the balmaidens used music in order to create a working beat, on the dressing floors. In 1878, Darlington, when describing the work of the bucking girls, remarked that 'in Cornwall it is customary to keep time with the blows'. [44] Visitors often remarked that the women and girls sang spontaneously while they worked:

'The females select the best portions of ore and occasionally relieve their labours with low, soft, and melodious choruses which surprise the stranger.' [45]

It would appear then, that the balmaidens may have worked in unison and used music to provide a regular beat. Most of the 19th century reports describe the women and girls singing hymns. While it is quite possible to use hymns to work to in this way, they may have sung other work-songs which have not been recorded or handed down.

Up until the 20th century, there were no long holidays in the mining communities, but the few festivals and feast days were occasions of great celebration. Special 'mining' celebrations included St. Piran's Day[46] and Chegwidden Day (White Thursday) held on a Thursday before Christmas.[47] On Whit Monday, Midsummer's Day and the Parish Feast Day there were also special markets, parades, competitions and games. In 1844, one such fair at Truro was described as follows:

' The Whitsuntide Pleasure Fair had about the average number of shows, which are stationed in High Cross, the Market Place, and Boscawen Street, and these all proved very attractive to the miners and the bal-girls, who on these occasions have been accustomed to pour into the town in large numbers from time immemorial.' [48]

These fairs and feast days were great occasions for balmaidens to be seen with their 'intended', or to find one. The expectation was that balmaidens would eventually marry, and, although they were usually free to choose husbands, there were unwritten expectations about marrying within the mining community and within 'one's status'. It was not usual for a balmaiden to marry one of the mine officers, for instance, and this is made clear in the novel *Norah Lang - the Mine Girl*. It was very common for cousins to marry, or for a marriage to take place within the extended family. Most balmaidens married between the ages of 19 and 24 years old, and usually to local miners. As there were so few holidays, Christmas Day or Boxing Day were popular days for getting married. Once married a balmaiden was not expected to continue to work at the mine, but to take on the responsibility of running the new household.

Cartoon sketch of a balmaiden meeting her sweetheart, entitled 'After Work',
by George Seymour Jnr. Note her work apron over her arm.
Courtesy of the Mining Journal

Chapter 4

BALMAIDENS AT THE COPPER MINES

Mention has yet to be found of women or girls at the copper mines in Cornwall before they became independent of the Mines Royal in 1689, and the first definitive records of females being employed come from the 1720s. However, copper mining was beginning to develop under private ventures before the end of the 17th century, when over 1,000 tons of Cornish ore were being shipped each year to smelters in Swansea and Lower Redbrook in the Forest of Dean. It is probable, therefore, even at this early stage, that female labour began to be used in the ore-dressing process.

At the turn of the eighteenth century the protracted wars with the French were creating new demands for copper armaments, so many new mines opened in West Devon and Cornwall, to supply this market. The most successful of those early mines were at Tolgus Downs near Redruth, and Poldice near St. Day. By the 1720s, the copper mines in West Devon and Cornwall, the most productive of which were Dolcoath, Cook's Kitchen, Relistian and Bullen Garden, were producing 6,000 tons of ore per year, which was half of the national output.

Over the subsequent 150 years, there were two major booms in copper trade in the South West. The first occurred in the 1740s, after the installation of better pumping machinery to enable mining at depth, and newly-designed horse whims for bringing the ore 'to grass'. As greater quantities of ore were won per month than ever before, a much greater workforce was required for the dressing operations. Most of the copper ore mined in the South West was soft and easily lost by over-crushing, so mechanisation was not necessarily the solution to the accumulating quantities of ore-stuff at the surface. The manual crushing and separating operations did not require great strength, but rather dexterity, patience, and a good eye. The most obvious and cheapest candidates for this work, therefore, were women and children. They were employed in the copper mines in ever-increasing numbers, and during this time many families migrated from the rural parishes of Cornwall into the mining areas to take up this type of work.

In the 1770s, however, there was a catastrophic slump in copper prices because copper was also found at Parys Mountain in Anglesey. As this copper could be obtained by the opencast method, it was much cheaper to extract than the copper from the deeper Cornish mines. As a result many copper mines in Cornwall had to be abandoned - even Dolcoath in 1787 - with the subsequent dismissal of a large proportion of the workforce, including the women and children. This was a time of desperate poverty and deprivation in Cornwall, as it coincided with some of the worst consequences of the *Land Enclosures Act*, when many rural families were left landless and with no means of economic support.

Eventually, with the exhaustion of the Parys deposit around 1800, coupled with an increase in world copper prices, some of the mines in Cornwall were able to re-open, or new ventures made. The largest employer by 1806 was Dolcoath again, with a total of 1,600 workers. How many of them were women or girls is not known exactly, but probably it was at least 400.

Over the next four decades, until about 1855, there followed another time of boom (the second peak of production) for the copper mines of Cornwall and West Devon. The total number of mines operating, as well as their output, continued to increase during this period. By 1838, 151,000 tons of copper ore was being raised per year. Although there were continual improvements in the technology of the underground operations at this time (e.g. the introduction of safety fuses, etc), there was very little change in the methods used on the dressing floors. These processes, using a combination of hard manual labour and some fairly simple labour-intensive technology, were still much the same in 1855 as they had been when William Pryce described them in the 1770s. This was a time, then, when the cheap but dexterous manual labour of women and children was still required, and the demand was increasing.

This lack of technological development on the dressing floors can be seen by studying the illustration of Dolcoath Copper Mine (c. 1831) reproduced on page 7. It shows the various stages in the dressing procedure, clearly recognisable as those described by Pryce in 1778, and yet not so different from later accounts of 1842, or of the carefully observed drawings of James Henderson (c. 1852).

The dressing floor

The copper-dressing processes were divided into two distinct phases. The first was the physical breaking down and separation of ore from waste rock as it came from underground, and the second was the use of water to separate out these components further, by using different sedimentation techniques. The physical layout of the dressing floor in the early years was usually determined by two main factors: the most efficient in terms of human carrying capacity, and the availability of water. To minimise human effort, and therefore wages, the first dressing processes tended to take place nearest to where the ore was landed.

Originally, ore was brought to surface in kibbles. Subsequent processes would take place downhill from there, wherever possible, so that movement of ore was by a system of gravity and chutes, or by hand barrowing. From about 1830, ore was moved in wagons on tramways, when the layout of the dressing floors often needed to be redesigned to allow for appropriate angles and gradients. Water was needed for the initial washing of the ore-stuff, and then for the various sedimentation and separation techniques used later in the process. Water was a vital commodity, and the dressing floors had complex systems of launders and leats to provide the necessary quantities. The water was often brought many miles by launder in order to ensure constant supplies. For instance, at Devon Great Consols it was brought in a leat for two miles, from the Tamar at Latchley.[1] It was such a precious commodity that it was re-used wherever possible, and carefully conserved. Even so, it often failed, especially in the summer months.

In the early days, the majority of the tasks were performed in the open air. From about the 1840s onwards, some of the activities were carried out under primitive shelters with no sides, but referred to as 'sheds'. As late as 1864, the Kinnaird Report remarks on the inadequacy of provision at Fowey Consols:

'The greater number of females employed on the surface work are in the open air. There are some sheds, but as they are only provided with roofs, without any sides, there is such a strong draught of air through, that the girls prefer being out of them. In case of wet weather, inasmuch as the mine is not working very extensively, the females stop work, they being able to dress all the ore in fine weather. There is a good house in the eastern part of the mine which is used for dressing purposes in wet weather.' [2]

The dressing process

The aim on the dressing floor was to remove as much waste as possible, with minimum loss of ore and the least expenditure. At each stage of dressing, the material was usually divided into three different grades of components - prills, deads, and gangue or drage. The pieces of pure ore (prills) would need no further dressing and would be moved away from the dressing floors ready for sampling and sale. The poorest materials (deads) would be rejected as waste, even though they might contain small amounts of ore. Gangue or drage, the medium-quality ore-stuff, was either sent on to a more refined dressing process, or recycled again through previous processes, depending on the richness and nature of ore remaining in it. The amount of ore discarded as deads would depend on the current market price. When prices were low, it was not worth the cost of extracting very low concentrations of copper. In times of high prices, it would be economic to retrieve copper from material at quite low concentrations. The average amount of copper ore retrieved for sale was usually not more than 8% of the original volume.

Because the nature of both the ore and the waste would vary from mine to mine, each would develop their own unique systems of dressing. Darlington eloquently makes the point in 1878 in his paper on ore dressing:

'It is scarcely possible to observe the same system in any two distinct concerns.' [3]

Despite variations in the detail of processes from mine to mine, two 19th century writers give us a very useful overview of what happened on the dressing floors at that time:

'The ores, or, as the miners term them, 'hures' are all dressed by women and boys, who cob them, pick them, jig them, buck them, buddle them and splay them as they may require. In order to prepare copper ores for market, the first process is to throw aside the deads, or rubbish; and this operation is very cleverly performed by little girls of seven or eight years of age, who receive threepence or fourpence per day. The largest fragments of ore are then cobbed, or broken into smaller pieces by women; and after being again picked they are given to what the Cornish miners term 'maidens' that is girls from sixteen to nineteen years of age. These maidens buck the ores; that is with a bucking iron, or flat hammer, they bruise them down to a size not exceeding the top of the finger; and the hures are then given to the boys, who jig them, or shake them in a sieve under water, by which means the ore or heavy part, keeps at the bottom, while the refuse is scraped from the top. The part which passes through the sieve is also stirred about in water, the lighter part is thrown to the surface, and the ores, thus dressed, being put into large heaps of about a hundred tons each, are ready for the market.' [4]

'The youngest girls are employed in picking out the best fragments, which they soon learn to do with much dexterity - the ore being spread out on a table, and receptacles being provided for the good and bad portions. The riddling is done by the elder girls and young women. Larger

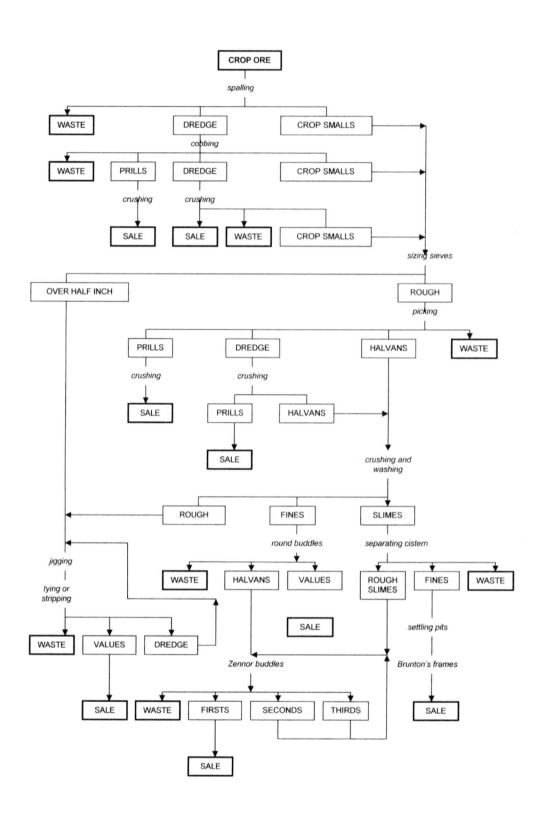

Diagram 1. Typical copper ore dressing procedures, based on Devon Consols, c. 1864.

masses are ragged by men, those of somewhat smaller size are spalled or broken by the elder girls and with hammers that are not quite so heavy. The youngest boys wash or clean the stones in a trough, through which a stream of water flows. The fragments are next cobbed, being broken still smaller by girls of medium age who use a short handled hammer. The ore is then bucked or broken into pieces an ounce or two in weight, by girls who stand at a sort of bench, having several iron anvils fitted into it, this is done with a broad square hammer 2-3lbs in weight, and is considered to be the hardest work at which the mine girls are engaged. The crushing mill is now coming extensively into use, as a substitute for the laborious bucking process. Machinery is now employed to keep the sieves jigging, and children are well able to supply and remove the material. When the ore is brought to a great degree of fineness it is collected into a heap sometimes weighing many hundred tons, and, when at intervals, varying from 2 weeks to two months in different mines, the ore is sampled for the smelter to inspect and buy it in lots, girls are employed to wheel barrowfuls of it into distinct heaps each to form one lot or parcel on the day of sale.' [5]

Due to the different levels of skill and strength needed for the various dressing processes, as noted above, there was a rough division of labour by age and gender. This is illustrated in this description of 1862:

'On the outskirts (of the mine) may perhaps be seen a great number of fine healthy children (boys and girls) of tender years, engaged at the buddle pits, or in jigging, screening, picking and dressing the ore; a little further on may be seen a number of stout girls and women, occupied in cobbing, breaking and assorting ores.' [6]

Generally speaking, the younger girls were involved in the lighter work of sorting and washing, while the older girls and women would carry out the heavier work of breaking down ore, and barrowing it around the site.

Spalling

Copper ore was originally brought to surface in iron kibbles (buckets), but by about 1830 these had been replaced in some of the larger mines by waggons. Once landed, the largest lumps (spalling stuff) were broken into smaller pieces by male surface labourers using ragging hammers which weighed about eight to ten pounds.

Two spalling hammers from the Helston area. Both are badly worn, but one is almost completely worn away with use. Spalling hammers varied in length of handle (presumably to fit the person or the task), however the longer one of the two has a surprisingly flimsy handle.
Courtesy of Helston Museum

The next stage in the physical separation of the ore-stuff, spalling, was nearly always done by women. The object of spalling was to break the gangue into an appropriate size for bucking, or for the stone crushers, and to remove as much waste as possible at this early stage. This reduction in the volume of material going to the crushers, or onto other manual operations was crucial to the economy of the mine. As no adequate mechanical means of performing these tasks was developed, hand ragging and spalling continued right into the 20th century. Both ragging and spalling required a firm base on which to break the ore, and areas of cobbles were usually set immediately around the landing area for these tasks.

In the 1831 engraving of Dolcoath Copper Mine, on page 7, a young woman can be seen spalling ore. Ore has been brought to her by one of the 'surface labourers', in a wheelbarrow, and tipped out into a heap. She is working in the open air, near to where the ore had been landed. She is using a long handled hammer with a blunt end, to break up the larger pieces of ore in the pile. The picture below of spalling maidens, drawn by James Henderson, shows clearly the style of hammer used by the spalling maids. The hammerhead was made of iron, and latterly, cast steel, and weighed about 1 lb. This was fixed on a light, slightly pliant handle, giving a total weight of about 3 lb.[7] Later, spalling was sometimes done in covered shelters built near the pit shaft, as at South Crofty[8], but generally it continued to be done in the open air, right up until the time that the last spalling maids left work in 1920.

Women spalling ore, by James Henderson, c. 1852.
Courtesy of the Royal Institution of Cornwall

This very demanding task, which required wielding hammers for hours at a time, was normally thought to be only suitable for girls over about 16 years of age. In reality, younger girls were often involved. Of six girls interviewed in 1842, who had done any spalling, only two were 16 or over. Christina Pascoe[9] and Martha Buckingham[10], who worked at Consolidated Mines, had sometimes been called on to spall ore when they were as young as 13 or 14 years old. Similarly, Mary Buller at Fowey Consols[11] and Mary Johns at Tresavean[12] were only 15 and 14 years old, respectively, and were regularly spalling ore.

Even in the late 19th century, it was crucial to minimise the amount of waste going to the crushers and Darlington, writing in 1878, still advocated hand spalling as one of the most economic way to do this. He also believed that an experienced spaller could produce about a ton of ore-stuff per day 'but the quantity must necessarily depend on the hardness and nature of the stone'.[7]

It is not clear whether the spallers actually carried out any sorting of the ore they broke, or whether it was just left for the sievers. It is probable that they may have carried out a very primitive level of sorting. It may be that at some mines they also carried out all the riddling and sorting of the spalled material as well, before the gangue was barrowed away to the pickers.

Riddling or griddling

Riddling was usually the next process, when the smallest of the spalled ore was separated through a sieve leaving the largest pieces needing to be re-spalled. The sieve used was made from an oak hoop eighteen to twenty inches in diameter, with about a one inch iron or wire mesh. This sieving was also usually carried out near to the shaft and, in 1842, was still being done in the open air. The smaller material retained in the sieve (the picking rough) was sent on to the washers and pickers. That which passed through (the shaft small) was sent on to be bucked. Any waste was discarded.

It was mainly women and girls over 16 years of age who were employed at sieving. At Fowey Consols in 1841, there were twenty-seven girls employed as 'riddlers'.[13] Of those, only four were under 16 years old, and the rest were between 16 and 18 years old. By the late 1850s though, this gruelling task had been partially mechanised, and the ore was separated on a hand cranked revolving griddle, with young girls and boys picking the best ore from a trommel.

In addition, riddling or sieving were also done at other stages during the dry dressing processes. Henderson's drawing of girls at a bucking table includes two girls sieving the newly bucked ore. They would return the larger pieces which had escaped crushing to the bucking table for reprocessing.

Washing

If the larger ore needed washing, it was done in a strake with an iron plate in the base. One girl would load the strake with ore-stuff, and another girl would stir the material with a Cornish shovel or rake, so that the mud and fine ore-sediment was washed through into collection tanks. Of the large material left in the strake, the good ore would be raised to the top due to its relative density. Another girl or surface labourer would empty the strake, separating the good ore from the mixed gangue, ready for further dressing.

Smaller material was sometimes washed in a short-legged trough with water running through, by the youngest girls or boys. They would throw out waste material on to the ground to be carried away. It may be that the washing was done using hot water from the mine engine outlet. This was certainly the case at Devon Consols Mine.

Picking

Picking the spalled and riddled ore was one of the first tasks that the young boys and girls were given when they came to the copper mine to work. Girls as young as 7 or 8 years old may be brought to this work, but generally they came to the tables at the age of about 9 or 10. It seems that, although boys would start at the picking table alongside the girls, they would very soon be moved to other jobs, usually at the buddles or underground, whereas the girls could remain for several years at this one task. The dexterity of the younger

Young girls picking ore, by James Henderson, c. 1852.
Courtesy of the Royal Institution of Cornwall

children meant that they were well suited to this type of work.

Most of the copper ore mined in Cornwall was in the form of chalcopyrite, and was fairly easy to identify due to its bright, golden colour. However, not all copper was in this form, and it was often brought to the surface mixed with other types of ore, so the sorting task could be quite difficult and complex. When Murchison visited Devon Great Consols in 1850, he had this to say about the young ore-pickers:

'When the ore is mixed with a good deal of mundic, spar and other materials it is first picked by young women and boys, who show great proficiency in their knowledge of their business.' [14]

De La Beche also remarks on the skill required by such young people:

'When ores are mixed with much foreign matter they require to be picked with care, and to the stranger the little picturesque groups of children thus employed, and the practical judgment they have usually attained, are generally subjects of interest.' [15]

Because the ore being brought had usually just been washed, this work was incredibly wet and cold. Apart from sorting the ore, the girls would also be responsible for carrying the full picking boxes on to the next stage in the process, probably to the bucking mill or crusher.

In the early days, the women and children would sit on the ground in the open air to sort the larger pieces of washed ore, which would just be tipped out in front of them. Later, the spalled and sieved pieces of washed rock and ore were tipped out onto picking tables, under very primitive shelters. As easy access was required for supplying material to the tables, and for the removal of the various sorted portions afterwards, these children worked with only minimal protection from the weather.[16] They were usually seated before a low bench, over which they leaned, to pick out the best ore (prills). Sometimes they stood up in order to reach, or just to ease stiff joints. The prills were thrown into special boxes placed on the top of the picking table. These picking boxes were made of 1" thick deal, 16" long, 7" wide at the base and 10" wide at the top, and 7" deep. Sometimes they would also have a wooden handle. When the pickers had finished picking out the pure ore, they would then sort the good quality mixed ore-stuff, and the remaining waste material was thrown under the table to be collected and barrowed away.[17]

Of the five girls interviewed in 1841, who had spent time at the picking tables, Martha

Buckingham[9], and Mary Verran[10], both from Consolidated Mines and 14 years old, had spent the longest time picking ore at about four years. 11 year-old Caroline Coom, at Fowey Consols[11], and 13 year-old Christina Pascoe, at Consolidated Mines[10], had both been picking ore for two years. At the United Mines (Gwennap) a total of fifty-three girls were employed picking ore, most of whom were under 13 years old. In comparison, of sixty girls at the picking tables at Fowey Consols there was a more mixed age range. Twenty-three were aged 10 to 12 years old, three were 13 to 15 years old, and twenty-four were 16 to 18 years of age.[13]

It was not just very young girls who were put to this work. Minnie Andrews, described as the last balmaiden, was one of two women, herself and an elderly woman, who were employed at picking copper at Carn Camborne in the 1880s:

'I helped an old lady called Anna Sincock pick over copper ore at Carn Camborne. They used to pull down the thing and the water would come down in the strip and wash the copper. We was picking out all the bad ones and letting the best ones there.' [41]

Cobbing

Writing in the 1770s, William Pryce described how cobbing took place at a stone anvil with a 'flat-polled hammer'.[18] This, presumably, was very like the process shown in the 1831 Dolcoath engraving. Five young women are shown kneeling, each at a stone block measuring about twelve inches in each dimension. On it they are breaking down ore-stuff with a short-handled hammer.

Although the 1831 Dolcoath engraving shows cobbing taking place in the open air, by

Two girls cobbing copper ore, by James Henderson, c. 1852. Note the protective wear on the left hand.
Courtesy of the Royal Institution of Cornwall

1842 it seems that it was mostly was done under cover in a 'hutch' or 'cobbing shed'. Cobbing sheds were occasionally built much earlier, e.g. by 1809 at Wheal Towan.[19] The girls, instead of kneeling at a primitive anvil, usually sat in a more comfortable position, on low benches. These benches had an iron anvil set in at the end, on which the girls broke the ore with a short-handled hammer with a sharp end. The heads of these cobbing hammers were four to eight inches long, and weighed between 2 and 4 lbs. In some cases, the cobbers had their feet and legs protected by a screen, but as in James Henderson's sketch of about 1852, often the damp, cold debris was left to gather around their feet and legs.

Girls of about 16 or 17 years old were set to this task, and they separated out and rejected any waste rock, and broke the mixed ore to hazelnut-sized pieces, ready for bucking. At Dolcoath, in the mid 1850s, the cobbing shed was known as the 'Roarer' on account of the terrific noise generated by the sixty girls working there.[20] Cobbing was not considered a light job, but was not quite as demanding as bucking.

In 1841, five girls were interviewed who were cobbers, and all were 16 years old or over. Elizabeth Curnow and Christina Pascoe, at Consolidated Mines[10], were 24 and 17 years old, respectively. Grace Bowden, at Trethellan[21], Jane Sandow, at Wheal Gorland[22], and Jane Uren, at Tresavean[12], were 18, 17, and 16 years old, respectively. Although cobbing was considered only suitable for older girls, Fowey Consols reported one girl at this work who was under the age of 13, and three girls between 13 and 15 years old. At Fowey, only four were the generally accepted 16 years or over.[23]

In 1841, Jane Uren, at Tresavean, reported she usually cobbed about 2.25 cwt of ore-stuff per day. This is probably the weight of dressed ore she produced.[12] In 1878, Darlington, estimated that an expert cobber could 'prepare about 10 cwts of tolerably hard stuff per ten hours'. In contrast, this is probably the amount of undressed material brought to be cobbed.[24]

Bucking

Bucking was considered the hardest task carried out by the women and girls on the dressing floors, and involved reducing the cobbed ore-stuff to small granules and powder. The bucking girls and women stood at a bench or a mound of stone packed with earth, into which was set an anvil. In the 18th century, a flat stone was used, set at slight angle to the bench or mound, but this was later replaced by a cast iron block about 16" square and 1.5" thick. The material to be bucked was delivered to the table from above, either from a hand barrow (see Henderson's drawing) or down a chute. Sometimes the girls stood on a small platform at the bench in order to keep their feet clear of the debris. Some wore 'kitty bags', a kind of leg protector, to keep their legs dry.[25]

A cobbing hammer (above) and a bucking iron.

Girls bucking copper ore, by James Henderson, c. 1852. Note also the two girls barrowing cobbed tin-stuff to the bucking mill, and the two girls sieving the bucked ore ready for the buddles.
Courtesy of the Royal Institution of Cornwall

The girls would sweep the ore-stuff from the accumulated heap onto the anvil with one hand, and beat and pound it with a 'bucking iron' with the other. This hammer weighed 3 or 4 lbs. It had a wooden handle inserted into a stirrup of iron, and a flat end about 6" square and 1" thick made of cast iron. Once the material had been crushed to powder, the bucking girls would then sweep it away with their left hand onto the floor. Other girls would shovel up the bucked ore and sieve it. They would then return the coarser material to be bucked again, and barrow away the finer material to the buddles. Darlington hinted that it was the custom for the bucking girls to keep up a rhythm of working, hammering in time with each other.[27]

As hand bucking was so difficult and demanding, it was one of the first processes to be mechanised. Crushing rolls were introduced, but in the first instance they were only suitable for the harder ore types. John Taylor installed such machines in the Tavistock area in the early 1800s, at Wheal Crowndale in 1804, and at Wheal Friendship in 1806. Reputedly the former action was to break a strike by balmaidens, however, Taylor's own account of a lack of females prepared to work at the mines, in an area unused to mine employment, seems more plausible.[26] By 1830, De la Beche reported that the best ores were being broken by steam-driven crushing machines in most of the principal copper mines. This was confirmed by Henwood in 1832, and certainly one was in use at Trethellan Mine in 1841. Unfortunately, it was found that the crushers generated even more dust on the dressing floors than the conventional bucking.

Bucking iron from the St. Just area, showing considerable wear.
Courtesy of the Wayside Museum, Zennor

In the 1831 Dolcoath picture, it seems that bucking took place out doors, but by about 1855 at Dolcoath it was being done inside, along with the cobbing. It was generally reported that was being done under cover by 1841.

Bucking could only be carried out by the biggest and strongest girls and women. By the time of the 1842 report, not many mines were still employing females for the bucking process, so only three of the girls who were interviewed had been employed in this type of work. Two of them were Elizabeth Carkeek[28], aged 18 years, and Sally Fall[29], aged 19 years. Both were buckers at Tresavean Mine. The third was 17 year-old Jane Sandow of Truro, who had only been at the bucking tables a very short while before she was unable to continue, as it had been too hard for her.[22] The total employment numbers at United Mines in 1841 indicated that there were thirty girls working in the bucking sheds, of whom two were actually under 16 years old, and the remaining twenty-eight were between the ages of 16 and 18.[13]

Jigging

In the early days of copper mining this very laborious task was done by boys or women,[30] and was also referred to as 'hutch work'. The work involved shaking brass wire sieves, holding gangue, in wooden boxes of water. The lightest material washed through and the material left in the sieve would settle into layers. By the end of the 18th century and beginning of the 19th hand jigging was done almost entirely by boys, and was found to be very injurious to their health. When Pryce wrote in the 1770s, he described how a girl would throw ore into the jigger, while a boy held it. After the shaking process, done by the boy, the different grades of sediment would be shovelled and separated by them both. The heavy purer ore was sent for sampling and sale, the medium mixed ore for reprocessing, and the poor ore was rejected.

However, from about 1830, mechanised jigging boxes were introduced, which could be operated fairly easily, by either girls or boys. They consisted of large wooden boxes, in which the jigging sieves were set, but which were shaken by means of a very long-handled horizontal lever. Even though jigging with the machines was so much easier than jigging

Two girls at semi-automated jigging machines, by James Henderson, c. 1852.
Courtesy of the Royal Institution of Cornwall

by hand, the operators still reported back pain.[31] Later, by the 1860s, jiggers had become fully mechanised and were belt driven, using water or steam power, and only required to be manually filled and emptied. It was then usual for boys to be responsible for these machines.

Buddling

In early part of the 18th century it seems that both boys and girls worked at the buddles. It was here that the very fine waste from jiggers and settling pits was taken, to extract some more of the remaining ore. The early buddles were long, rectangular sloping pits or wooden troughs where waste was washed out from ore-stuff, leaving heavier copper ore to settle at the 'head' of the frame. To aid separation, the boys or girls agitated the mixture with a heather broom, or by standing up to their ankles in the buddle and using their feet. Pryce said these children were called 'lappiors' (dancers) in the earlier part of the 18th century.[32] By the 19th century, the actual 'buddling' was done primarily by boys. However, girls were often responsible for 'serving the buddles', i.e. controlling the water flow through the sluices and launders to the buddle, or helping to barrow, load or unload the increasingly purified ore from the buddles. The Cornish buddle, with its mechanised sweeping arms was introduced from about 1860, and boys tended to be responsible for these. By the mid 1870s, when it was illegal to employ children full time, women sometimes would fill and empty the large round buddles, under supervision of the surface captain.

Barrowing

The efficient transportation of the ore-stuff, waste and copper ore around the different areas on the dressing floor must have been one of the most difficult logistical challenges for the surface captain. In order to keep the flow, teams of men and girls were employed continually just to barrow material from one place to another. Even after the introduction of waggons onto the dressing floor, there were some areas where it was still necessary to hand-carry materials, and hand barrows were still being used in the late 19th century. Apart from the regular barrowing teams, girls were also called away from other tasks to help on an 'as needed' basis, when there was a bottleneck at one of the processes. Generally, it was the male surface workers who used wheeled barrows, and the women and girls who were given hand barrows.

In the early days, it seems that the hand barrows used at the copper mines held 3 cwt of ore. It was estimated that, allowing for the weight of the barrow, the ore plus the water held in the ore, the weight to be carried could total as much as 4 cwt. In 1817 it was observed:

'This is an enormous burthern, which is borne by all descriptions of persons who are employed in dressing and weighing. Labour so disproportionate to the degree of strength possessed by ordinary individuals, has given rise to a most pernicious custom, generally adopted by persons, women as well as men, who are employed in mixing, dividing and weighing ore; that of drinking large quantities of spirituous liquors, from the false idea that they are thereby invigorated to perform the labour required of them.' [33]

It seems that, historically, the hand barrow was designed with the same capacity as the sacks used for transporting ore to the smelter, which was 3 cwt. One mule could carry two of these sacks, one on each side. By about 1780, it was decided to halve the sack sizes used on the tin dressing floors, due to the number of injuries incurred by the surface men and carriers in lifting them. As a result, the corresponding barrow size was also halved to contain

1.5 cwt as well. The same observer wrote:

'What has been done in the case of the load of tin ore will, I hope, be shortly accomplished in that of weighing copper ore.' [33]

As all references, both in tin and copper mines, in the 1842 Commission are to hand barrows with a 1.5 cwt. capacity, it seems that this change was made. These hand barrows were shallow wooden boxes made of deal 1.25" thick. The total length, including the handles, was 5'6" long, and the carrying box being 10" x 18" at the base, 18" x 24" at the top and 9" deep. The girls and women used a Cornish shovel to fill them. This had a curved and roughly triangular blade about 11" wide at the top and 13" from the shank to the point. It was made of hammered iron initially, and later pointed with steel. The hilt was normally of ash, and also slightly curved. The whole shovel weighed about 4 lbs.[34]

In his *Mining Journal* article on balmaidens in 1858, Henwood describes how two women were called to barrow ore when there was a shortage of male surface labourers and observes that they were carrying a weight of 3 cwt between them. It is not clear whether he had mistaken the size, or whether at this particular mine the larger hand barrows were still in use:

'There being a scarcity of hands (men) on the floor Mary and Nanny were called. On which two amazons rushed forward. Hand barrows filled with copper ore contain 3 cwt, 7 to the ton (21 cwt). These girls were employed to fill these barrows with the long handled Cornish shovel, and to carry them several yards to the scales. Then further to the heap, where they upset the ore, and returned to the pile to refill.' [35]

It seems that any strong adolescent girl or woman could be called on to barrow at a moment's notice as with Mary and Nanny above. In the *1842 Commission Report* we are told that Martha Buckingham and Mary Verran, both aged 14, were occasionally called on to barrow at the Consolidated Mines.[10] As a full-time task, however, it was often allocated to girls in their early to mid-teens. In 1841, for instance, 17 year-old Fanny Francis was a full time barrow girl at the United Mines.[22]

Sampling

Once every two months or so, activities on the dressing floor changed dramatically in order to prepare the ore that had already been dressed for sampling and sale. This sometimes took up to two weeks to complete so at some mines extra women and girls were drafted in. For instance, Sarah Michell was employed at 'weighing up' at Dolcoath in August 1789, and was paid 1s 2d.[36] At East Wheal Crofty in the 1840s, a designated team of women and girls were 'shared' with an adjacent mine, and were employed just for sampling for a month at each mine, alternately.[37] In most other mines, some of the normal dressing activities were stopped, and those workers sent to help with the sampling.

Sampling proceeded in different ways, depending on the dressing arrangements at each individual mine. Where ore was raised and dressed by separate tribute teams, each tribute team would prepare their own ore for sampling. Where ore from the different teams had been mixed at surface, then it would all be prepared together.

Either way, the principles involved were the same. Each heap of dressed ore would be thoroughly and carefully mixed to try to ensure complete uniformity of content. Because some of these heaps would be very large indeed, sometimes consisting of many hundreds of tons, the mixing could take a long time.[38] The thoroughly mixed ore would then be shared out as fairly as possible into 'parcels' or shares, according to how many people had an interest in the ore (which would include the tributers, shareholders, mineral lord etc). Within each parcel the ore would be barrowed and laid out into neat 'doles', flat-topped circular piles about 2-3 feet thick, ready for the assayers to sample.[39] Once sampling was over, and ore was transported, it was usually barrowed into rectangular doles, as at Morwellham Quay, which was more economic with regards to the storage area required.

This complicated procedure of sharing out into doles at sampling was sometimes directed by one senior woman or girl, appointed by the surface captain. The rest of the women and girls were organised into groups of four, one pair shovelling and the other barrowing. At allotted times the two pairs would change over tasks.[40]

Waste picking

During the tin mining operations of the early 18th century, the value of copper was not necessarily recognised, and copper ore was sometimes discarded as worthless along with the other waste. In the late 18th and early 19th centuries, copper ore was subsequently retrieved from these waste heaps, sometimes at great profit. When copper prices were high it also became economically viable to re-dress the waste heaps from previous copper mining ventures, for the copper that had been left when prices had been low. Mine adventurers would either employ their own dressers for this task, or sometimes lease out the work.

The final copper years

New technologies were already heralding the reduction of the use of manual labour on the dressing floors when, in 1855, there was an enormous slump in copper prices. Many copper mines in Cornwall, previously in their heyday, closed, resulting in huge job losses. Some copper mines found tin at depth and were able to convert to mining tin. This occurred at Dolcoath, Tincroft, and Cook's Kitchen. However, the transition process was slow and, as tin dressing was usually less labour-intensive than copper, job losses for the women on the dressing floor, even in the surviving mines, was inevitable. As a result, women and children were never again to be employed at the Cornish copper mines in such numbers as in the 1850s.

In 1866 there was another depression in the copper market, which heralded the final decline of the Cornish copper industry. Copper production in Cornwall had halved between 1860 and 1870, and halved again between 1870 and 1880. Also many of the most successful copper mines, which had been in continual production for sixty years or more, were becoming exhausted. As a result, by 1885 only 35 mines were producing any copper at all. By the turn of the century, the only copper being produced in Cornwall was as a by-product of the tin mines. Over the border in Devon, Great Devon Consols continued to extract some copper, although its main product by now was arsenic, and even this major mine closed in 1901. So from 1866 onwards there were huge job losses on the dressing floors of the copper mines, with many women and children thrown out of work. The mining parishes that depended almost entirely on copper mining were the worst affected, and there was desperate poverty and hardship.

However, the contribution of these copper mines to the world economy should not be underestimated. During the eighteenth and nineteenth centuries Devon and Cornwall gained four times as much revenue from copper as it did from tin, and at the peak of production it provided 50% of the national output. The impact on the course of world economics, history, and trade is impossible to quantify. This copper provided the nation with high quality domestic ware and copper coinage in the 18th century. It also had its darker side, providing much of the copper necessary for commodities for the transatlantic slave trade and armaments for the long-term war effort against Napoleonic France. It formed an important component of Britain's 19th century colonial trade. During all these years of production, the dressing of copper ore was hardly mechanised at all and relied almost entirely on armies of women and children and their corporate manual effort. They were one of many crucial links in the booming economy of mid 18th and 19th century Britain, which, for better or worse, had such far-reaching consequences around the world.

Chapter 5

BALMAIDENS AT THE TIN MINES AND SMELTERS

Cassiterite (tin ore), like copper, is found in lodes and deposits where the sedimentary rocks meet the granites of the South West. Unlike the copper ores found in Cornwall however, it is relatively hard and heavy and can survive in very small dense particles, even after the minerals in which it was deposited have been physically or chemically eroded away. This means that viable amounts of tin ore have been found in stream beds and even on the sea shore, often far away from their point of origin, when the parent rock has long since been washed away. The tin in this form has been weathered over many years and is very pure, making it relatively easy to access and requiring very little dressing. This kind of tin has been collected over the centuries, sometimes by comparatively simple methods, without the need for complicated equipment or the investment of large sums of money. These types of tin recovery are known as tin streaming, sea tinning, and blown tinning. When these sources of relatively pure tin from rivers and streams were exhausted, deposits began to be exploited from underground, by shode, drift, or deep mining. However, tin from these sources is less pure, still being incorporated in the parent rock, and requires far more preparation and dressing before it is ready for smelting.

Tin streaming, shode tinning and drift mining

Evidence of tin stream workings have been found out on the Cornish moors from very early times. It is believed that tin has been extracted in this way and smelted for at least two thousand years in Cornwall, more or less continuously through the Roman and medieval period, right up to the first half of the 20th century, often with little change in technology.

The simplest early process of obtaining tin was similar to that of panning for gold. Tinners would collect a small quantity of sandy river deposit in a wooden bowl of water, and swirl the mixture, allowing the 'values' to settle to the bottom. Repeated discarding of the lighter waste would eventually concentrate the small quantity of ore in the bottom of the bowl. This method could be used by men, women, and children, alike.

When the tin in the recent deposits of a stream was exhausted, the prospecting for tin deeper in the river bed would begin. Owing to the heavy nature of the ore it would collect, over many years, in pockets on the granite bedrock under the stream or river, having been washed there as the parent rock had been eroded and carried away in the water. Sometimes these pockets were a considerable distance from the source of the mineral, collecting where water movement was significantly reduced.

Stream works, to exploit the deeper deposits, were built at the downstream side of the location where tin was suspected to lie. A shallow pit would be sunk to the stanniferous gravel layer, and then drained by buckets, or simple water-powered pumps. Work would progress back up the watercourse. Ore was collected by building a series of wooden leats and strakes, whereby river deposits were washed in a current of water. In the very early days, the tin ore was raked up onto a piece of turf at the top of the strake, which acted as a sieve. The turf was then carefully rolled, and carried to a large wooden bowl, usually about two feet in diameter, where the ore was washed out and collected. Latterly the tin-stuff was worked against the current with a rake or brush, by a person standing in the strake. The heavy ore then separate out at the top, while the lighter waste and ore was washed away into collection pits for further separating. From this simple strake the first buddles evolved, being larger rectangular troughs sometimes built out on trestles, and sometimes sunk into the ground. The ore that was extracted from the stream beds tended to be very pure, and therefore needed little dressing. Coarser gravels would be dug out separately, and left in piles for picking over. When the ore from one area had been removed, the waste would be back filled into the hole.[1]

As work proceeded, material from the streambeds would become exhausted, but, with diligence, miners were often able to locate and expose the tin lodes which had been the source of the stream tin. They did this by looking for the 'shode stones' (stones found in the river bed, containing tin, but with little sign of being rounded into pebbles by water erosion) indicating that the parent lode was not far away.

On discovering the tin lode, which was the source of the stream tin, a drift mine would then be driven into the valley sides. The material mined in this way had not been exposed to the elements and broken down in the same way as the stream tin, so needed more dressing to remove it from the substrate in which it was found. Originally, all the picking, sorting and crushing that was required was done by hand. The crushing was done by placing the tin-stuff in hollows in granite blocks, or in specially made mortars, and beating with hand-held rocks, until it was the consistency of fine sand. This was called crazing. Later, it was done using a hand operated 'crazing mill', not unlike a flour mill, where the material was ground between two flat rotating stones.

During the middle ages, hand operated crazing mills were replaced with larger horse- or water-powered versions. Eventually, by the 16th century, most of the crushing of tin-stuff was done by water-powered log 'stamps', which acted as huge battering devices. Even then, the 'leavings' were often recycled through the water powered crazing mill as well, in order to extract more tin.

The first detailed documentation of the tinning industry in Cornwall survives in court records from the middle of the 12th century, with the signing of the *Charter of the Stannaries* in 1201, which sought to regulate tinning in Cornwall. Mining was then under control of the Crown, and was organised in four stannaries. For instance, tin was being extracted from Fowey Moor, Hansborough Beacon, at Tywarnhaile, and in Kerrier and Penwith. From very early on, large areas of moorland in Cornwall were allocated to named tinners, and each small area or 'bound' was described and named.

Tin streaming and drift mining continued in this way for centuries, with varying degrees of success. Tin mining in Cornwall went through the doldrums in the 15th and 16th centuries, but began to pick up again when the Crown released its monopoly on the Mines Royal, and allowed the landowners to apply for mining rights. Private arrangements were then made between the landowners (mineral lords) and individual venturers who applied to search for tin. Even though tin streaming was to be largely overshadowed by deep mining during the 19th and early 20th centuries, new stream deposits continued to be discovered. The main areas of tin streaming were in the Cott and Kelynack Valleys of the St. Just Peninsula, Trevellas Valley, St. Agnes, and the St. Austell area. The largest tin stream works in Cornwall in the 19th century were at Carnon and Wendron. However, most had closed by the end of the 19th century. Many tin stream works were opened in the late 19th century to reprocess the tin-bearing waste that was washed from the deep tin mines, further upstream.

The degree of involvement of women and girls in the tin streaming and drift mining ventures over the centuries is unclear. Certainly many of the simple dressing operations, such as picking, buddling or straking, and crazing, are all activities which could have been done by women or girls, and all of these tasks, or their equivalents, were definitely performed by them from the early or mid 18th century onwards. Whenever these tin streams or drift mines were being run by family units, or community groups, it would be fairly safe to assume that women and children would each have had their allotted tasks.

The earliest definite reference, however, to females as part of the tin mining workforce is in 1357, where Abraham the Tinner was employing three hundred men, women and children at mines and stream works at Crukbargis. Beare only mentions boys, not girls or women, at work at the tin mines in the mid-16th century, and the next definite reference comes from the early 18th century. Pryce describes how both boys and girls would work barefooted in the buddles, and were called by an ancient name 'lappiors'. By the end of the 18th century Pryce indicated that it was quite the norm for women and girls to be filling buddles and sieving or trunking.[2] Women and girls continued to work at the tin streams through the 19th century. For instance, in the mid 1830s, two women and sixty-six children were working at Carnon Streams, Redruth, and five children (gender not specified) were working at the Pentuan Stream Works at Mevagissey.[3]

Sea tinning

As considerable amounts of tin ore are continually washed down onto the beaches from streams and from the adits of tin workings, sea tinning was one of the easiest ways of all to collect tin ore. It required little more than some wooden frames, sieves and a shovel, plus a means of transporting the ore to the stamps. Collection of sea tin, however, was not usually a continuous occupation, and could only be done after allowing a sufficient amount of deposit to accumulate, probably over a period of several years.

Due to its greater density, after the tin was washed onto the beaches, it would slowly sink through the sands or shingles with successive tides and collect in pockets on the bedrock, in much the same way that it collected under the riverbed gravels. Once one of these pockets had been located, the miners would simply dig down to it, extract it and separate it from the sand and shingle in which it had collected. This was done using a series of sieves and simply-built washing strakes. It would then be transported by mule or cart to the nearest tin stamps for crushing and dressing.

There is very little documentation about sea tinning in Cornwall, but it is known to have taken place at Perranarworthal in the 18th century, also at Priest Hole at Cape Cornwall in the 19th century, and at Porthledden at Cape Cornwall, Portheras near Pendeen, Letcha Foreshore, Lelant, Loe Pool, Chapel Porth, Trevaunance, and Trevellas at St. Agnes, and Levant and at Perranporth at the end of the 19th or into the 20th century.[4]

Engraving of Botallack mine, showing considerable artistic licence. It may show sea tinning in the foreground.
This could never have occurred in this part of Cornwall which has a steep and rugged coastline.

A similar venture that took place on the shoreline was the collecting of 'blown tin'. This was opportunistic mining at its best. Under certain weather conditions, as ore washed down on to the beaches, it could be blown into concentrated deposits. For instance, the accumulation of blown tin at Porthrepta, near St. Ives, was usually seasonal, and depended on a north wind to give a good 'coat' of tin on the sand. Under any other weather conditions the sea remixed the tin with sand, making it uneconomic to collect. During the last half of the 19th century 'beachwork' there was taken to the six-headed stamps and dressing plant on the shoreline, for processing. In 1887, five workers were employed but their gender is unknown.[56]

The earliest reference of women or girls being involved in sea tinning comes from Pryce, when he reports that sea tinning was carried on at Perranarworthal in the 1720s. He describes how men, women, and children, who were destitute, worked on the shore collecting tin in order to earn themselves a few pennies just to survive.[7] In 1775, Cunnack gives even more detail:

'At low spring tides when the creek is low wash works can be seen. Some time ago the country people began to wash the mud, and poor people can often make 30 to 40s and up to £3 per month.' [8]

Deep mining for tin

By medieval times, some tin was being mined from deep pits, or by driving drift mines into the valley sides. The depth of a tin mine at this time, as with the copper, was limited by the height of the water table, and also by the efficiency of any primitive pumps, used to keep the mine dry. Medieval accounts of mining for tin in Cornwall, describe an all-male workforce, most of whom were employed in keeping the mines clear of water.

When tin and copper mines became free of Crown control by the end of the 17th century, landowners were allowed to lease out their mineral rights to private adventurers. This change was followed almost immediately by the development of improved pumping and lifting technology, so that, from the beginning of the 18th century, deposits could be exploited at greater depths than before. Improved tin stamps also meant a more efficient dressing of the ore. Although the initial emphasis was on opening up the copper mines for the escalating copper market, a few deep tin mines were developed, and operated on a far greater scale. Some of the earliest successful tin mines which opened were Rosewall Hill Mine (Towednack), Polberro (St. Agnes), Polgooth (St. Austell), and Great Work and Wheal Vor (Breage).[9] It was at this stage that the workforce at the tin mines began to expand rapidly, with the need for large numbers to work on the dressing floors. From about 1720, women and girls are believed to have been employed in increasing numbers at these deeper mines. Little documentary evidence seems to survive confirming their involvement before about 1770, but Pryce implies that their employment was quite normal by that date.

By 1770, when employment of women and girls was well under way, copper prices were falling, resulting in mine closures. The copper mine workers put out of work often offered their services at the tin mines, which enabled an initial increase in output. It was just at this time, though, that pewter for domestic tableware and kitchen utensils fell from fashion in favour of earthenware, so the price of tin then dropped, causing more mine closures.

Eventually, about 1800, both copper and tin prices began to pick up again, and mines in West Devon and Cornwall came back into production. During the first half of the 19th century, however, tin was never as important as copper, and it was to suffer the same vagaries of trade depressions, especially in 1837 and 1838, when many of those working at the tin mines, including women and children, were laid off again.[10] The total number of women and children at the tin mines was always much less than the number at the copper mines during the 18th and first half of the 19th century.

Tin eventually came into its own from the mid 1850s, and, after an alarming slump in tin prices from 1865-7, peaked in production around 1873. During this time, many women and girls were employed to work at surface, eventually outstripping the number employed at the copper mines as they closed from about 1856 onwards. Probably the highest number of females employed at the tin mines was between 1855 and 1860. A description from this time gives some idea of their working environment:

'Soon the scene presented another abrupt and extraordinary change. We had hitherto been walking amid almost silence and solitude; but now with each succeeding minute strange, mingled, unintermitting noises began to grow louder and louder around us. We followed a sharp curve in the tramway, and immediately found ourselves saluted by an entirely new prospect, and surrounded by an utterly bewildering noise. All about us monstrous wheels were turning slowly, machinery was clanking and groaning in the hoarsest discords; invisible waters were pouring onwards with a rushing sound; high above our heads, on skeleton platforms, iron chains clattered fast and fiercely over iron pulleys, and huge steam pumps puffed and gasped, and slowly raised and depressed their heavy black beams of wood. Far beneath the embankment on which we stood, men, women and children were breaking and washing ore in a perfect marsh of copper coloured mud and copper coloured water. We had penetrated to the very centre of the noise, the bustle, and the population on the surface of a great mine.' [11]

The dressing floor

As with the copper dressing floors, the layout at the tin mines was designed to minimise effort in transporting ore, but was also dependent on good supplies of water. In mines where there was no regular supply of water, ore was carried, by mule in the early days, or by waggon later, to nearby stamps, which had been built where the water supply was more reliable, for dressing. Even so, stamps could sometimes lie idle from May to October, for lack of water. These separate stamps were sometimes managed by the mine, but were frequently privately-owned. In the parish of St. Agnes, in 1790, so much tin was being raised that twenty-five different stamps were at work in the parish, employing a total of one hundred and fifty people. At about the same time, six different privately-owned tin stamps were operating in the Redruth area, all of which received tin-stuff for crushing from Wheal Sparnon. In the late 19th century, stone was sent down from East Pool Mine to be crushed at the stamps at Tolvaddon.[12] Where the stamps were at a distance from the mine, all the subsequent dressing took place there. The women and girls who worked at the separate stamps were sometimes referred to in the census records as 'tin stamps workers (or girls)' or 'stamps maids'.

The dressing process

In contrast to the tin extracted from the river beds or the sea, tin mined from depth had not been weathered, and therefore needed much more dressing and preparation. Also, unlike copper, which can be smelted as small pieces, tin needed to be reduced to the finest powder first. As a result, the mines had to set up extensive dressing floors to prepare the ore for smelting.

Some of the processes required for dressing tin ore were quite different from those used for dressing copper, due to the very different nature of the two ores. Even the words for the material brought to grass were different. At the copper mines it was referred to as ore-stuff, or 'hures'. At the tin mines it was called 'tin-stuff'. Although there were some processes in common, such a washing and picking, spalling, buddling and jigging, some of the processes were quite different, due to the much heavier and more robust nature of tin.

On landing, the tin-stuff was picked, and washed, with larger pieces being spalled, in much the same way as copper. Unlike copper, however, all the tin-stuff was then taken to stamps for crushing, instead of being manually cobbed and bucked. The stamped material was then separated by a series of sedimentation and separating techniques using kieves and buddles, and then trunked, jigged or racked. The tin stuff would be taken through these washes and sedimentations many times, and, depending on the exact nature of the ore and the equipment available, each mine developed its own procedures. As with copper, each process usually involved the dressers in recognising and separating three grades of material: the ore that required no further dressing and was pure enough to be sent for sampling and sale, mixed materials with some value but requiring further separation, and waste.

In some respects the women and girls working at the tin and copper mines would be learning quite different skills. It was often remarked that copper and tin mining were 'different trades', and that the skills of one were not necessarily transferable to the other. While these comments may have been made with reference to the miners and captains, it does not seem to have been so true of the women dressers. The women and girls regularly either chose to, or had to, change their places of work, which included alternating between tin, copper and even lead dressing. For instance, Minnie Andrews, 'the last balmaiden',

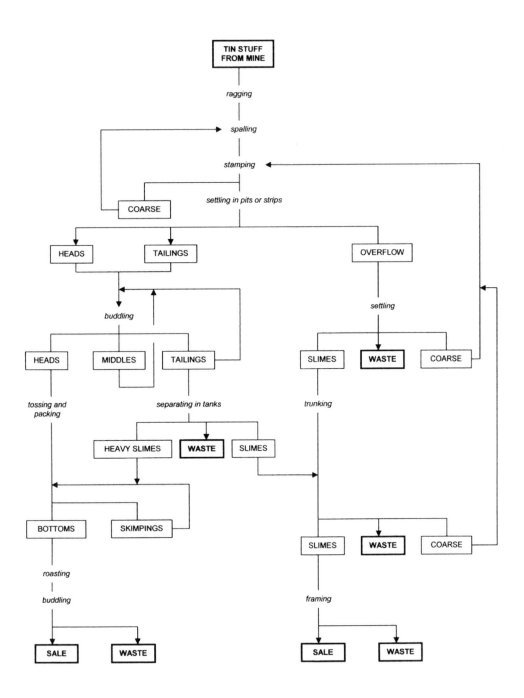

Diagram 2. A simplified diagram of typical tin dressing procedures.

worked at four different mines, sometimes picking copper, and sometimes working at the racking frames at a tin mine.[13]

As with copper, the main technological improvements in the 18th and the first half of the 19th centuries were made in below-ground extraction techniques. The introduction of mechanisation on the dressing techniques was much slower, the most significant development being the improved effectiveness of the stamps. Other innovations, such as self-acting frames, were not introduced until about 1860. These were followed fairly rapidly by other mechanisations in the 1880s and 1890s so that most of the female labour on the dressing floor had been replaced by the early 1900s.

Picking and washing

In the early days the tin-stuff, on being landed, was loaded into hand barrows and tipped into heaps to be roughly sorted and washed. This mixture of ore and waste was known as 'spaller'[14] and was generally hand-picked by young girls. They discarded the waste, and selected the good quality tin-stuff of a suitable size for crushing. The pieces which were too large, or had low ore content were left for spalling. This sorting was not an easy task, as the 'values' were very difficult to distinguish from the waste. It seems possible, that, due to the more difficult nature of this task, older girls were used than at the copper mines. For instance, at Charlestown Mines in 1841, the three girls who were employed picking were all between the ages of 16 and 18, whereas at the copper mines girls of 9 or 10 were commonly employed. Other girls or women would also be employed to wash the ore, if it was very dirty. One such ore washer, at Bassett and Grylls Mine, was a woman who had been deserted by her husband, and went back to work there to try to support her family.[15]

Tincroft Mine, showing a woman spalling the large pieces of tin-stuff raised from the shaft, prior to it being carted to the stamps for crushing.

Courtesy of Paddy Bradley

Spalling

The mixed tin-stuff, left after the pickers had removed the waste, and the large pieces of best ore, were broken (spalled) by hand with a long-handled hammer weighing between 3 and 7 lbs, into fist-sized pieces. As with copper, this would be done on special cobbled dressing floors near to where the tin-stuff was landed. The spalled pieces would then be re-picked to remove more waste, and the remainder sent to the stamps. Spalling was nearly always carried out in the open air, and sometimes under appalling weather conditions:

'On the hill at Dolcoath the girls had to face wind and rain, and soon had to 'touch pipe' as they were drenched and cold, and when standing before the fierce fire in the little shed the steam rose in clouds from their garments; yet they soon resumed their labours.' [16]

The quantity of material that balmaidens were able to spall varied with the quality and type of tin-stuff. At Dolcoath in 1893, it was estimated that one woman or girl could spall between three and five tons of rocks per day.[16] As spalling was a very demanding task, it was generally carried out by the older girls and the younger women. Herbert Thomas had this to say about the skills and strength required:

'Even for strong girls who have the knack of striking rocks at the right spot and breaking four or five tons a day to a size suitable for the stamps, the wages are decidedly well earned.' [17]

However, it was not just older girls who were put to this task. When 17 year-old Elizabeth Hocking was interviewed by the 1842 Commission, she had been spalling tin at the Charlestown Mines for three years.[18] Annie Roberts broke stone from East Pool Mine, ready for the tin crushers at Tolvaddon Stamps, during her teenage years in the 1890s.[19] Annie Martin, a spaller at Dolcoath Mine, was slightly older (23 years old) when she was involved in a quite a serious accident in 1892.[20]

Four spalling women in a posed photograph of the surface workers at Mitchell Shaft, East Pool.
Courtesy of Paddy Bradley

The family-run Glebe Stamps, Wendron, c. 1890.

© *Royal Cornwall Museum*

Stamping

After spalling, the tin-stuff was taken to the stamps or the crushers. In the earliest days the moving of stuff to the stamps, if on site at the mine, was done by hand barrowing by an army of girls and women. If the stamps were some distance away, material was carried on mules, or in carts. Latterly it was trammed in waggons. Ore was usually gravity-fed to the stamp heads. There the tin-stuff was forced through a fine copper mesh into collection pits. When settled, the fine particles of tin and quartz-rock sediment were dug out of these pits and sent for further processing. By the mid nineteenth century these pits were replaced by longer sedimentation areas called strips. Many women and girls were involved in the digging out of these sediments.

Buddling

The coarser sediments were separated by buddling, in much the same way as copper. Initially, in the late 18th century, square buddles were used, which were wooden boxes approximately 7 ft x 3 ft x 2 ft, with a 2 ft incline. A dresser stood or sat on a board across the buddle, and worked the ore with a broom or bare feet to help separate the different grades of particles. By 1850 square buddles were still in use, but were gradually being replaced by the Cornish round buddles with mechanised sweeping arms. It took about ten hours for each of these large buddles to be filled. As at the copper mines, boys usually looked after the buddles, but girls were sometimes involved. For instance, at Wheal Vor in 1841, three girls between the ages of 13 and 18 were employed in 'serving the

Four balmaidens posing for a photograph by the buddles at Basset Mine, Carnkie, c. 1900. This is one of the few photos showing balmaidens in their work aprons.

Courtesy of Paddy Bradley

buddles'.[21] After 1878, when child labour was restricted, it was older women who did this work. One of these was Minnie Andrews who worked at Tincroft, in the late 1880s:

'Then I used to buddly in the strip and used either to work with a shovel in the strip, keeping them going, water coming down, washing it all down and filling up the buddle. A buddle would go round with sweeps to it, and then the young men would clean un up and then I should fill un again. I filled twice a day.' [13]

Buddling required considerable skill, as implied by these comments of 1843:

'To the inexperienced eye, the various deposits left on the cone of the buddle all look the same, yet these young dressers were able to distinguish the line between the purer tin settled at the top of the cone, and the waste material, or sometimes other minerals such as copper or zinc, which settle further down. This process was repeated until much of the contaminating material was removed.' [22]

Tozing and packing

The medium coarse sediment from the stamps, or lower grade ores from second buddling, were shovelled into large kieves (barrels), about 3'8" in diameter, which had already been half filled with water. Two boys or girls would carry out this task, carefully tipping the sediment down the side of the kieve with a shovel, whilst a third child constantly stirred the mixture with a shovel. This stirring was carefully done in one direction, in order to assist separation of the ore from the lighter waste. Sediment would continue to be added until the water level had risen to within 2" of the top of the kieve. When this was done, one of the boys or girls would then strike the kieve with an iron bar, which was usually fixed into the ground at one end, to settle out the sediment. This could take between fifteen and sixty minutes, needing about one hundred blows per minute.

When the packing was finished, the surplus water was baled into a second kieve alongside, ready for the next trunking. Then the top thin layer of waste or mixed ore (not more than half an inch) was removed using a 'limp' (semi-circular piece of wood) and put aside to be rebuddled. The settled white sediment in the bottom of the kieve was ready for roasting, to remove any arsenic impurities.[23] This sediment was called 'whits'. After roasting, the whits were usually returned for re-buddling, or kieving.

By 1860, mines began to install water-powered wooden hammers to do this laborious task. Henderson said:

'This saves the time of the child who might be more usefully and certainly more comfortably employed. The occupation of packing being anything but a pleasant one during the winter season.' [24]

Jigging

In the 18th and early 19th century, the finest sediment from the stamps was taken for hand dillueing or jigging, as at the copper mines. It was passed through a very fine copper-based sieve, shaken in a hutch (barrel) of water, and the pure tin ore left in the bottom of the sieve was sent for sampling. The even finer sediment in the bottom of the hutch was sent on to be racked. Jigging was generally done by young boys, but occasionally by young women. This was very difficult, wet and heavy work. The process was semi-mechanised by the 1830s, and fully mechanised, except for filling and emptying, by about 1860.

Trunking

The finest of the slimes collected after stamping were dried and then taken to the trunks. These consisted of a circular strake, sluice and settling area, and was a variation of the buddle. The slimes were agitated with water in the strakes, and then allowed to flow out through the sluice into a rectangular settling box. The purest tin, settling out at the head, was then barrowed to the frames, ready for racking, and the rest was either disposed of as waste or retrunked. Trunking was usually done by girls. At Wheal Vor, in 1841, there was one girl responsible for 'trunking slimes' in this way, and she was under 13 years of age.[21]

Racking

This was also known as recking, ragging or framing, and was the process of separating out tiny tin particles from the very finest grade of waste. It was the most delicate process in the dressing of tin ore, and was usually carried out by women and girls. The skill required, as with buddling, was considerable. This separation took place in wooden frames, usually built in ranks. Each frame was made up of two flat portions, the head and the body, all inclined at a slope of about one in seven.

The fine tin-stuff was laid in ridges at the head of the frame, parallel to the flow of water. By careful management of the water flow, the tin particles could be made to collect at the top of the frame, while the waste sediment would run off at the bottom. The girl in charge of the frame would stand to one side and encourage this separation with a light brush, or feather, or, later, by a toothless rake. When the separation was complete, she would then tip

Cartoon sketch of girls at the
racking frames, by George
Seymour Jnr. c. 1870.
Courtesy of the Mining Journal

the frame over, using a brush or rake, and wash the tin concentrate into a wooden collecting chest underneath. A balmaiden can be seen emptying the racking frame in the drawing of a tin mine dated 1858, reproduced on page 8.[25] [26]

The first technological development of the frames came with a self-supplying design. Prior to this, one girl was required to operate each frame. These new ones were usually installed in two lines of eight, with one girl responsible for four at a time - four girls to each section.[27] However, by the end of the 1850s, self-acting frames were beginning to be used, which would tip up and empty automatically. This meant that one boy or girl could oversee twenty or thirty frames at once.[28] Among the first installed were at St. Day United Mines.[29]

Racking was usually carried out by young girls in their mid or late teens. Only two of the girls interviewed by the 1842 Commission worked at the racking frames. They were Elizabeth Hocking and Elizabeth Davey, both employed at Charlestown Mines, who started racking at the ages of 13 and 17 years, respectively.[21] Of a total of thirty-seven girls employed at the frames at Charlestown, all were between the ages of 16 and 18.[23] In the census it was unusual for particular dressing tasks to be recorded, however in 1861 Elizabeth Foy, aged 13 years, from Porkellis[30], and Peggy Phill, aged 61 years, and Margaret White, aged 18 years, of Amalebra[31] were described as a 'stamps framers'.

In the early days, when one girl was responsible for one frame, it seems that this work was done under cover, in open-fronted sheds, built in ranks. The later self-supplying and self-acting frames, constructed in large blocks, had to be built in the open air. Minnie Andrews gave a graphic description her outdoor work at the frames, in about 1882:

'*I first went to work when I was nine year old. I was turt (taught) to the frames and cleaning the holes and getting the water to run, and taking out gravels out from the holes; it did choke up the holes, you know, they things. Oh, I worked awful hours, mister, because I been dying with the cold, my hands, no wonder they go dead, I didn't, they don't go dead, my lor'.*'[13]

Balmaidens at the racking frames at South Wheal Frances, c. 1890. Notice the various forms of headdress, especially the woman who has pinned her gook to protect her face.
Courtesy of the Cornwall Centre Collection.

In addition to looking after the frames, the balmaidens also 'stanked widths'. This involved treading (puddling) the tin-stuff that had been separated at the frames into the collecting tanks underneath, so that the water rose up out of it and was drained away. The tin ore was then relatively dry for carrying to the calciner, or for sampling.[32]

Unidentified tasks

In some drawings and photographs, young girls are seen to be carrying woven baskets on the dressing floor of tin mines. It may be that the young girls in the pictures were delivering dinners to the mine. However, the older girls appear to be involved in the dressing process in some way. It is uncertain what they were doing, but possibly they were clearing blockages in the launders or channels.

Barrowing

As in the copper mines, a continual flow of tin-stuff, ore, and waste, through the dressing operation was vital, and so the effective barrowing between different processes was very important. Most of the barrowing was done by girls and women, using hand barrows of the same design as at the copper mines, with a carrying capacity of 1.5 cwt. Most of the hand barrowing was replaced by waggons, tramways or overhead 'telepherage' by about 1860. However some mines, for example Old Wheal Vor, continued to hand barrow beyond this date.[33]

Sampling

As at the copper mines, normal work on the dressing floors was suspended on a regular basis, in order to prepare the dressed ore for sampling and sale. At these times, the women and girls were often diverted from their normal tasks, in order to mix the dressed ores, and then barrow them into the separate parcels. This process was carried out as for copper sampling. Some of the women in the South Wheal Frances photograph appear to be involved in sampling, with one of the doles of ore being laid out in the background on the right hand side of the picture.

The complete process of dressing tin ore took from eight to ten days, during which time the concentration of tin was raised from less that two percent to over ninety percent, when it was then ready for sampling, sale and smelting.[34]

Second streaming

From the early 18th century, individual families or venturers often applied for leases to search riverbeds and streams for waste tin washed down from the deep mines. This was called second tinning, or tin salvage or recovery. Pryce was familiar with this type of tin extraction:

'(The) leavings from the stamping mills which are carried by the rivers to lower grounds; and after some years of lying and collecting there, yield some money to the laborious dressers.' [35]

In the 1850s it was calculated that between 17% and 33% of tin from the deeper mines was never recovered from the ore raised. It was this 'lost tin' which was the lifeblood of the second streamers. It became even more profitable to reclaim this tin during the early part of the 1870s. The deeper tin tended to be very fine-grained, and the newly designed Californian stamps liberated more tin from the tin-stuff raised, so that large quantities of fine tin were available in the 'slimes' collected after stamping. However, not much of this newly available fine cassiterite was recovered during the dressing operations. As a result, even greater quantities of tin found its way into the rivers and streams serving as outflows to the mines, and some estimated that as much as 40% to 50% of the tin was being lost.[36] Barton described it in this way:

'The only aspect of production which failed to keep pace with this technical revolution was tin dressing and a great deal of cassiterite stamped out of the ore was certainly being lost.' [6]

By 1879, one eighth of all Cornish tin came from stream works. They were often set up in sequence down a stream or river bed, and by this time no fewer than twenty stream works were to be found on the Red River alone, in Redruth and Illogan. Stream works continued to be in operation throughout the 1880s and 1890s, and some proved to be more profitable than the deep mines which had lost the same tin in the first place.[37]

Extraction of tin from these deposits required relatively low investment; the main equipment required being water-powered frames, buddles and settling pits. However it was a very labour-intensive process. Some stream works employed very large numbers, especially of children, and sometimes tin dressing continued around the clock, with the women and children working shifts.[38] Reskadinnick employed 210 people, mostly children, in the 1870s, and had three quarters of an acre of settling pits, buddles and frames.[6] When Relubbus Streams, in the Cober Valley, were put up for sale in 1881, there were eight water wheels, three scoop wheels, eight heads of stamps, one hundred racking frames, and fifty-seven dead frames for auction, giving an indication of the number of boys and girls who may have been employed there.[39]

Muriel Sara remembered visiting a 'courtesy aunt' who worked at the tin streams, probably either at Gwithian or Portreath, in the 1890s. This is how she describes the working conditions then:

'These tin streams were rather like a field of red water and sand, with wooden bridges or planks that led you over it, and at certain places there were big brush machines (buddles or frames?) that the bal maidens worked. Aunt Harris would show us how things were used and let us try at times to work the great brush, not so easy as it looked.' [40]

Cornwall's 'last balmaiden', Minnie Andrews, worked for short periods at two of these stream workings, Dick Hole (or Olds), and Rodda's, on the Red River, about 1890. Her sister, Bessie, also worked at Dick Olds on a regular basis. Some balmaidens were still working at W. G. Hocking's Tin Streams at Reskadinnick in 1915, and they were described in this way:

'There were about a dozen balmaidens working there then. They were all good maidens. Some of them was strong, like men. … They worked hard, wheeling barrows to the buddles and keeping them tidy. The also looked after the round frames, there was one maiden to each. One of their jobs was 'stankin widths', that is treading heavily on a width of tin stuff that had been through the frames. All the water would then come up from it so that it was pretty dry before it went to the burning house.' [41]

Re-picking of tin waste (second tinning)

As with copper, there were occasions when it became economically viable to re-pick over old tin waste. For example, Emma Jane Jenkin, 18 years old, was recorded as working at the tin 'burrows' in the Marazion area in 1861.[42] The waste burrows at Balleswidden and Ding Dong Mines were re-sorted and stamped round about the time of the First World War. New Cornish Stamps were installed at Ding Dong and nearly 14,000 tons of ore, yielding 51 tons of black tin, were extracted between 1912 and 1915.[43] Similarly, during World War Two second tinning was carried out at a number of mines, such as Wheal Reeth, Dolcoath and Drakeswall. These tasks may have been carried out by women or girls, as was the re-dressing of the lead waste heaps at Wheal Mary Ann during World War One.[44]

Apart from formal employment at these waste heaps, second tinning had probably been the source of money through the informal economy for as long as mining had occurred in Cornwall and West Devon. Unemployed miners and their families would eke out a living from re-picking tin and selling it to local tin stamps. This was particularly true in times of high unemployment such as during the 1880s and early 1890s. Small groups of tributers were working in this way at Poldice and Gwennap, where they sold over 5,100 tons of tin stone to stamps at Bissoe or on the Red River in 1890. Similarly, an amazing 120,000 tons of tin stone was believed to have been collected and sold from old burrows at Clifford Amalgamated Mines, after its closure in 1870.[45]

Tin smelting

Until the turn of the 18th century tin was smelted in blowing houses or 'ore hearths' usually built near the tin works. They required charcoal or 'moor coal' (peat) for fuel. They were usually built in exposed places that could provide good ventilation to the furnace, in order to achieve the very high temperature required to melt the tin ore. It is not known whether women were involved in these early smelting processes.

By about 1700, finding wood, for charcoal, or suitable moor coal, was becoming increasingly difficult, with much being brought by mule from distant places, such as Dartmoor. As a result, in 1703 the first iron furnaces were built in Cornwall. They used fossil coal from Wales, and could also process larger quantities of tin quickly. The first furnaces were in operation in Newham by 1703, at Calenick by 1711 (both near Truro on the Fal) and at Angarrack, near Hayle, by 1704. These smelters, in contrast to the hill and moorland positions of the blowing houses and ore hearths, required easy access to the shore or a harbour to enable delivery of coal and other commodities. Hamilton Jenkin reports that at Newham:

'The work of landing coals, clay, lime, brick and sand from the River Fal was done almost entirely by barrow women'. [46]

From cost and receipt books for Newham Smelter from 1704 to 1707, it appears that a similar system was in operation. There are regular entries for women carrying coal 'into yard from the shore', for which they appear to have been paid between 2d and 2.5d per ton:

'Twenty second day of November 1704 received by the barrow women for carriage of thirty two tons weight £3 5s 6d, signed (mark of) Martha Crips, Elizabeth Traffon.' [47]

On 31st May 1706 Ann Stevens was paid three shillings for carrying 1,500 bricks ashore.[48] If these women were using the standard 1.5 cwt hand barrow for carriage, this means that they were being paid 2d for about seven journeys, which presumably would involve the filling and emptying of the barrows at either end. If their round trip from the smelter to the shore took as little as fifteen minutes, they may be able to earn about 6d to 8d per day.

Specific entries indicate when women were paid for barrowing from the ships to the smelting yard, when they were paid by the ton. Other entries show that women were also barrowing ore, coal, lime etc. at the smelter, but for this they were paid a daily rate. This barrowing was usually combined with sifting slag, culm and cinders, and the going rate was 6d per day:

'29th July 1704 3 women barrowing and sifting 1s 6d'. [48]

Presumably these tasks involved sieving the coal on arrival, to remove fine dust and particles before it was used to fuel the furnace. Sieving of the slag and cinders could only be done when they were cold, and this would be to recover re-usable coal, or ore which would be re-smelted.

There is very little subsequent information about females employed at tin smelters. However, in the 1891 census there is a record of two women working at a tin smelter in the Hayle area. They were 40 year-old Amelia Rowe, and her 17 year-old daughter Kate, from Chenhalls, St. Erth. [49]

The final years of tin

From the 1850s onwards, innovations on the tin dressing floors meant fewer people employed. With public feeling growing against the employment of women and children at mines in general, it was hardly surprising that it was the girls and women who were often the first to lose their jobs. For example, when a new water wheel was installed at Great

West Wheal Seaton, c. 1890, showing six balmaidens working in pairs, two of whom are hand barrowing. The neatly laid out dole behind them suggests that this is sampling time.

Courtesy of the Cornwall Centre Collection

Wheal Busy, in 1859, to work a set of thirty self-acting frames, one small boy was employed to do the work of six or seven girls. [50]

As copper prices fell, some copper mines struggled on and eventually found tin at depth, such as Dolcoath, West Wheal Basset, West Wheal Francis and South Condurrow. They installed tin dressing equipment to replace the existing machinery, including new stamps, and continued to employ some girls and women at spalling, picking and to operate the racking frames. At Providence Mine the improvements included roofing in the entire dressing floor, giving shelter to all one hundred and fifty working there, although providing shelter was not a universal feature at this time.[51] Another mine which offered covered-in working areas for dressing in the 1870s was St. Ives Consols. The advertisement listing items for sale, when the mine closed in 1875, gives an indication of the equipment used at this time:

'Tin floors, together with the excellent and lofty woodshed covering the same, 21 large centre headed buddles, 6 square ditto, 124 self-acting and other tin frames, Brunton's Calciner and waterwheel, 4 water wheels for dressing machinery, tin kieves and all the necessary dressing tools for a large mine.' [52]

Tin production stayed at reasonable levels from 1870 until 1890, but tin prices started to drop again from about 1873, resulting in more closures. In 1873 there had been over 230 mines producing tin in Cornwall but only 98 remained open in 1877, with massive loss in the jobs of both underground and surface workers.[53] Those tin mines that stayed open found it economically expedient to remodel their dressing floors yet again and install improved or semi-automated equipment, so that although the total amount of tin produced did not radically alter, it was raised and dressed by half the number of people. This reduction was mostly in the number of children, especially in the younger age group, because they could no longer be employed after the passing of the *Factory and Workshop Act* of 1878. Sixty young people were dismissed from Dolcoath at this time.[54] However, Dolcoath was to continue to employ balmaidens for spalling in fairly large numbers, with 745 surface workers employed at the peak of its tin production in 1893.

In 1893 there was another drop in the price of tin, so by 1897 only nine tin mines remained open in Cornwall. In 1895, for instance, the 70 surface workers were laid off at South Condurrow.[55] Between 1891 and 1898 the number of surface workers employed at the tin mines in Cornwall had fallen from nearly 6,000 to 2,500, most of these losses being women. At Dolcoath in 1908, the tasks left for women were spalling, (still considered by some to be the most economic way of reducing waste at the point the tin-stuff arrived from underground), sorting and racking.[56] In 1910 Tincroft was still employing a few women, but just 67 out of the total workforce of nearly 1,000.

Eventually even these tasks were mechanised. Hand sorting was replaced by automated shaking and separating tables, Californian Stamps and Husband's Stamps replace the spallers, and frue vanners were used to separate the finer wastes, replacing the women and girls who attended the frames.[56] These processes only required one or two employees to oversee them where, previously, dozens had been needed. Training to operate these machines was always given to male employees. The last women at the tin streams seem to have finished by the end of the First World War and the last spalling maidens at the deep mines were dismissed from Dolcoath in 1920.[57]

China Clay Workers 1840

Bonneted, they billow through my thought;
stand there in the chaste, transparent wind,
white-aproned, with their sleeves down to their wrists,
averted at their tables on the moor.

Half-covered by their shelters, thatched with reeds
that shadow out their features. At their backs,
white-painted by the clean slime of the clay
the men pick at the pits, and wash the sands.

then lead away the slurry, soft as milk,
to settle in a thick consistent cream
and dry out in the shallow moss-lined pans
beneath the summer sunlight. Even now

their dream-like shapes reform, compose in air,
arranged still with their sober elegance,
their ankles in a waste of powdered dust,
still turning around the cut and lifted lumps.

and scraping clear the residue of grit
that tarnishes the bottom. Pass them on
to stack then, clean of all impurities,
as modest, stainless blocks of solid light.

John Gurney
Courtesy of Peterloo Poets 1977

Chapter 6

THE 'CLAY MAIDENS'

Although the majority of women and girls employed in the mining-related industries in Cornwall and West Devon were employed in the tin and copper mines, a considerable number also worked at the various clay pits. A few also worked at the soapstone quarries and glass (potash felspar) mines. These women were also referred to as 'balmaidens'.

China clay and china stone

The granites of South West Britain have, in places, been extensively altered. China clay and china stone have been extracted where felspar, one of the chief minerals in the granite has been broken down by fluids and vapours and converted into kaolinite. Commercial china clay is made up almost entirely of kaolinite, hence its alternative name, kaolin. This kaolinised granite is often found in association with veins of tin, but was little used before the second half of the 18th century. For instance, Carclaze, which was to produce significant amounts of china clay, was initially mined for tin for well over a century, with the china clay being discarded as waste.

When well-kaolinised ground was soft enough, it was washed out as a thick slurry of mineral particles, the finest of which was kaolin. The coarser waste particles of mica and sand dropped out of the suspension in successive settling pits, and the remaining fine clay was settled in pans and slowly dried before cutting into blocks, ready for sale as china clay. In harder ground, where the granite was only partially kaolinised, the mineral was quarried and sold in lump form as china stone, or ground and sold as china stone powder.

It was not until the 1760s that the full potential of these products in the manufacture of fine porcelain was realised. The Bristol, Worcester, and Staffordshire potteries took both china clay and china stone in equal quantities. However, during the 19th century, many other uses were found for the clay, especially as a filler in fabrics and paper. During this time production expanded enormously.

China clay

Whilst china clay working is mostly associated with the St. Austell area, the first commercial exploitation in Cornwall was at Tregonning Hill between Helston and Marazion, in 1746. Good quality clay was then also discovered at Carloggas near St. Stephen in Brannel. Prior to this, only very small amounts had been dug out by the farmers or landowners, and sold to local potters for earthenware production, or used for making bricks, fireboxes for mine steam engines, or casting moulds.

China clay was quarried in a small way in the 18th century, but during the 19th century it became a large scale industry. By 1809, 3,000 tons of china clay and stone was being exported through the Charlestown Docks. The earliest mention of women and girls working at the clay pits is in 1812, and refers to Trethosa Clay Work, along with others:

'It is probable also that from time to time, and in other small works then active, women and children were also employed on the simpler and lighter tasks.' [1]

Some surviving cost books record women and girls employed in small numbers from the late 1820s onwards. At Ninestones two women worked from May until September 1828, and five or six women in March and April 1831.[2] An unspecified number of women worked at Goonvean for the equivalent of 160 to 190 days per month from March to August, and for 30 to 80 days from September to December 1834.[3]

Although the word 'bal' was not applied to the clay works, it is interesting that the term 'balmaiden' was applied to the women and girls who worked at the clay pits, as well as at the mines, and was certainly used in the latter half of the 19th century. In census returns more functional descriptions were used such as 'clay worker', 'china clay labourer', 'clay scraper', 'clay cleaner' or occasionally 'china clay girl' or 'clay refiner'.

An intriguing reference also suggests that women were involved in working at the pumps at the clay pits, a task that was assumed to be done by men or boys at the mines:

'An early form of pump was usually worked by women' and *'probably women working at the pumps ceased about 1865-1870, I remember seeing them when I was a lad.'* [4]

By 1845 at least forty five pits were open, and by 1851 the volume of clay produced had increased to 98,000 tons. By 1852, it was estimated that the total number of employees at the West of England Clay Works, operating in the Hensbarrow area, north of St. Austell, was about 7,200, of whom a proportion would have been women and girls. In 1864, the five 'china clay' parishes of St. Austell (St. Austell, St. Stephen, St. Dennis, St. Mewan and Roche) employed a total of 1,700 clay labourers out of a total population of 30,000, but no separate figure was given for balmaidens.[5] When Esquiros travelled through Cornwall in 1865 he noted that:

'The china clay works in the St. Austell area employ a large number of men, women and

children.' [6]

From about 1865 the clay pits often offered employment when other mines in Cornwall were laying people off, but, even so, there were times when there was desperate poverty in the clay-mining areas. During 1868 corn prices were so high, and the wages at the mines and clay pits so low, that soup kitchens were set up at Blowing House Hill, Wrestling Green, for the china clay workers. This 'Parish Relief' was available three days per week, at 1d per quart.[7]

During the 1870s the china clay industry was actually expanding, at a time when the copper mines were in very deep trouble, and employment levels at the lead, iron and tin mines was also dropping, either due to closure or increased technology. As the market developed for the china clay, new clay pits opened. According to Hunt's annual *Mineral Statistics*, 1874 was the peak year for the number of active clay works, when 119 enterprises were reported for Cornwall, and 10 for Devonshire. Most of these were in the St. Austell and Par area, but some also opened in other parts of Cornwall, such as Breage, Germoe, Towednack, and Ludgvan. In Devon there were some pits which opened on Dartmoor.

Initially, the china clay 'matrix' was dug up and dumped into pits using manual labour. In the pits it was thoroughly agitated with water, so that the clay could be decanted in suspension. By the end of the 18th century most producers were using the less laborious technique of breaking up the clay in situ, and diverting streams of water over it. The finer particles were washed out, leaving the coarse material behind. This was then drawn up onto the waste heaps (sand-burrows). The stream of 'fines' was then channelled in such a way that the coarser particles would sediment out sequentially into the sand and mica 'drags' (pits). These preliminary separating tasks were normally carried out by male employees, however, in the 1841 census 70-year old Jenepher Jacob of Barbellingey was described as a 'sand settler'.[8]

Eventually, only the lightest clay remained in suspension. This fine clay slurry was run into shallow tanks, usually about 40' by 12' and 14"-18" deep, called sun pans. Each pan was lined with granite blocks and, before the clay slurry was poured in, it was made waterproof by lining the cracks with moss. A young child was paid to go out on to the moors to collect the moss and to fill these cracks. The bottom of the pan was then covered with sand prior to being filled.[2]

The time it took for the settling and drying of the clay depended on the weather, but generally the clay collected in the summer and left to dry over winter (called the 'winter saving') took about eight months, and was ready for lifting sometime between March and May. The clay collected in the spring months (the 'summer saving') took about four months to dry and could be lifted in the late summer or autumn.

This seems to have given a seasonality to the work done by the females, whose task it was either to carry out the clay blocks to be dried, or to dress or pack the blocks of dried clay. Surviving cost books show that there was usually higher employment from March through to August or September, with very few women employed in December or January. The numbers employed in the spring and summer months fluctuate, and presumably were dependent on weather conditions. It seems that work was offered on a much more casual basis than at the mines, with workers being called in at short notice, and presumably laid off at short notice as well.

Two women clay cleaners. Although this is a back view, it shows clearly the sort of reed hurdles which were used, both to work under, and to protect the china clay blocks as they dried.
Courtesy of Wheal Martyn

When the clay was dry enough to be moved (between 15% and 20% water content) it was cut up by two men using a special knife with a blade at right angles to a long handle. In the early years various shapes were cut, including prismatic shapes and nine to twelve inch blocks.[9] Latterly they were standardised to twelve inch blocks. The men would throw these blocks out onto wooden boards placed at the side of the pans. In good weather, they would be carried out onto the hillsides to dry:

'The diggers fling the lumps on a board, and boys and women carry these to the drying ground … watching the women and boys as they spread their burdens on the drying ground, all as white as only clay workers can be.' [10]

If the weather was not good enough for drying on the hillsides, the clay was carried straight to the 'reeders'. The women and girls would build the blocks into an airy tower, separating the blocks with layers of sand or straw to prevent them from adhering to each other. These towers were usually protected by a thatched roof or thatch-covered hurdle over the top and, often around the exposed sides as well, hence the name 'reeders'. In 1852, a visitor described the scene at a clay pit on the day that the sun pans were being emptied:

'The scene was animated by the constant passage of women with white bonnets, aprons and sleeves carrying cubes of clay for placing beneath reeders, in sheds or in their hundreds on drying grounds on the surrounding hills, by the comings and goings of heavy sand wagons, the creak of pump and horse whim and the sound and motion of countless water-engines about their endless tasks.' [11] [12]

When dry, it was the job of the balmaidens to scrape the sand, straw and algae off the blocks, clean them generally, and load them into casks. Charles Thurlow suggests that it was only the better grade of china clay that was scraped in this way.[13] The cleaning was usually done in the open air, or under a simple movable shelter made from three thatched hurdles. The girls or women stood at slatted trestle tables, working on individual blocks. They used a triangular iron scraper to remove the dirt and sand. Walter White, during his

Three women dressers at a clay works, showing china clay blocks stacked in the air to dry behind them.
Courtesy of Wheal Martyn

travels of 1854, describes the blocks being scraped with an instrument like a Dutch hoe. Alternatively, the women placed the blocks on a board held against their chests, and cleaned them by dragging a special sort of knife towards themselves, over the surface of the clay.[14] Stoker made the following comment about these groups of women:

'As they surround their scraping tables, (they) present a formidable appearance.' [14]

The scrapings and other waste were collected and rewashed. Although not an onerous task, the hands of the women and girls who were scraping must have become very coarsened and sore, and the work would have been unpleasant in cold weather conditions. As the clay had to be kept dry, presumably the women did not work in wet weather.

China clay extraction has continued to the present day, but with inevitable closures, amalgamations, and mechanisation. From 1845 coal-fired dries, or pan kilns, began to be used at the clay pits, instead of the sun pans. This meant that it was possible to dry the clay more quickly and that clay could be ready for market all the year round. As a result, where these changes were made the women and girls were no longer required to scrape clay blocks. They were now dried in a clean state and were loaded straight from the dries into wagons by men.

Some clay works, however, continued to use the sun pan process for drying into the 20th century, as at South Carloggas, but eventually it was replaced by pan kiln drying in all the clay works, so that the women were no longer needed. Nearly all the balmaidens involved in the drying and scraping processes were laid off by the beginning of First World War.

This was not the last time that women were employed at the clay pits, though, as some were recruited to take over the process of extracting clay when there was a shortage of employable men during World War One. They actually worked in the clay pit, often several hundred feet down from the surface. They would hose out the clay matrix after it had been loosened by men setting charges in the side of the pits. Some women were also employed to mill and pack the waste china clay sand for sandbags during World War Two.[15]

China stone

Where the granite was only partly weathered it was possibly to quarry the china stone, rather than extract it as a suspension in water. This china stone was also known as 'white granite'. It was mostly quarried from the north of St. Stephen's parish, although Finton reported that 'most china clay works have a stone quarry. The stone so hard as to be wedged or blasted. The hardest is preferred for easiest carriage'.[16]

After the stone was quarried, the blocks were carried to the dressing floor for storing. The natural joints in these blocks were often discoloured with green vegetable stains, and brown iron oxide or black manganese oxide deposits. It was these blemishes that need to be removed, as the Potteries, the paper and the textile industries required a very high grade pure white product. The blocks often became stained during storage, so they were not cleaned until the stone was sold and ready for shipment. This was done by the balmaidens, who chipped over them with a kind of axe, or used a scraper to remove the stains and any dirt that may have accumulated.[17]

Working conditions

Most of the Clay Works were run on the Cost Book System, like the other Cornish mines, and used the same employment practices. So the 'maidens' were paid monthly, either one or two months in arrears. The women and girls seem to have been paid in different ways according to the task and varying from works to works; whether laying out clay on the hillside, stacking clay in the reeders, or scraping or packing the clay blocks, once they were dried.

The child who collected moss to seal the granite blocks in the sunpans at Lower Ninestones in 1828 was paid 7d per day.[2] At Goonvean, the women and girls who carried the clay blocks out on to the moors to dry worked in teams of about eight. They appear to have been hired by a subcontractor, who was paid by the number of yards of blocks that the women had laid out, normally 1d per yard. In some cases it seems there was a woman in charge of the group, for example Kittey Grigg and Ann Brook, who received payment for the group.[3]

Some women were paid for their work by the ton, 4d or 5d per ton at Goonvean, for instance, in March 1835. This seems to be the rate for stacking clay blocks in the reeders, or packing them in the casks. Other women were paid by the day, and these were probably the women who cleaned the blocks; for instance the women 'scraping clay' at Goonvean, from 1833-36, were being paid 4d per day.[3]

A decade later, in the 1840s, the boys and 'maidens' at the clay works were still earning much the same - 4d to 6d per day. By the 1880s the rate had increased to about one shilling. This was still comparable with the rates of pay at the tin and copper mines. Mary Ann Bray and Elizabeth Fisher were paid this amount for scraping clay at Wheal Henry Clay Works between 1882 and 1886.[18] There was no increase in this rate over many years, and the clay balmaidens were still earning one shilling per day in the early 20th century.

The number of days worked by the balmaidens varied greatly, especially over the course of the year. Sometimes they are recorded as working only a few days in the month, but there are other months when they appear to have been employed full time, and even doing overtime. For instance, at Ninestones, Elizabeth Grose was recorded as working a total of 31 days in August 1833, about 65 hours in the week, which must have required her to work time and a half for most of the month.[2]

All of work carried out by the women and girls could only be done in dry weather, and every opportunity had to be taken to complete the tasks before the weather broke. Sometimes work continued long after dusk, both in winter and summer, and this would be done by the light of lanterns or candles. There was some recompense for having to work late, it seems, as this entry in the cost book for Ninestones for November 1832 shows:

'12 quarts of beer on scraping by night - 10s 10½d.' [2]

Although the tasks performed by the balmaidens at the clay works were very different from those undertaken by the balmaidens at the mineral mines, the clothes they wore for work were recognisably the same. Esquiros describes them in this way:

'The women are in white bonnets, white sleeves, white aprons and it is curious to see them carrying to the surrounding hills a clay whiter still.' [6]

Photos show the cotton 'gook' with stiffened brim, the hessian apron, and one balmaiden wearing removable protective sleeves. In another picture the women look cold despite wearing thick woollen skirts, thick stockings and warm shawls. Surprisingly, they appear to be working bare-handed. They seem to be wearing lighter shoes than some of the balmaidens who worked at the copper and tin mines.

The proportion of women and girls employed at the clay works was not ever as great as at the copper, tin or lead mines. Generally, the greatest numbers employed seemed to be at the time that the clay was being laid out to dry, and for scraping. Most clay pits just employed a handful of women, with the maximum probably being between 20 and 30. In the 1861 census for Cornwall the total number of females recorded as working at the clay pits was 144. (72 in Treverbyn, 35 in St. Stephen and 20 in Roche). By 1891, however, less than a dozen women or girls are recorded as working at the clay pits in the two parishes of St. Austell and St. Stephen.

With quite low numbers, it seems that it was only older women and girls who were recruited. There is no written evidence of very young girls working, and surviving photos seem to confirm this view. In 1861, the youngest girl recorded at the clay works was 12 year-old Georgiana Poad of Washaway. One of the oldest women recorded as working at the clay pits was 70 year-old Jenepher Jacob of Barbellingey, who was described as a 'sand settler' in the 1841 census. It is thought that she worked at Ruddle Pit.[8]

The cost books record that there were women employed at the clay works who were involved in tasks other than cleaning, carrying, stacking and packing the china clay. For instance, female waggoners were contracted to cart china stone (probably from Wheal Prosper Quarry to the railway at Burngullow). A few were working in 'husband and wife' team such as Mary Ann Williams, working with her husband William, and Catherine

Boundyn, working with her husband James, in 1858 and 1862 respectively. Some, however, seem to have been working in their own right, such as Nancy Phillips and Ann Key who were transporting loads of 7.5 or 15.5 tons of china clay in 1864. They were being paid between 2.5d to 3d per ton.[20] In the 1891 census 21 year-old Ellen Pearce of Boscell Farm is also recorded as a 'clay waggoner'.[21]

An unusual feature of the china clay and china stone business was the number of women who appear to have become involved in management, and who sometimes took significant steps in the development and progression of the industry. For instance, Sarah Michell managed Carbeen, Bluebarrow (Bunny), and Yondertown Clay works from 1848 until about 1868 after the death of her husband.[22 23 24] In 1851, she sent samples of her clay to the Great Exhibition at Crystal Palace, which appear in the catalogue described as:

Michell, Sarah, St. Austell - Producer 'White china-clay, for manufacturing china and earthenware, also for bleaching paper, calico etc.' [25]

Phillipa Lovering also took over management of her husband's business interests at Lower Ninestones, when he died in 1834. Phillipa was in her late forties, and continued to manage these works until her son, John Lovering Jnr., was of age (by about 1845). The Lower Ninestone Cost Books 1828-1836, which survive at Wheal Martyn Museum, were written by Phillipa, so it seems that she was working as her husband's book keeper before his death.[2] Phillipa and her son subsequently took leases on Stents in 1850 [23], West Goonbarrow in 1868, and Carbeen and Bluebarrow in 1870.[22] It seems that Phillipa was a very able women, described as 'a lady of great strength of character and activity' and 'a capable business woman.' [24]

Mrs. Thriscot managed Caudledown after the death of her husband, from about 1858 [22] [24] and Mrs. Margaret Spargo was described as a China Clay Merchant in Gunnislake in 1893.[26] However, the most notable female 'clay baron' must have been Rebecca Martin who managed several large clay works and was largely responsible for initiating co-operative practices in the clay industry, in the mid 19th century.

Women were sometimes called in to replace male clay washers who had joined the armed forces during forces during World War One. This certainly happened at Rocks and Bluebarrow Clay Works. Two photographs in a Pochin's manual of about 1920 also show pairs of women working at the monitors at Gother's clay pit, indicating that the practice was more widespread. Their work required them to handle the heavy water jets under very wet and slippery conditions, on the clay pit sides or at the bottoms. The hoses could discharge up to 750 gallons per minute, at a pressure of 100 lbs per square inch.[27]

Soapstone

In Cornwall, soapstone, or soap rock clay, was found uniquely in veins of serpentine on the Lizard peninsula, and was exploited briefly from the mid 18th century until about 1818. It was an important constituent of soft porcelain, but was quickly superseded by china clay, which enabled the major potteries to produce the more desirable and better quality hard porcelain.

One of the earliest references to the mining of this product is from Dr. Richard Pocock in 1750,[28] who describes soapstone being shipped from the Lizard to potteries in Bristol. Majendie lists soapstone being extracted at Trethvas, Predannack Downs, Mullion

Churchtown, on the North West Coast of the Lizard, as well as Gew Graze, in 1792.[29] In 1801 Britton and Brayley described the soapstone in this way:

'The serpentine is occasionally intersected with veins of steatites, most contained in the celebrated soap-rock situated between the Lizard and Mullion. Its colour is whitish or straw yellow, with streaks or veins of green, red and purple. It is found in three degrees of purity. The first is called best-best, and is most beautifully white. It possesses an absorbent quality, and will imbibe spots of grease or oil from silk without injuring its colours.' [30]

Gew Graze Mine, situated in a deep valley three miles south of Mullion, had been worked by the Worcester Potteries from about 1757 until 1775. In 1780, the lease was taken over by the proprietors of the Caughley Manufactory. Although Paris describes Josiah Wedgwood as one of the lessees, there are no supporting documents for this[31], and it is from this mine that the only reference to women being employed has been found. It comes from the writings of Rev. Richard Warner as he travelled through Cornwall in 1808.[32] He describes the operations at Gew Graze, the mine then being leased by Messrs. Flight and Barr, who owned potteries in Worcester.

At this time, five men, who dug out about five hundred pounds of soapstone per week, were employed at Gew Graze. This was graded into fine and coarse steatite at surface. It seems that the steatite at Gew Graze came in mixed colours, with the white being in great demand, and needing to be separated from the red and other colours before sale.[33] It was graded, and then packed into casks, by 3 or 4 women working in a nearby building. The casks were then shipped from Mullion Cove to Worcester. Gew Graze Mine was still being worked in 1818 but only producing about twelve tons per annum, and by 1819 it seems to have ceased production altogether.[34] It is not clear whether women were also employed at the other soapstone mines on the Lizard.

Potash felspar

In Cornwall there were at least two orthoclase mines operating during the 19th century in the St. Austell area. One was Tresayse Mine, locally called Polpuff Glass Mine. It was open for ten years from about 1870 but closed when the best material was thought to have been mined out, leaving the quarry unable to compete with good quality ore imported from Norway and Sweden. Very little is known of the workings of this mine in the 19th century, and it is not known whether women and girls were employed at that stage.[35]

Despite it being thought that only lower grade ore was left, it became necessary to re-open the mine during the First World War, in order to obtain the felspar for specialist glass production, as supplies from Norway could no longer be guaranteed. Glass was needed for such vital items as clinical thermometers and, the workers believed, for periscope glass. On re-opening it was found that Polpuff still had considerable quantities of very high-grade material. Although Russell reported that the mine reopened in 1917, John Tonkin believes it may have been functioning as early as 1914 [36], and continued in production until about 1921, with at least 50 women or girls working there at its peak. Most of the information about the working of this mine in World War One has been preserved by the foresight of John Tonkin, who started archiving material and interviewing individuals in the 1970s. Without this, we would know almost nothing about Polpuff, its employees, or the processes involved.

The rock being worked at Polpuff contained quartz, tourmaline and mica, as well as the potash felspar. After being quarried, the potash felspar needed to be separated from as much of the waste as possible, and this was done by women and girls. The material was brought from the quarry to the picking table in waggons, along a bank about twelve feet above the pickers. The teenaged male trammers would tip the material from the waggons down onto the bank. The women and girls would pull the ore-stuff, as required, down the chutes onto their picking table. Each balmaiden used a small cobbing hammer for separating the waste from the felspar.

From the photograph below, taken of the women at work, and dated about 1918 [37], the picking table looks about forty feet long, and two or three feet wide. Approximately thirty women and girls are shown standing at the bench, under a crude iron roof, about six feet wide, with no shelter on any side. The women in the photograph are all working bareheaded, in long skirts and blouses, or dresses. Some seem to be wearing long aprons, and protective sleeves.

The picture was taken at Polpuff (Tresayes) Glass Mine. Taken from above, it shows the waggonway along which the felspar was delivered, and the slope of ore from which the women and girls worked.

Courtesy of China Clay Review

There are two other known surviving photographs of these women. In the photograph of 48 women, believed to have been taken in the autumn of 1918, the women and girls are all wearing a variety of overalls or aprons, over long sleeved dresses or blouses. They are mostly bareheaded. In a photograph of a smaller group of six, several of the same women can be identified, and they are wearing much the same as before, and are all holding their cobbing hammers. They are photographed with two men, presumably the two surface

Forty-eight women and girls who worked at Polpuff Glass Mine. Probably taken in 1918.
Courtesy of John Tonkin

captains. Both photographs must have been taken before they started work, as they are all
in beautifully clean clothes, and in summer time, as they are wearing light summer cottons.
Most of the young women look as if they are in their late teens or early twenties, but with
a small number looking as if they are of school leaving age, about 14 or 15 years old. Many
of these women were interviewed by John Tonkin in the 1970s, and of six for whom a date
of birth is available, the youngest would have been 15 years old, four of them 16 years old,
and the eldest 20 years old in 1914.

The women were paid piece-work for a given number of boxes filled with sorted and dressed
ore each day. Each woman had a box number, and on completion of the box would have
the box tallied against her name. The ore-stuff would be sorted, with clean potash felspar
being placed straight into the box, and the quartz and other waste being thrown as 'deads'
into a pile behind. The dressed boxes would then be taken by a male surface labourer who
emptied the box into the leat which ran behind the women. After the ore was washed in the
leat, it would be raked out onto the concrete wharf to drain and dry, ready for shipment.
It is thought that this team of 40 or 50 women could probably dress about one ton of ore
per day.

Periodically the pile of 'deads' was graded through a sieve by a young boy, and the larger
waste returned for cobbing and re-sorting. As this task gave much lower returns, and very
often the material was wet and cold, the job was the least popular, and the women took it
in turns.

During the summer months, two or three of the most skilled of the women were selected
to work out on the wharf, where they broke some of the dressed ore into two inch cubes.
This was a slow job, and they would only finish a few boxes per day, and were on a different
rate of pay. This dressed ore was shipped to South Wales to be used in the coal washing
process.

The women were generally superintended by the two 'treatment captains' who literally 'over saw' from the top and bottom levels of the dressing floor. Mary Higman from Luxulyan was the 'shift manager', and 18 year-old Gussie Retallack, who was the daughter of the surface captain, was the tally checker for the women's boxes. Trammers sometimes favoured particular workers, and would deliver better quality ore to them. As a result, some women finished their allotted task much more quickly than others, with the older or unpopular women often finishing last.

The working day began at 7 a.m. The women travelled from such places as Enniscaven, Whitemoor, and Luxulyan, involving a walk of two to five miles, across very exposed countryside, in all weathers. Hazel Glanville, (née Mary Hazel Varcoe) worked at Polpuff, and lived in Enniscaven. Her father was responsible for the 'dry' at Polpuff. When she was interviewed at the age of 78, she was able to boast that she had never been late to work despite the three-mile walk in all weathers. Annie Andrew who lived in Currian Road, Nanpean, used to leave home at 6 a.m. with five of the other women to reach work in time. She described how sometimes, if she worked hard, she could finish her allotted task for the day by 2 p.m. and then would be allowed to go home early.

Some women were conscripted against their will to work at Polpuff during this time. Beatrice Jenkin described how she had trained as a music teacher when she was called to work at the mine. When she arrived she was issued with clogs to wear, but because the dressing floor was so uneven, she found it more comfortable to wear her own shoes. She remembered how quickly clothes wore out at the picking table. Several of the women remarked on the difficulties of dressing the ore under winter conditions. The winter of 1920-21 was particularly severe, when the ore-stuff froze to the galvanised chutes, and to itself. Polpuff Mine eventually closed in 1921. Varcoes, who owned the mine, also owned a knitting factory in Newquay, and it seems that some of the women were offered alternative employment there.[36]

Chapter 7

BALMAIDENS AND OTHER MINERALS

Despite tin and copper mines being the major producers of minerals in Cornwall and West Devon during the 18th and 19th centuries, other mines were in operation which employed a considerable workforce of women and girls and which were making a significant contribution to the economy of the nation. These mines, or quarries, were producing lead, zinc, manganese, wolfram, and slate. Some other mines also seem to have employed small numbers of women or girls, such as the iron, and uranium mines.

Mines producing mixed ores

A good number of mines were producing more than one mineral, which required careful separation, often dependant on the careful judgment, not just by the surface captain or agent and underground miners, but also by the ore dressers themselves. For instance, other secondary minerals, mined in conjunction with copper or tin, included arsenic, silver, gold, and cobalt. Silver was invariably mined with lead, as was zinc. Sometimes these ores were raised separately from different shafts, in which case they were dressed totally separately, but in many instances, they would come to the surface mixed. For example, in 1854 Great Wheal Baddern Lead Mine was producing 'mundic (arsenic), jack (zinc) and lead' from one 3-foot wide lode, while silver and copper were being extracted from other parts of the mine.[1]

The stage at which mixed ores were separated from each other depended on the relative quantities and type of ore. Some could be separated by feel or by eye, depending on texture, colour, or density. In such cases they could come to the surface already roughly separated by underground workers designated to this task. They could be further separated at the picking table, and subsequently by the spallers, cobbers and buckers. Some minerals were much more difficult to distinguish from each other or from the parent rock, but the ore dressers soon became skilled at discerning one from the other. Wolfram, for instance, was very difficult to distinguish from tin, and in the early days was rejected as waste. It was only in later years that it was exploited for tungsten. Henwood described wolfram as:

'So nearly in appearance when in the stone, that none but the experienced tinners can tell the difference.' [2]

No doubt an experienced balmaiden would be expected to be able to distinguish wolfram from tin. Others minerals were not easily distinguished by eye, but could be separated out by gravity at the buddling stage:

'The purpose of the revolving arms with their drags was to distribute evenly the slime, so that

the minerals could arrange themselves according to their specific gravities. Casserite (tin oxide), being the heaviest, would settle in the head of the buddle. Then following outwards would be the copper, zinc, iron and arsenic sulphide, and the lightest quartz as the tailings. The sulphides and tin oxides were calcined. The other oxides were buddled again, then the copper oxide treated with sulphuric oxide and precipitated out of solution using scrap iron. Zinc oxide was removed by buddling.' [3]

The problems involved with separating mixed ores were mentioned in a report to the Boiling Well Mine in 1858. It is not clear whether the 'expensive and tedious' separating methods in place were at the picking or buddling stages, but the recommended remedy was to install specialist machinery:

'Your mode of separating lead from the blende and copper is very expensive and tedious. It may be much facilitated in time and with less expense by a Vian's separator.' [4]

Others were either so intermixed, or had such a similar density, that they could not be separated either by appearance or by gravity, and could only be separated by differential treatments during smelting and refining. This included such mixtures as cobalt and nickel, or silver and lead.

Because of the complexities of dealing with mixed ore, each mine would have to develop its own sequence of processes to exploit their ores to the best. The complicated process of separating ores is summed up in this description by Henry Boase in 1819:

'Iron ores are rejected as far as possible, and tin and copper completely separated from each other. But sometimes they are so intimately intermixed that much judgment is required to decide whether they can be dressed with greater advantage as tin or as copper.' [5]

The major decisions regarding these processes would be made by the surface captains or mine agents. However, the efficiency of separation also depended on the skill, eye and dexterity of the picker, cobber, bucker and buddler. Depending on the ore raised, they would sometimes need to discern several different types of ore. Not only would they be selecting for the main Cornish ores such as tin, copper, lead, silver and zinc, but might also need to identify such minority minerals as cobalt, manganese, wolfram, or molybdenum.

Arsenic

In Cornwall and West Devon, the element occurring most frequently in combination with other minerals and in significant quantities, was arsenic. Most of the tin and copper ores in the South West contained arsenic as a naturally occurring impurity. In the early years its commercial value was not recognised and it was treated as unwanted waste, as it interfered with the smelting process. This removal of arsenic was usually an integral part of the dressing process.

Where the arsenic occurred with copper, the best copper ore was picked out, and the copper and mispickel ore that had high arsenic content was sent to be roasted, originally in open hearths, and later in special calciners. Where the arsenic content was lower, the ore-stuff was sent to the rolls and jiggers for further separating first. In the same way, if the arsenic was found with tin in high concentrations it was roasted in road-stone sized pieces, and then stamped for tin and roasted again. If the arsenic content was low it went straight to the stamps and then on to the calciner. In some mines it was possible to remove the recognisable arseno-pyrite ore at the picking stage.

By 1830, it was realised that there was a commercial market for arsenic in the manufacture of pesticides and medicines, for instance, and methods were required where this by-product could be collected. Brunton's calciners were designed and developed, whereby the 'whits' (ore concentrate) could be fed from an upper floor through a hopper onto a revolving hearth below, in the top of the furnace. The arsenic fumes were then carried away through lengthy flues, sometimes for several miles, where the arsenic eventually deposited out in a white powder form on the flue sides. These residues were then carefully collected and sold. The purified roasted copper or tin ore which remained in the calciner was then cooled and dressed in the usual way.

James Henderson's 1850s drawing of a Brunton's calciner suggests that older girls or women were responsible for feeding the ore into the hopper. Similarly, when Esquiros describes the mining operations at Botallack in 1865, he describes women and children as being involved in 'burning'. It seems from Robert Hunt's description of the calcining process in 1878, that the hopper was actually charged with a mixture of 6% salt and ore, presumably prepared by the balmaiden responsible for filling the hopper:

'The furnace is charged with ore and salt by means of iron hoppers placed immediately over the centre of each of the hearths. For the supply of each hopper, a heap of about 14 quintals of ore (one quintal = one cwt), with 5 or 6 per cent of salt, is prepared from time to time upon a small platform on top of the furnaces, and a few shovels-ful thrown in occasionally as required.' [6]

About one quintal of ore and salt needed to be fed into the hopper per one revolution of the hearth, and it took fifteen to twenty minutes per revolution. This would need the balmaiden responsible to shovel about five to eight pounds of ore per minute. This would not be a very arduous task, somewhat boring perhaps, but needing the greatest of care. Where several calciners were installed together, she presumably would be responsible for charging the hoppers for each one.[7]

In 1879, there is a note in a Penhalls and Blue Mines Minute Book which indicates that the man working at the calciner was to be replaced by a woman or child, in order to reduce labour costs.[8] Langsworthy also refers to women being involved in the loading of the calciners at Levant:

'Bal-maidens spread the ores to dry on the upper floor of the calciner house, before shovelling it down vertically through a cone in the centre of the floor onto a large iron plate.' [9]

As the tin and copper mines began to fail from the 1870s onwards, some mining was carried out specifically for arsenical ore instead, as at Devon Consols, Gawton, Okel Tor and Lady Bertha in the Tamar valley, either by redressing the waste heaps, or by revisiting the galleries below ground to retrieve what had previously been left as worthless. At Devon Consols, for instance, it was found that where four or five feet of material had been removed from a copper lode, there was another similar depth of mispickel to be exploited on either side. Total production of arsenic peaked in Cornwall between 1880 and 1890, at about 1,400 tons per year. By 1903 however, only two mines were still producing. There was a temporary recovery in 1907, but then the industry closed completely.

In the census records there are very few references to females working specifically with arsenic. There is a reference to a female 'Mundic Miner' in Gwennap in 1881.[10] In 1891, 82 year-old Eliza Kellow, an inmate of Truro Workhouse, had also been a 'labourer in a mundic mine'.[11]

At what stage the dangers of working with arsenic were appreciated is hard to judge. Pryce, writing in the 1770s, describes the utter devastation of the surrounding countryside when arsenic was burnt in the early calciners, and the agents at Wheal Vor reported how employees became ill when the fumes from the arsenic furnace were discharged into the centre of the mine.[12] However, photos from the end of the 19th century of men collecting arsenic show the only precaution taken is the placing of cotton wool plugs in their noses and ears. Similarly, according to Henderson's diagram of about 1852, the woman filling the calciner hoppers is not wearing any protective clothing of any kind. However, in Robert Hunt's description of arsenic calcining in 1878, the care required, to avoid the hopper filler being overwhelmed with arsenic vapours, is mentioned:

'A few shovels-ful (are) thrown in occasionally as required, taking care, however, always to have enough ore in the hopper to prevent the ascension of acid vapours, etc. from the furnace.' [7]

Lead, silver and zinc

Interestingly, the very first accounts so far found of female involvement in the mining industries of Cornwall and West Devon relate to women at the lead-silver smelters in Calstock in the early 14th century. At this time a considerable deposit of silver and lead was found at Bere Alston on the Devon side of the river Tamar, and the Mines Royal developed mines there from 1295, eventually employing about 700 people. By 1302, the ore was being transported over the Tamar to Calstock for smelting because there was an ample supply of wood and charcoal to fuel the furnaces. The white and black ores, containing lead carbonate and galena respectively, were initially smelted in a traditional 'bole', but often the white ores did not fully separate, forming a black slag instead. This slag was retrieved and subsequently re-crushed and washed. It was then smelted again at a higher temperature, in a separate ore furnace, which burnt charcoal and brushwood. At Calstock, it seems that some sort of horse-powered mill was usually used to crush this 'black work'. Unfortunately, detailed surviving accounts relate only to the smelting operations at Calstock. They do not give the names of women dressing or washing ore at the Bere Alston end of the operations, although almost certainly they would have been employed in considerable numbers there.[13]

However, detailed accounts do record the names of women working at the Calstock smelters. Although some breaking of slag was done by hand, usually by men, Mattillid de Suthecon was paid '3d for breaking black ore' on two and a half days in July 1304.[14] The most common task carried out by the women, though, was the washing of the slag (confusingly also described as black ore). This washing was done in the watercourse next to the boles and furnaces at Davypulle.[15] No details are given of the method of washing, but each washer had an 'assistant' or 'servant', which sounds like the equivalent of the 'server' at the dressing floors of the lead mines in the Pennines. Presumably they used some sort of sieving or grading pans, which the women would wash and shake under a stream of water. Their assistants would help load the crushed slag, and then remove the cleaned residue ready for drying and re-smelting. The women were also sometimes employed washing and sieving tan bark ash which was used in separating silver from lead in the smelting process.[16]

These women appear to have been working up to six days a week. During the summer months of 1306 about four or five pairs were normally at work. Agnes Oppenhulle seems to have been the first woman employed at the smelter in May 1302. Mattillid de Suchecon began work initially as an 'assistant' but eventually was employed in her own right. Others working there during 1306 were Isabelle Cutard, Gunhilde de Bonn, Dyonis and Desiderata de Milleton, Emma de Falling, Matilda Bate (whose father was the furnace man), Joanna Cole and Agnes Sludde.[15] It seems they were all employed by the Mines Royal, and were supervised by an 'overseer'.[17]

When Pryce was writing about mining in Cornwall in the 1770s, he referred to the oldest known lead mines in Cornwall being at Perranporth, and that they reached out under the sea. He does not indicate a date for these. However, of the two major lead deposits in Cornwall, by far the more substantial was between Perranporth and Newlyn East, and several mines of note developed in this area during the mid 19th century.

Although some lead was being mined in Cornwall in the 18th century, the mines were small, and ore dressing presumably very simple. The major period of lead production was from 1830 to 1880, peaking between 1850 and 1860, with East Wheal Rose being the largest and most famous of the mines. Other lead mines producing significant amounts during the 1850s were Trelawny, Mary Ann, and Callington in the east of the county. All of these began to decline after 1860. The major producers after that date were West Chiverton (in Perranzabuloe), and Cargol and Lanescot (in the east). From 1845 until 1913, there were about 170 mines producing lead in Cornwall, but mostly in conjunction with tin or copper.

Lead, being the most dense and the softest of all the ores mined in Cornwall, required its own combination of dressing processes; its main quality being that it was easily separated by weight. The relative densities of galena to the rock in which it was found was at most about 7:4, enabling good separation by gravity, when washed in water. The softness of the ore, however, meant that it was easily lost in the stamping process, so in many respects the dressing procedure was similar to copper (which is also very soft), and involved manual or very careful mechanical breaking down of the ore, prior to sedimentation. However, because lead ore very often needed to be crushed or bruised to a smaller grade for smelting, compared with copper, it generally took longer to dress. For instance, in 1841 lead dressers at Old Cornubian Mine were dressing only three barrows of ore per day, about half of the amount processed at most copper mines in the same amount of time.[20]

Because lead ore was invariably impure and contained traces of other valuable ores with it, various techniques were used to separate the minerals. Zinc, for instance was separated at the buddling stage, when it could be found in the lower sedimentation zones in the buddle, whereas the lead which would accumulate around the cone.

The earliest dressers in the very small mines operating in the late 18th or early 19th century hand sorted and hand crushed the ore-bearing material.[21] This was then separated from the waste by sieving in water, the larger ore being picked out. The lighter waste, and ore that passed through the sieve, was then separated out in a stone-lined buddle. Many of these processes were done by women and children. Initially, as with tin and copper dressers, the lead dressers were employed by their own tribute team to dress the ore that they raised.

From the early 1800s the dressers began to be employed by the mine, each tribute team being charged for the dressing of their ore. By the 1850s dressing was still the province of female and child labour, with some male labourers carrying out the heaviest of the work, and all supervised by the surface captain. The ore-stuff was raised in kibbles or rolled out of the levels in wagons and would be deposited in piles or hoppers and then taken for dressing as needed. It would first be spalled or put through stone-crushers to break it down into manageable pieces. In lead mines in Scotland a young boy was responsible for supplying the crushers with ore[22] so it may well have been the task of a child at the lead mines of the south west. After crushing, the ore-stuff would then be barrowed (in the earlier days) or trammed to a hopper and sent down a chute onto a picking table were it was washed and picked, in the same way as copper and tin ore. By about 1860, the picking was fairly mechanised, with ore being sized in a rotating trommel or sieve, and with a final hand picking out of waste, by boys or girls, from a rotating table. Pure ore needed no further treatment and was taken away to be stored, ready for sampling and sale.

The medium quality ore would then be cobbed into pieces about half to one inch across, and the waste discarded. This illustration shows a girl bucking lead ore at the bucking mill whilst standing on a stone or box to keep her legs and feet free of the dressed ore-stuff. The cobbed pieces which still contained waste would then need further separating by hand bucking or at the crushing mill. Some ore was too hard to be bucked easily, and as early as the 1790s stamping mills must have been used for this purpose.[23] Although crushing machines were used from early on, even as late as 1878, bucking was still being done by hand at the smaller mines. As with copper, the ore was bucked at a bench, sometimes brick built, with a slab of iron used as an anvil. Where the lead ore was very soft, it was sometimes carefully dry-stamped or sent through a roll crusher, rather than being hand bucked. In 1841, the dressing captain at Cornubian Lead Mine reported that the females on his dressing floors were able to buck 4.5 cwt of material per day. Nine girls were involved either in bucking or cobbing at this

Girls picking lead from a rotating trommel (1884)

time, of which one was under 13 years old, the others being between 13 and 18 years old.[24] Similarly, at Cornubian Mine there were 10 females recorded as cobbing or bucking ore, one under 13 years, and the rest under 18 years.

The fine sand-textured material from the bucking mill or the stamps would be separated by jigging. In early days this was done by boys. After the development of semi-mechanised jigging boxes, several tasks were still done manually - the filling and emptying, the operation of the lever to shake the boxes, and, where appropriate, the continual removal of the lighter waste from the surface.[25] Sometimes girls were employed at this task. Wheal Betsey lead mine was one of the first mines to install these improved jigs in about 1830.[26]

The sediments from these processes were continually rewashed and cleaned, and the very fine slimes would be sent to the buddle. Most of these latter processes were done by boys, but after 1876, when full time child labour was illegal, older girls and women replaced them. Other lead slimes were trunked and treated at the racking frames, in the same way that tin was separated. Girls and women were responsible for this part of the process, and at the frames one girl could wash 30 cwt of lead slimes per day, using as much as 600 gallons of water.

Statistics of the numbers of women and girls working in the lead mines are difficult to find. Mr. Spackman reported only 21 females working at lead mines in Cornwall in 1827, but this was before any of the major deposits had begun to be exploited. In the *1861 census for Cornwall*, approximately 200 females were recorded. No other total figures for the county are yet available. In the returns sent to the 1842 Commission 57 females were working at three lead/silver mines in Cornwall, and 33 in two lead mines in Devon.[18] In the parish of Menheniot there were 140 women and 152 children recorded at the lead mines in 1851, 260 women and children in 1856, and 132 surface workers in 1868.[19] This gives us an estimated picture of perhaps 500 or 600 women and girls working at the lead mines at the peak of production in the middle of the century, but the numbers dropping to probably about 300 by the end of the 1860s.

Although the lead mines were fewer in number and generally smaller than the copper and tin mines, some employed a reasonable number of women and girls. One of the earlier lead mines, Trewavas (in Breage) was employing 42 females and 17 children in 1836.[27]

East Wheal Rose seemed to employ very young girls in 1841. There were a total of 19 girls under 13 years old (of whom 6 were under 10) and 27 between 13 and 18 years old. The youngest worked at trunking slimes or at the picking tables; the older girls were cobbing or bucking, with one child under 13 years old also at the cobbing bench.[24]

At the South Tamar Lead Mine in the summer of 1856 the 130 surface workers (men women and children) were dressing an average of 100 tons of lead ore per month between them. Sadly, that autumn the mine was flooded, when the waters of the Tamar broke through into the levels, and all the hands were laid off. The mine never reopened.[28]

There are few surviving cost books or records, and census material does not always designate the women and girls as working at the lead mines, so information about named lead ore dressers is sparse. During 1867, about 9 girls or women were employed on the dressing floors at New Trelawny Silver and Lead Mine, and their names appear in the cost book. In addition, Mary Peak, was employed at New Trelawny for 'making sacks for underground work' at one shilling per sack. Also, a Mrs. Elizabeth Hill was paid for carriage. Her donkey and cart collected 'oils from Callington to the mine' for 1s, and on one occasion made 'four journeys to Liskeard and two to Callington' for 4s 8d.[30]

Other than the early Calstock records, little mention has yet been found of women or girls working at lead smelters in Cornwall, but in 1861 two were recorded. They were 34 year-old Grace Richard of Come to Good, and 56 year-old Mary Ann Martin of Quenchwell, both in Feock.[31] They were almost certainly working at the lead smelter at Point.

Invariably in North Cornwall, lead was found in conjunction with silver. The mines around Newlyn East were particularly rich in this valuable ore, sometimes yielding up to 35% silver. One of the most famous silver mines was at Huel Mexico in St. Agnes, but no employment records survive.

All Cornish silver was extracted along with lead ore. From 1870 to 1880 there were eleven mines producing silver in any quantity, the main mines being Newton and Prince of Wales (St. Mellion) and Great Crinnis (Charlestown). As the silver was separated from lead at refining, the dressing procedures were as for lead. In mines where valuable quantities of silver were retrieved, security must have been an issue. A 16th century picture of a German silver mine shows workers subjected to body searches, but no information has been found about the security measures taken in the Cornish lead and silver mines.

About fifty Cornish mines extracted zinc, either on its own, or in conjunction with copper, tin or iron. The main producers in these combinations were Great Retallack and Budnick Consols in Perranzabuloe, and Penrose Consols (British Silver and Lead Co.) in Sithney; the output being greatest between 1850 and 1860. There were about forty mines which extracted zinc with lead, and these chief producers were West Chiverton and Cargol. Creegbrawse (in Kenwyn) was another mine which produced good quantities of zinc in the first half of the 19th century, along with copper and tin.

Zinc was separated out from the other minerals during the buddling or jigging stages.[32] Very little information is available about employment of females at the mines producing any quantity of zinc. However, Creegbrawse was employing five women and ten children in its dressing operations in 1838.[33] At the same time, Pembroke Mine (in Par) was producing zinc with tin and employing a total of 12 women and 52 children. Zinc dressers were very rarely recorded as such in the census returns, however, nineteen women and girls are described as 'blende (ore) dressers' in the parish of Perranzabuloe for 1861. They were living in the Goonhaven and Carnkie areas. The youngest among them was 9 year-old Georgianna Manadue of Polvenna, but most were aged between 12 and 18 years old.[35] Later in 1865, at Rosewarne United (in Gwinear), 20 females were employed in the dressing of zinc and silver.[34]

Manganese

Very little is known about the mining of manganese in Devon and Cornwall, but it is believed that it was first mined in the Tamar region from about 1805, when small mines were worked in the Launceston and Tavistock area, especially in the five parishes of Milton Abbott, Marystow, Coryton, Lifton and Brentor. Between 1805 and 1820 the manganese from the Tamar area was the main source of this mineral for use in glassmaking in the UK. Later it was also used in steel manufacture and chlorine production. Such was the local impact of these mines that the population at Lifton, Coryton, Stowford and Lewtrenchard doubled between 1801 and 1851.[36] [37]

Manganese was found in this area in irregular nodular masses, and usually at very shallow depths, so the earliest operations were often very simple excavations made by farmers, as they discovered these deposits in their fields. As these surface deposits were exhausted, the manganese was then worked by very simple methods, either by open cast mining or sinking very shallow pits.

By about 1845, as the surface deposits and open cast workings were also worked out, some of the mines developed into more extensive underground mines. The largest working was at Hogstor, near Chillaton, where over 50,000 tons of ore was produced. Other mines operating on a fairly large scale were at Monkstone (Brentor), Coryton, Dippertown (Marystow), and Ramsdown (Milton Abbott).[38] Manganese was also mined in a small way in parts of Cornwall. One such mine was Falmouth and Sperries in Kenwyn, where manganese was mined with copper, tin and lead. It was also mined with iron and tin at Ruthers in St. Columb.[39]

When brought to the surface, the ore readily lent itself to hand picking, the black manganese ore being easy to distinguish from the slate and chert usually brought up with it. The 'fines' and 'dredge' ore were then treated by jigging and the finest portions buddled, in the same way as copper ore.

Women and girls were employed in the picking and dressing process at these mines. Manganese mines at Milton Abbott (probably Chillaton and Hogstor) and Lewtrenchard were mentioned by the 1842 commission. In 1841, they were employing ten girls under the age of 13, and thirty-three girls between the ages of 13 and 18. No figures were given for women working above that age.[13] The *1841 Census* gives little information on women's occupations, but two women living at Brentor, and one girl living at Milton Abbot were recorded as working at the manganese mines or stamps.[40] The *1851 Census* gives more detail and records five women in Coryton and twenty in the Lifton and Tinhay area as 'at the manganese mines'.[41] It seems that because manganese dressing was relatively simple, a much smaller proportion of the mine workforce were involved in dressing than at the tin, copper or lead mines.

After the ore was partially dressed by the women and children, it was transported by mule, or later by horse and wagon, down to water-powered mills in the river valleys. There were

Morwellham Quay from Calstock Church c. 1868. Numerous copper doles are laid out ready for sale on the quayside. The manganese mill is the building at right angles to the tallest building beside the further quay.
Courtesy of the Morwellham and Tamar Valley Trust

manganese crushing mills at Shillamill (Tavistock) and Slimeford[42], but the largest mill was at Morwellham.[43] Here the mill and manganese quay were constructed away from the copper quays, in order to prevent contamination. Manganese was exported from Morwellham from at least 1820.[44] Hearder, in his travel book about Devon and Cornwall, makes this comment about the manganese mills at Morwellham in 1841:

'At Morwellham Quay, which developed as the chief port for Tavistock and the mines of that area, there were also mills for crushing manganese ore, certainly in the 1840s. After crushing, the ore was carefully packed in large casks which are then stored on the quayside. It is almost certain that women in Morwellham were involved in this dressing and packing of the manganese.' [45]

At these mills, the women or girls fed the roughly dressed manganese into the mill where it was crushed to a fine powder. They then packed the powder into 4 cwt casks ready for export. Unusually, in 1845, a three-shift system was operating at the mill, so that there was a continuous supply of dressed ore for shipping.[46]

Wolfram

Wolfram was almost indistinguishable from tin, and up until about 1900 was discarded as waste, despite being recognised as a potential hardener for steel as early as 1785.

With a developing market for steel, from 1900 some of the waste heaps of the Cornish Mines were reworked for wolfram, as at Clitters Mine in Gunnislake. Wolfram was probably also extracted from Wheal Mary Ann (in Menheniot) when reworking for lead

Twelve women and girls employed dressing wolfram from the spoil heaps at Wheal Mary Ann, Menheniot, during World War 1.

Courtesy of Brian Bawden

between 1900 and 1908.[47]   Whether females were employed at this time is unclear.

Wolfram was certainly recovered from the spoil heaps at Wheal Mary Ann during World War One, when it was desperately needed for steel-making for the war effort. A surviving photograph shows twelve women were working there at this time, under two foremen. The women in the photograph are named, and all appear to be in their late teens or early twenties. At least four of them were married, and sisters Nancy Bawden and Pol Pomeroy were both working there while their husbands were serving in the forces. They would have been 25 and 31 years old respectively in 1914.[48]

The very nature of their work meant they were working in the open air at the spoil heaps, so these women and girls were dressed accordingly, with long overcoats, long boots, and warm hats. Interestingly however, as with their contemporaries at the clay pits, they appear to be working bare-handed. A photograph shows them with cobbing hammers and a short narrow type of rake, presumably used for dragging down material from the heap. One of the foremen is leaning on a long-handled rake for the same purpose. They do not appear to work at tables, as at the glass mine, but seem to be equipped with buckets for collecting the material they have dressed.[49]

Other metalliferous mines

The census records also report females working at the iron and uranium mines, although little is known about the nature of their work. In 1861 Eastelle and Eliza Jevens, 12 and 10 years old respectively, were described as 'iron ore workers' and Elizabeth Ann Sussier, 17 years old, as 'iron ore dresser'. All were living in the Rejarrah area of the parish of St. Colomb Major.[50]   In 1891 27 year-old Janie Minors was recorded as a 'uranium mine girl', and seems to be part of a small group of people employed at a mine in Coombe, in

St. Stephen in Brannel.[51] Most of the uranium obtained from Cornwall in the late 19th century was recovered from spoil heaps, as its use had not previously been recognised at the time of the first working. Janie's work, therefore, was probably very similar to that carried out by the women at the wolfram mines.

Slate

Although there were many slate quarries in operation in Cornwall during the 18th and 19th century, with 130 granite and slate quarries recorded in Cornwall in 1829, there are very few records surviving. The largest complex of quarries was at Delabole, on the north coast, and slate is still extracted from there today.

In one of the earliest references, tribute teams seem to have worked at Delabole under much the same system as at the copper and tin mines.[52] Although the presence of women in the workforce is not mentioned, we may assume that wives and daughters were probably part of the tribute team, dressing the slate brought out of the quarry by the men and boys. Certainly women and girls were being employed as slate dressers at the quarries during the first half of the 19th century. The tribute system seems to have still been in place in 1864, long after the women and girls had ceased to work there.[53]

The following description, of 1850, gives us an inkling of the environment in which these women and girls lived and worked:

'Two villages owe their origin to the Delabole quarries, Pengelly and Medrose. These quarries present one of the most astonishing and animated scenes imaginable. The traveller suddenly beholds 3 enormous pits, excavated by the uninterrupted labour of centuries, slowly encroaching on the domain of the farmer. Upon the edge of each quarry is the Papote Head or platform from which guide chains are stretched like the shrouds of a ship to pit bottom. The slate, after blasting, is placed on a truck, which being attached to a wheel traversing a guide chain, is drawn up to the Papote head by steam engine. Moveable hatches are run out 14 ft over the face on to which the truck lands and is then drawn away by horses to the workshops.' [54]

The exact nature of the work done by the women and girls is not clear, although they were described as being 'of equal ability to the men'. This implies that some of them were actually involved with dressing the slate. When Jenkin describes the work on the dressing floors in 1888, he mentions boys being responsible for dressing 'scantle', small-sized slate of various sizes, usually about 9"x 5", 8"x 6" or 7"x 7". This small slate was sold for roofing outbuildings, such as mine engines and boiler houses.[55] Turner, writing in 1854, also mentions 'cullers', or 'hullah bobbers' searching the waste heaps for good slate. These were usually young boys, who were able to make a living from dressing the scraps. Although there is no evidence of women or girls working at the quarry at Delabole beyond about 1855, these tasks ascribed latterly to boys, may also have been done by women and older girls.

It would be at the 'workshops' that the female dressers worked. In early days they would probably be working out in the open air, or in crudely erected sheds, the sides of which would be made from rejected slate, and roofed over with wood or iron. These sheds were only open at the front, giving more protection from the weather than their counterparts in the copper, lead and tin mines. In 1864 the dressing houses were described as having two sides at an acute angle with a roof over the top.

Once the blocks of slate reached the dressing area they would be trimmed roughly to standard sizes ready for splitting. The process of making slates from these blocks involved three steps. The first step was the splitting of the block into fine sheets about one fifth of an inch thick. This was done by the 'river', using a beetal (mallet) and chisel. These split portions were then squared off by the dresser. Dressers sat on a wooden horse, and, using a 'travel iron' (goudge) to mark a groove, the slate was laid over an edge and tapped sharply with a beetal to break off the surplus. Finally the slate would be shaped at the top, and a hole made for the nail, by the 'whittler'.[55][56] Those slates which were left uncut at the top were called rags. In expert hands 100 slates could be dressed per hour.

It seems that in 1839 each tribute team had its own particular storage and dressing area.[57] By 1864 the finished slates were stacked in a communal 'show yard' where they were marked with the tribute team's symbol, and recorded by the tally clerk. The slates were taken to the yard by 'pitchers' who carried them in V-shaped receptacles on their backs. Slates were usually stacked in rows of one hundred dozen (1,500 to allow for breakages) and each five dozen would be marked by a slate turned on edge.[58] The younger girls employed at the slate quarries were perhaps involved in carrying, or stacking and counting the slates.

As well as dressing, women were also involved in the transporting of slate. About 1836, one of the Delabole quarry companies bought six donkeys to carry the slates to the 'slate depot', presumably Port Gaverne. They then employed a woman to drive the donkeys. Apparently this method of transport was quite successful, and soon most of the carriage was done in this way.[59] By 1850, bullocks and horses were being used instead, but these were probably driven by men. Women also packed slates from Delabole into the ships at Port Gaverne. These women were employed by the ships' captains, not by the quarry managers and so fall outside the brief of this book.[60]

Although the *1841 Census* for the Delabole area does not identify any women as working at the quarry, other than possibly two widows who are recorded as 'labour women', Delabole Slate Quarries were clearly employing females at that time.[61] According to the *1842 Employment Commission Report* there were nine girls under the age of 13 years, and seventeen between the ages of 13 and 18 in 1841, a total of twenty-six. No figures were given for adult females. These women and girls were usually hired as daily labourers, with their wages ranging from 2s to 5s per week, depending on age.[62] As at the copper and tin mines, a deduction was made from their earnings for their tools.

The *1851 Census* for St. Teath gives much more detail than the census of 1841, mentioning twenty six 'quarry women' or 'quarry girls'. In ten years, the average age of girls employed at the quarry changed, with girls under the age of 13 years no longer recorded. The youngest, Mary Tremaine and Elizabeth Lane, were just 13 years old, but most were between the ages of 14 and 17 years. The oldest was 48 year-old Catherine Killow, who was a widow. Of the twenty-six female quarry employees, twenty-five lived in either Pengelly or Medrose, almost adjacent to the quarry.[63]

Balmaidens at Pednandrea spalling floor.
Courtesy of Paddy Bradley

Chapter 8

THE COUNTHOUSE WOMEN

Apart from the large number of women and girls working on the dressing floors and at the stamps, there were usually other females at work at the mine counthouse. These 'counthouse women' were not often mentioned, but were an important part of the total workforce, and had significant parts to play in the smooth running of the office management. Not only were they rarely included in descriptions of the mine, but they were not necessarily recorded in the cost books, sometimes just being included under 'general office costs'. Neither were they always named in the census material, probably alternatively recorded just as 'housekeeper', 'domestic servant' or 'employed at mine'. In the *1861 Census for Cornwall* a total of 41 counthouse women and girls are recorded, mostly in the parishes of Camborne, Redruth, Phillack and St. Just. They were variably described as mine or counthouse servants, or counthouse women. Occasionally their work was described in more detail, such as 'cook', or 'washing and cleaning at account house'. Due to the scarcity of information, it is very difficult to find much out about individual counthouse women, and most of our information about their work comes from general reports of events at the counthouse. It seems that there were not the same arrangements made for a central office on site at the clay pits, so counthouse women were not employed there.

The mine counthouse had developed from very humble origins, to become, by the turn of the 18th century, the organisational centre of a mining venture. In early days, or in very small mines, its equivalent was probably no more than a hut, where stores were kept and paperwork done. At remote mines or workings, it would sometimes be necessary for mine officers to remain overnight, so a multipurpose counthouse would then have been built. In Bottrell's 1870 *Traditions and Hearthside Stories of West Cornwall* there is the following description of one such house on Trewey Downs:

'The streamers built a much larger moor-house than was usual for such sized tin-works, because many men lived down in Ludgvan or Towednack: besides, as some always remained on the place by night, when there was much liquor to be disposed of. They soon got up a house more than 30 feet long and 12 feet wide, with a broad deep chimney in one end, and a wood corner that would contain a cartload of turves, and enough furze to do the cooking for the week. Between the fireplace and the end wall of the house, there was a place contrived to be entered from the wood corner, large enough for storing away a score of ankers or more, besides other goods which required to be kept dry. When the wood corner was full of fuel no person could see that the chimney end wall was double. Planks on stakes stored heath, rushes, ferns or straw for bedding along one side of the house'. [1]

This particular counthouse was obviously used for more than just mining activities.

Although it seems that the men were fairly self-sufficient at such a place, catching rabbit, game or fish for their food, it is not clear whether women were involved in the upkeep, or the smuggling activities, of these remote counthouses.

At the larger mines, from about 1750, permanent residential buildings, which served as an office as well, were often built on site by the managers. These buildings would be placed in some prominent position where the agents could keep an eye on the workforce, but far enough away from the worst of the noise and dust of the mining operation as to make life bearable. As mines expanded around the house, or managers became wealthier, they generally moved away and built more extensive properties some distance from the mine. The old residence was then often used entirely for business purposes and termed the counthouse (account house):

'In the centre of this hive of activity (the mine) is seen the counthouse, replete with comfort and convenience for the mine agents, clerks, and other officials, and where a most hospitable welcome is ever awaiting the curious visitor'. [2]

The counthouse would have an office, or offices, for the manager and purser, where all book-keeping was done, and business visitors received. In addition there would be a large dining room, probably upstairs, where visitors and shareholders were entertained, and some had a separate 'map room'. There would also be the kitchen and various store rooms. Sometimes there was sleeping accommodation for captains on duty at night, or for emergencies.

In the early days, when the mine office and reception area was just part of the mine manager's residence, the domestic work was probably done by the manager's own household staff. Where the counthouse was independent of the main house the management of the domestic arrangements in the counthouse were the responsibility of the counthouse woman. This was usually a woman of mature age, as shown in an advertisement in the *West Briton* in 1889 where the minimum stipulated age was 40 years old.[3] The qualities required were 'a good character' and 'experience of household work and plain cooking'. Depending on the number of staff and visitors, the counthouse woman may have had one or two women or girls to assist her. In these situations the senior counthouse woman usually fulfilled the duties of cook and housekeeper, with the others responsible for the general cleaning, laundering and kitchen duties. Unlike most other domestic servants and housekeepers, the counthouse women were not normally resident, and were usually drawn from the local mining community.

Daily routine

The main duties of the day were to prepare a dinner at mid-day for the agents, purser and captains at the mine, and to keep the counthouse room clean and tidy, despite the amount of dirt and dust that must have been brought in throughout the day. Other duties revolved around the mine officers' tours of the mine. In one of Seymour's cartoons of 1877, three men are depicted, almost certainly mine officers, in the washing sheds. They are soaking their feet in hot water and being provided with a drink, while their discarded underground clothes are being picked up by a maid and carried off to be washed. We are left to read into this cartoon picture what we will, but this picture fits well with a description of events in the wash-house that come from Moonta in South Australia:

'At nine-thirty every morning the captains began the ritual associated with their daily visits to the underground workings. This would begin when they entered their special changing-room,

where white duck coats and trousers, flannel shirts and drawers, thick woollen socks, leather boots, and safety helmets had been laid out by the attendant. By the time they returned at two p.m. the boots they had removed before they went underground would have been polished by the attendant, who would also have sharpened matches ready for them to clean their nails, and would be ready to start laundering their towels and their underground clothes in readiness for their next visit. When they reached the changing room on their return they would strip to the waist, wash the upper part of their bodies, then put on their shirts before they washed their feet and legs in a bowl.' [4]

In Moonta, apparently the 'attendant' as mentioned was a male, but the Seymour cartoons show a female doing these duties. In Cornwall it seems that the counthouse women were responsible for having ample supplies of hot water ready for the agents and captains on their return from their underground tours, or when they had been involved in dirty tasks at surface. Hot water for baths was probably obtained from the engine house outflow, or possibly heated in cauldrons over the fire in the kitchen. It would then have to be carried to the dry or washing sheds, or to a designated part of the counthouse.

The women probably also kept the mine officers supplied with a fresh supply of clean protective clothes. This would involve continual laundering of duck jackets and over trousers. This was probably done at the engine outlet, where other women from the locality often gathered to do their washing. The clothes were probably dried in the 'dry' or the counthouse kitchen. The women would also have the men's boots and helmets to clean after each visit underground. It seems that they were also responsible for the general upkeep and repair of these clothes. One person was paid at total of 6s at Wheal Comfort (St. Ives) in 1834 for 'washing and mending agents' clothes' over a period of eleven months.[5]

The counthouses were most famous for their provision of very liberal hospitality, especially

Cartoon sketch, by George Seymour Jnr., c. 1870, depicting a counthouse assistant collecting managers' clothes from the mine bath house for laundering.
Courtesy of the Mining Journal

Cameo sketch of the same counthouse assistant, by George
Seymour Jnr., c. 1870.
Courtesy of the Mining Journal

in the early part of the 19th century. According to George Henwood, people took advantage
of this:

'*Counthouses were more like regular hotels, with a bottle on the table, dinner open to anyone,
with wine and punch.*' [6]

However, he reported that by 1857 most counthouses were more restrained in their
expenditure:

'*Counthouses are now what they were originally intended and ought to be - the proper offices
for the keeping of mine accounts, for the meeting of the adventurers, for the receipt of persons of
business, for the temporary residence and sleeping apartments of the captain when night captains
were employed, or in cases of emergency.*' [7]

Nonetheless, even in the days of a more closely controlled budget, the counthouse women
still had to be ready to receive unexpected visitors at a moment's notice. At the very least,
'visitors' meant the preparation of extra food for the mid-day meal. For those wanting to go
underground it would also involve finding suitable protective clothing and the provision of
adequate washing facilities afterwards, as indicated in this conversation, reported by George
Henwood, between a mine captain and the counthouse woman:

'*Well, then Mary, … get out and air three suits in three minutes … send off the maid at once for
a few pounds of beef steak, and a bit of fish, if she can get it; and some new bread, and tell her
to go to my house for two bottles of wine and a bottle of brandy. These strangers ought to have
something when they come up; and be sure and have plenty of hot water to wash. We shan't go
down until twelve, and we come up at three; have'n all ready by four, tha'al do; have't all nice,
now.*' [8]

Leifchild was appreciative of the attentions and preparations of the counthouse staff in this
way, after a visit to Botallack Mine:

'*At the counting house, gallons of water are awaiting us, and tallow, mud, ooze, and iron-rust,
all give way to the application of soap. Off go our miners' caps, and woollen jackets, and wide
inexpressibles.*' [9]

Unfortunately, in mine records the names of the counthouse women are rarely given, and
where they are recorded in the census returns, the mine at which they worked are not

usually mentioned, so it is difficult to associate individuals with any particular mine. In the *1861 Census*, however, two women are described as the cooks for two of the most significant mines in the St. Just Peninsula. They were 52 year-old Matilda Grenfell of Tregeseal (at Botallack)[10] and 57 year-old Elizabeth Johns of Bosvargus (at Boswidden).[11]

Setting Day, Sampling Day and Mine Account Meeting

Apart from the daily routine and visitors to the counthouse, there were other special days for which the counthouse women had to prepare. Among then were Setting Day, Sampling Day and the Mine Account Meeting.

Setting Day usually occurred every two months and coincided with the payday for that month. This was the occasion when miners bid for new pitches at the mine. The auction would be conducted by the mine captain, outside the counthouse. If there were gentry visiting the area, Setting Day was often considered a good time to have a tour of a mine, as it was one of the few occasions when working miners were to be seen above ground. It was also of great interest to the visitors to see how the bidding was done. Once the setting was complete and all the employees had been paid, guests would then be taken on a tour of the mine, including an underground visit if required. When all was done, the mine officers invite their guests to a meal. Henwood described such a scene at Great Hevas Mine:

'A neat, tidy, elderly woman appears to lay the cloth, which is soon done in the plainest possible manner. Savoury smells assault the nose, provoking an already keen appetite, seeing it is three o'clock; and the neat little woman re-appears with a goodly, plain sort of roast beef, accompanied by potatoes and cabbage. A jar of ale is brought from the public house two miles off, and a little bread and cheese completes the welcome repast.' [12]

Sampling Day, like Setting Day, occurred about every two months, and was the day when the assayers and managers of the smelters would come to sample the ores for sale. These visitors may have several mines to visit in one day, so it was customary for the mine to provide dinner for them in their travels. There could be as many as thirty people attending. Henwood, again, described a typical meal:

'Roast beef, and a leg of mutton with wine. Followed by rice pudding, bread and cheese and then brandy.' [13]

However, the major event at the counthouse appears to have been the quarterly Mine Account Day. Under the cost book system, used throughout Cornwall and West Devon until almost the end of the 19th century, adventurers (shareholders) met every three months at the counthouse to receive reports, approve the accounts, and make decisions about the running of the mine over the next quarter. Each mine had its traditional day of the quarter for this meeting, for instance at Bosom and Bollowell it was the third Friday, and at United Mines it was the Saturday before the second Monday of the month.[14] The meetings usually started at midday, and dinner was not served until the business had ended. After the two-course meal, the meeting continued with drinking into late afternoon or early evening.

In the early years, these meals were famous. In fact, some people invested just the minimum amount in the mines in order to attend the counthouse dinners. These people were known as 'knife and fork' shareholders.[15] This probably romanticised and exaggerated view of the 'old times' was recorded in 1872:

'The old school of mine managers' creed was that a lode could not be found without proper dowzing of the ground, and dowsing of themselves with the strong contraband from the other side of the channel, that the cost-book could not circulate for signatures, unless the bottle, with a good drop of 'something short' in it accompanied it round the table - and the next six months' work would never be fortunate unless every equestrian, as he climbed on his nag, hours after dinner, fell over the saddle half a dozen times ..., and every pedestrian had three or four snoozes ... on his way home from the counting house.' [16]

A typical scene at the Counthouse Meeting was also described by Hamilton Jenkin:

'Thus as soon as the business part of the meeting was finished, a dinner consisting of roast beef, giblet pie or other delicacies would be served by the count-house woman and her assistants in some long low room adjoining, where the trestle tables covered with rough but snow white cloths, and the clean, holystoned floor set scenes of homely festivity hard to describe.' [17]

In 1838, a special counthouse dinner at Fowey Consols, was arranged to celebrate the sale of a large quantity of lime, and was described as the 'Lime Feast'. Seventy people sat down to dine in the dining room, and a further twenty-six dined in the map room. The menu included boiled and roast beef, as well as legs of mutton. Cider was supplied, and the ninety-six guests also drank seven gallons of gin, rum and brandy. Little wonder that the mine purser began to suggest that the adventurers should look into the 'Counting House Expenses', and the 'Wine and Spirits Expenditure' Books! [18]

Preparation for any of these special dinners would have required a very early start for the

The impressive pewter dinner service from Botallack Mine Counthouse. It was made with tin from the mine.
Courtesy of the National Trust (Cornwall)

counthouse staff. All the rooms to be used would require thorough cleaning and the laying of fires from early on. The dining room needed to be prepared; laying the trestle tables with coarse white cloths, and often using tin, copper, or pewter plates and dishes made from ore from the mine. At Botallack, for instance, the table would be set with the dinner service made from tin from the mine, a set of silver decanters used at one of the royal visits, along with a 'gigantic' punch jug.[19]

In early days all the cooking was done over a fire in the open hearth in the kitchen. The joints of meat were turned on a spit, with potatoes and vegetables roasting in trays underneath. Meat and vegetable stews would also be prepared in cauldrons over the fire. Alternatively, a giblet pie might be baked under the ashes, on a baking stone covered by an inverted iron pot or dish. This might be followed by a dessert of apple pie, rice pudding, cheese and biscuits, or fruit.[20]

In some mines, the counthouse kitchen was 'open house' during the morning and early afternoon, and, if the weather was particularly bad, guests might be given a dish of warming soup taken from the stew. Sometimes, during the business part of the meeting, adventurers would go out to the kitchen to collect a bowl of soup, if the dinner seemed a long time coming.[21] Eventually, the business part of the meeting would end, and the counthouse women would be called on to serve the dinner.

After the two courses had been served and consumed, the counthouse women would 'clear the board' and the drinking would begin. Meanwhile, in the kitchen, the women could begin the clearing away and washing up. In cold weather they would have to make a hot punch ready to serve to the visitors before they went home, and this would be simmering in a cauldron over the hearth.

The end of the meeting was probably the most difficult part of the day for the counthouse women, having to enable the adventurers to get on their way, often in a less than sober state. It was only after the party had broken up and people were on their way home, that the counthouse staff could finally clear away whatever debris was left from the carousing, before they could go home. It must have been a very long day.

Henwood reports that, towards the middle of the 19th century, the money spent on these mine account meals was beginning to be limited, and the meetings were less riotous. However some mines continued to be quite extravagant, on food at least, as this account of 1872 indicates:

'A real old-fashioned meal, - plain but good, tummels of beef and mutton, vegetables piled up like little haystacks, wholesome beer; followed by steaming punch.' [22]

Although the mine was not identified, this particular feast was prepared, served and then eaten in terrifying circumstances:

'The manager holds that the mine will never be a success unless there is a bit of grub and a glass of punch once a quarter, but he will not expend much on the old rattle trap of an account-house. It is a land of storms, on the very edge of the cliffs, and catches the full force of the gale; while, from its windows, a magnificent sight, of wrathful sea and stern cliffs may be witnessed. Chains - passed over the roof, and secured by iron bars to the cliff - keep the frail and rocking tenement in its place. The windows were buttressed by pieces of timber, nailed to the floor and jammed diagonally against the wooden framework.' [22]

Botallack Counthouse 2003

Photo by Lynne Mayers

It is difficult to imagine the conditions under which the counthouse women had cooked the food, or indeed carried out any of their duties, at this particular mine.

Other mines, by this time, had completely phased out their sumptuous feasts. The author of the same article of 1872, having reminisced about old style account-house dinners, was very scathing of what generally began to replace them. This was usually a more simple fare of bread and cheese, which he called a 'Captain Teague' in honour of the mine agent who had first instigated them at the Counthouse Meeting he attended.

With the advent of limited companies taking over the cost book companies during the 1880s, the quarterly Account Meeting became a thing of the past. Big dinners continued to be provided at the mines for directors and shareholders, but usually now on an annual basis, or on special occasions. For example, the following was prepared by the counthouse staff at Wheal Emma in 1899:

'Boiled leg of mutton at the head of the table, ribs of beef at the bottom, two steak pies in the middle with plain dumplings after, and apples, pears and grapes for desert, all washed down by a liberal supply of claret.' [23]

Parish Feast Days and special events

One of the annual holidays was the Parish Feast Day, celebrated on or near the Saint's Day to whom the church was dedicated. Quite often, part of the celebrations would take place at the mine. Special church services would be held on the Sunday, and then on the Monday there would be a carnival procession, usually followed by a communal meal. At the Wendron Feast Day held at Porkellis Mine in August 1859, seven hundred miners with their friends and families sat down outside the counthouse to share tea and cakes, while the guests of the adventurers had refreshments inside the counthouse. This was another mammoth organisational task for the counthouse women, but no doubt they were aided and abetted by other women of the parish.[24]

One of the other major events at the mine, which would involve the counthouse staff, were the beginnings of new ventures, such as the opening of a new shaft, the 'christening' of a new mine engine, or the restarting of an old one. These, too, were all-day events and involved the whole community. Generally, the counthouse and other mine buildings would be decked out in evergreen and laurel decorations, and great evergreen bowers built around the area designated for where the miners and their families would eat. Considerable numbers of important guests would be invited including local landowners and JPs, plus the parish vicar who would perform the blessing ceremony. We have this description of the festivities that took place when the engine was re-started at Wheal Helena in 1891:

'In front of the blacksmith's shop an ox was being roasted whole, and in the account-house a whole sheep was undergoing a similar process, while a long row of boilers suspended over an open fire in the open air contained the vegetables for the dinner. The account-house, carpenter's shop, and a few other places were decorated with flags, the carpenter's shop being fitted up as a dining room, while four rows of tables were laid outside for the workmen. 150 guests partook of a champagne dinner.' [25]

Because celebrations of this kind were of such proportions, they were beyond the capacity of the counthouse kitchen and kitchen staff alone. Frequently some of the catering for the special guests was done at the mine manager's house, by his domestic staff, and then carried in crates and boxes to the counthouse when ready. The food that couldn't be easily moved, such as the vegetables, punch etc., was prepared at the counthouse. Catering for the miners and local people would not be done by the counthouse staff, but probably by a local butcher and licensee.

Such a day would begin with the special guests gathering for a breakfast at a tavern in a central place, and then being driven to join the local parade at some place along its route. This would include mine employees and their families, local residents, and a band. As the parade wound its way through the streets, the numbers would increase until, by the time it had reached the mine, it would have swelled to great proportions. On arrival, the dignitaries would be given a conducted tour of the new engine or new part of the mine, by the captain and engineer. Eventually when all was ready the vicar would give the blessing, and the engine driver would start the new engine.

Meanwhile, the counthouse staff would have laid out the food for the special guests, and at the appropriate time rung the mine bell to signify 'quarter of an hour to dinner on table'.[26] The special guests would make their way to the counting-house, where the celebrations would continue all day, with food, champagne, brandy and gin. Outside, the mine employees would be provided with a roasted ox, and plenty of beer and cider, whilst they enjoyed various sports and games.

Similar large-scale celebrations were also arranged at times of national celebrations, presumably involving the counthouse staff in much the same way.

First aid post and morgue

From time to time, the counthouse women had to turn their hands to much more sombre occupations than preparing dinners and banquets for the mine adventurers, or the gentry of the parish and county. When there were the inevitable accidents at the mine, casualties were often brought to them at the counthouse.

Where possible, injured miners were taken home, but in some cases this was not appropriate or possible, and so the counthouse became a first aid post or morgue. The counthouse women would administer what care they could, while waiting for the mine surgeon, which could take several hours. This would be particularly true of accidents where victims were burned or scalded, or too seriously injured to survive a long journey home on a stretcher. For instance, when the boiler exploded at Boiling Well Mine in 1858, it seems that the injured were carried to the counthouse there. The engineer was killed outright, and nine others were seriously scalded or burned, among them two women. It was at the counthouse that Mary Webster died shortly after the accident. The other woman, Alice Jones died later in the evening, but it is not clear whether it had been possible to move her, or whether she too died at the counthouse.[27][28]

The dead were also carried to the counthouse, and one of the rooms would be cleared to become a temporary morgue. The bodies would remain there until the inquest which was usually held the following day. Thus the counthouse staff would be involved in the preparations for both the appropriate laying out, and for the inquest itself. For instance, at Poldice Mine in March 1789, the cost book shows an entry of 6s 6d for a shroud for 'Enylew', followed by a payment to Martha Higga for 'striping him' (presumably stripping him).[29]

Other tasks

Brief mention has been made of other tasks relating to the more domestic tasks at the mine. Mary Peak was paid 1s for making sacks at New Trelawny Silver and Lead Mine in 1867.[30] From 1832 to 1834 'sack washers' were employed at Wheal Comfort Mine in Carbis Bay.[31]

Recruitment

From the limited census information it seems that, generally, the counthouse women were older than the balmaidens on the dressing floor, with most being over 40 years old. (Twenty-four of the thirty-eight with identifiable ages in the *1861 Census for Cornwall* were over 40). Many were widowed, with or without dependant children, or single with elderly or disabled dependants. Among the oldest were 71 year-old Ann Richards[32], a counthouse cook and 73 year-old Sarah Goldsworthy[33], both of Camborne, and 72 year-old Mary Hosking[34], of Connor Downs. One of the youngest was 12 year-old Elizabeth Martin from Lower Dimson, working with her mother at a counthouse in 1851.[35] It seems that the offer of this type of work was often viewed as a charitable act on behalf of the mine venturers, and was given to women perceived to be in the most need.

Pay and conditions

It is unclear how many 'counthouse women' were employed at any one time at the mines, as they were not often clearly designated or named in the cost books. There are surviving records of counthouse women for Wheal Basset and Grylls, and Wheal Agar. At the former, Susan Jenkins was 'account house woman' from 1866 to 1871. During this time she was paid £1 per month, two months in arrears, with the exception of the month of June 1866, when she received £1 5s 0d. From November 1871 the name Susan Moyle appears, at the same rate of pay. We do not know if Susan Jenkins had married, or whether she had been replaced by this Susan Moyle.[36] At Wheal Agar, in the early 1890s, there were usually two 'accounthouse women' employed at any one time, but they were unnamed. One received about £1 per week (and paid 6d per week into the sick club) and the other was only paid £1 5s 0d per month.[37] It looks as if one counthouse woman was full time, and the second was employed on a casual basis for the accounthouse meeting, or other special events. Alternatively, she may have been paid on a casual basis to do the counthouse laundry. At Rosewarne Herland United Mine In 1856, Ann (Nanny) Cock was paid either 5s or 10s per month for washing and cleaning at the counthouse.[38]

Even where mines were not so large as to have regular women as counthouse staff, there were still tasks to be done on a piecework basis. At Wheal Trerew Lead Mine in 1859, for instance, an 'E. Tippett' was paid for washing 'underground clothes'.[39] In the 1880s, at Wheal Goole Pellas (Towednack), Ann Williams was sometimes employed at 20s per month, but otherwise at 10d per day, usually for 15 or 24 days in the month.[40]

In the latter part of the 19th century, as many of the mines became less profitable, the amount of money spent on the counthouse hospitality began to decrease. The expenditure had almost always come out of the mine's accounts and often to excess in the early days. It was not unheard of in failing mines for sick club money, or money earmarked for outstanding bills to be used to fund a final dinner for the adventurers. By the 1860s, the amount was usually closely regulated, and the number of women needed at the counthouse was much more closely scrutinised. The total numbers employed at the mine office would probably have been considerably reduced. When mines ran into difficulty, counthouse women were also among those who remained unpaid, or were laid off. For instance, in 1874, when Boscaswell Downs Mine was failing, counthouse cleaners were among those listed as not receiving their wages.[41]

Counthouse women continued to be employed at the mines, long after their sisters on the dressing floor had gone, and as late as the 1950s women were still employed there. However, their daily tasks must have been very different from their counterparts a century

Poor quality copy of a photograph showing counthouse staff and managers at Condurrow in the late nineteenth century, including two counthouse women.

before, with quarterly Account Meetings replaced by the Annual General Meeting, tighter accountability of the hospitality budget, and labour-saving devices for use in the kitchen and office. Gone were the days when the mine would provide a sumptuous meal. However, Cornish ranges were often still in use in the kitchens of the counthouses, and visitors could leave their Cornish pasty on arrival, and find it warmed through and ready for them, when they returned to the kitchen at the end of a cold and damp mine inspection. [42]

Our last words on counthouse women, perhaps, should come from Levant Mine. In a lengthy traditional song about the various personalities associated with the mine, two verses are dedicated to their counthouse women. The sentiments expressed indicate that, although they were the sort of women not to be trifled with, they must also have had a sense of humour or the men would not have dared to have made up the verses[42]:

> *'Then next comes Cappen Fanny*
> *And also Cappen Grace;*
> *Among the other Cappens*
> *They too must have their place.*
>
> *They cook the beef and mutton*
> *And serve the bread and cheese,*
> *They do not care a button*
> *Whether they vex or please.'*

Chapter 9

BALMAIDENS - THE COST

During the 18th and 19th centuries, young women or girls could well have worked for up to twelve years at the mines, and this in their most formative years, both in terms of their physical development and in their educational opportunity. For instance, sisters Hanna, Susan and Ellen Lance, daughters of a copper miner in the parish of St. Agnes, were recorded as working 'at the mine' both in 1841 and 1851. Their respective ages were stated as 15, 9 and 8 years old in 1841[1][2] and their careers as ore dressers spanned at least another ten years, and quite probably more.

Although some may have worked for a comparatively short time or intermittently, generally these young women were severely disadvantaged by their lack of schooling, and also had to live with the medical consequences of their demanding work for the rest of their lives.

Education

Even though formal full-time schooling was not provided by the state until 1876, the school movement had been growing in momentum in Cornwall from the early nineteenth century. Prior to about 1800, it seems that balmaidens would not have had much opportunity for any type of schooling. From about 1800 'dame schools' began to open, and, from about 1840, schools run by the church or other educational charities were established in most sizeable towns or villages. This gave the opportunity for a handful of children from working families to obtain some very basic education. Children could generally attend for about a penny a week. Within mining families education was usually highly valued, so miners would often struggle to send at least one child to school. However, this was dependant on the money being available, and, with large families and intermittent earnings, the chances of any child from the mining community receiving continuous education remained very small, especially among the girls.

Sometimes philanthropic mine managers provided some basic education for the mining children. As early as 1811 Wheal Alfred Mine, being a Quaker concern, was providing a Sunday School for their 250 to 300 mine girls and boys.[3] By 1842 some mines, such as Wheal Friendship and Wheal Betsey, Devon, were providing day school education for the children of their employees.[4] Others provided places at a local school for a levy on the miners' wages (as at North Roskear).[4] In 1841 there were twenty-seven day schools open in the central mining district, of which nineteen were co-educational. In the eight girls' schools, the teaching (unfortunately) was described as 'scarcely passing the boundary of the merest elements'.[5] Because of the great value placed on education, however, much informal teaching was done within the mining community, and many taught themselves. For instance, during the 1830s William Murrish 'The Miner of Perranzabuloe' who was self-taught, went on to teach the children in the hamlet where he lived to read and write.[6] Similarly, Patty Tremellin, having had the benefit of some schooling paid for by an aunt before she went to work at the mines, taught the young children of Wrestling Green from her sick bed in her later years, from 1833 to 1837.[7]

Any schooling that the girls did receive was severely disrupted when they started work at the mines. Continued attendance at day school was no longer possible, as mines did not generally provide schooling during the day for their young employees. In 1864 though, the commissioners were impressed with the exceptional provision at North Roskear Mine:

'Many of the girls are being taught to write by the clerk of the mine, under the auspices of the manager, who gives prizes monthly for the best copybook, and best reading.' [8]

Those girls who went to the mines as young as 7 or 8 years old, would have had virtually no education at all. Those who went at the average age of 10 or 11, may have received up to four or five years of schooling at best. Once at the mine, the only opportunities to continue with some education would be to attend one of the local Sunday Schools, or to be taught by someone in their family or local community. Of the mining parishes surveyed in 1841, only 25% of the balmaidens under 18 years old attended Sunday School, but this varied from parish to parish. St. Just had by far the lowest attendance at only 8%, and the St. Agnes area and West Devon had the highest at 36% and 29% respectively. The level of attendance for the girls was approximately twice that for the boys. When asked, one of the most common reasons given for non-attendance by girls at Sunday School was the lack of suitable clothes for them to wear, presumably only having their working clothes and maybe some other very old clothes to change into while they were being laundered.

At the Sunday Schools girls were taught the basics of reading and writing, usually through Bible teaching, and 'a little sewing'. In 1841, balmaidens attended Sunday School, on average, until 17 or 18 years old. This was longer than the boys, who left at about 15 or 16 years. It was commented that the girls who attended Sunday School commonly achieved a higher level of education, and developed a keener understanding of its importance than the boys. In 1841, 35% of balmaidens could 'read a little' compared with 17% of boys, but very few wrote their names on the data collecting sheets (0.2% compared with 10% of boys).[9] This trend was echoed at a later stage of life, when very few balmaidens signed their names on the marriage register. Barham suggested caution in interpreting the attainments of these young people, and despite being described as being able to 'read a little' he said: 'many read so badly that no pleasure or interest can be derived by themselves from reading'.[10] By 1855 however, the number of children who could read and write had risen dramatically to about 80%, at least in Gwennap:

'It was stated that in mines in the parish of Gwennap, about 18 out of forty of the children could not read or write; that on mines in the parish of Redruth, at least 20% of the children could not read or write; and that on Wheal Basset Mine, out of two hundred and four children employed, forty eight could not read or write.' [11]

Although in some parishes evening classes were also available, in addition to Sunday School, it seems that girls did not normally attend them. These classes were far more expensive than the Day or Sunday Schools, sometimes costing 3d per week plus a candle.[4] Presumably it was not considered appropriate to invest this much money in the education of girls.

The benefit that balmaidens would have gained from their limited education was often lost through lack of sustained learning. When schoolteachers were asked about the effect of early removal from school they replied:

'What little they have learned is soon forgotten', 'education is not continued long enough to fix in the mind what may have been acquired', and 'they have not learnt to read with ease … and they soon give it up altogether'. [10]

Most Victorian commentators placed much store on the ability of girls and women to manage the domestic chores in the home. Of all the concerns about the well-being of balmaidens at the mine, it is this area of neglect that they seemed to lament the most. In 1836 Dr. Richard Lanyon remarked: 'We may observe how desirable it is that the wives and daughters of miners should be better acquainted with culinary and other domestic affairs'.[12] Only four years later the Royal Commission in 1842 concluded:

'The slenderness of the stock of domestic knowledge possessed by the females employed in the mine is attested by all parties. When they come to be wives and mothers, the consequences are very injurious to the husband and children.' [13]

Thus these young women, denied the opportunity of education and achievement for themselves, were also then blamed, in part, for the subsequent ill health of their husband and family.

From 1876, schooling was compulsory for all children under fourteen, and so by the 1880s most young women coming to work at the mine had received some degree of basic education. Suddenly the scene changed.[14] When visiting a copper mine in the Carn Brea area in 1880, Rideing remarked that all the young girls could write, and spent much of their spare time reading. He described how they eagerly spent their pocket money, as soon as they were paid, on penny instalments of popular fiction. For generations, the vast majority of the girls and women who had worked at the mines had never been able to read or write. This was the end of a long dark era.

Health and mortality

With growing public concern during the 19th century for the plight of miners, from about 1830 onwards much was researched and written about the health of men and boys working underground. In contrast, virtually nothing was written about the health of surface workers or, more particularly, about the health of the women and girls. There is one recorded experiment involving the working conditions of women and girls, but the results were then applied, not to their situation, but to improve the working conditions of the men and boys underground. [15]

The most detailed information on the health of balmaidens in the 19th century comes from the *Royal Commission Reports of 1842 and 1864*. The *1842 Report* includes interviews with nineteen girls or women who were working at the mines, in which there are indications of their general state of health. These interviews were published in full in an appendix to the report.

In the 19th century, illness was rife, not just among the mining communities, but among the population as a whole, due to poor housing, diet and sanitation and almost non-existent healthcare for the poorer classes. It is difficult to assess how much ill-health was due to the general living environment of the balmaidens, and how much to their working environment. However some trends do emerge from these reports.

Neurological or skeletal problems

The unnatural and demanding postures of many of the tasks undertaken by the balmaidens, along with their repetitive nature, took their toll. In addition to the physical strain on the structure of the body, these girls and women were also exposed to extremes of weather, many working with no shelter at all, or at best working in an unheated shed open to the elements. This in itself could exacerbate arthritic and rheumatic complaints. The *1842 Commission Report* comments on the effect of these damp working conditions:

'Some of the girls are liable to get wet, especially in the feet in their employments, and all are so in coming to the mines. No provision is ever made for the change of shoes or stockings under these circumstances and the liability to injurious chill is consequently great, particularly to those (a large majority of the whole class) whose labour gives little or no exercise to the lower limbs.' [16]

Spalling was carried out for the most part in a semi-stooping posture, whilst wielding a long-handled hammer weighing 3 lbs for hours at a time. In 1841, 17 year-old Christina Pascoe, working at Consolidated Mines, had to be taken off spalling because of pains in her back, and shortness of breath. She was moved inside to work in the cobbing shed.[17] Elizabeth Hocking, also 17 years old, working at Charlestown Mines, found spalling by far the hardest work on the dressing floor. She suffered pains in her limbs and her back, which continued even when she had stopped work and had laid down.[18]

Balmaidens at Carn Brea Mine, c. 1880, spalling, and loading copper ore-stuff into waggons to be taken to the crushers.

132

Neither Charles Barham (1841) nor Kinnaird (1864) considered that picking and washing, the tasks done by the very youngest children, would cause health problems in themselves. However they recognised that when the children were exposed to bad weather they could then be at risk:

'The work is in itself but little laborious but there is much exposure to cold from the openness of the sheds and the wetness of the mineral and the posture constrained, the lower limbs having little or no exercise.' [19]

'This employment (picking by young children), when carried on under cover is not found to be prejudicial to their health.' [20]

However, 14 year-old Mary Verran, a picker at Consolidated Mines, did find picking hard and complained of pain in her back and side towards the end of the morning session. The dinner break seemed to give her a chance to recuperate, and she usually felt less pain in the afternoon.[17] Some of the girls who operated the new mechanical jiggers, which required moving the sieves up and down in their boxes by means of a long lever, also complained of pains in the back.[21]

From about 1840, cobbing and bucking was usually carried out under shelters, or in sheds, giving the girls and women a little more protection from the weather. Even then, their legs and feet were vulnerable to severe chilling from the accumulated debris around their ankles. In 1841, Christina Pascoe, having been moved from spalling to the cobbing sheds, found her legs became very cold, especially when the ore-stuff was wet. She also described how the rain came into the sheds, so that their feet were soaked, even if the ore-stuff was dry.[17]

Of all the tasks on the dressing floor, Barham considered bucking the most physically demanding task:

'The less robust are usually obliged to relinquish it after a short time, and many apparently strong girls are unable to continue at it. Pain in the back and side is the most frequent complaint. Giddiness and faintness now and then occur.' [22]

Only three 'bucking girls' were interviewed for the *1842 Report*, and all had some difficulty when carrying out this task. Eighteen year-old Elizabeth Larkeek, a bucker at Tresavean, described getting pains in her left arm, especially in damp weather.[23] Nineteen year-old Sally Fall, at Gwennap, reported pains in her side.[24] Most severely, 17 year-old Jane Sandow at Wheal Gorland did not have the strength to continue at the bucking table, and had to be moved to work in the cobbing shed.[25]

One of the other most strenuous and demanding tasks on the dressing floors, for the women and girls, was barrowing. When barrowing, two girls would carry over 1.5 cwt between them. Each hand barrow was constructed to hold 1.5 cwt of ore, but the total weight could exceed this by a considerable amount, as it did not account for the weight of the barrow itself, or for the weight of water held in the ore, if it was wet. Martha Buckingham, 14 years old, at Consolidated Mines, complained of back pain after barrowing all day.[26] In his report of 1842, Charles Barham seemed to imply that this employment had the most potential for serious injury, and had this comment to make about the balmaidens who carried barrows at sampling:

'The latter have, during their turn, by far the harder work (carrying usually about 1.5 cwt). It

is hard work and is often complained of as causing pain in various parts, and not infrequently, occasioning more permanent injury from sudden strains or falls.' [27]

He reported that the balmaidens, despite the many very heavy and strenuous tasks they had to perform, were remarkably free from physical deformation or serious orthopaedic problem. This is at odds with the observations of a visitor to Fowey Consols. Having observed that the girls who filled the buddle strips might shovel as much as 15 tons of tin-stuff in a day, the following query was raised:

'Why they should choose this heavy work which often caused deformation in the shoulders by the continuous use of the shovel?' [28]

Interestingly, although there seem to be no written references, there is a common understanding that balmaidens (especially cobbers and buckers) regularly suffered permanent damage to their left hands, due to misdirected blows from the hammers. Bruising and cuts to the fingers, and even fractures must have occurred despite wearing protective padding or gloves.

General neurological and orthopaedic complaints would probably manifest themselves years later. Christina Morom, who had been working at the Gwennap mines in the early 19th century, believed that the lumbago she suffered in mid-life had been caused by her work at the mine as a young woman. Two of the girls interviewed in 1841, thought that the chronic pain from which they suffered had begun when they had strained themselves lifting too heavy a weight at the mine.[29]

Respiratory and circulatory problems

Apart from the cold, damp environment on the dressing floor potentially causing problems with muscles and joints, there was also the risk of aggravating or triggering respiratory disease. This in turn could also be affected by high levels of dust in the atmosphere. This was particularly acute in dry weather, especially in proximity to the stamps or crushers, and in the cobbing and bucking sheds.

In 1839, Samuel Moyle carried out some interesting experiments in the bucking shed of one of the copper mines. He discovered that 4.5 grains of copper was deposited on an area one foot square per day, when the bucking house was in full use. This compared with just over half a grain per day, when only one person was working there. The results of this experiment were then used to illustrate the potentially hazardous levels of dust below ground, and to indicate the pressing need for improved ventilation down the mines.[30] Despite these findings, there is no evidence that there was any attempt to reduce the levels of dust pollution for the women and girls working in the bucking sheds. However, at this time mechanical crushers were already beginning to perform the tasks which the bucking girls had previously done, so that they were gradually being replaced. It was subsequently observed, in 1842, that the amount of dust created by the mechanical crushers, brought in to replace the buckers, was even greater than when the breaking was done by hand:

'The working of this machine is attended with the suspension in the air of a great quantity of mineral dust, often of a very suffocating nature when inhaled cursorily, but producing serious ill effects with the lungs exposed to it during many successive days.' [22]

In the report it is observed that it was usually boys who attended this machine, and that they were the ones affected most by the dust. There is no indication as to how much the other workers on the dressing floors were affected by this pollution of the air.

Of the very small sample of girls interviewed in 1841, four reported respiratory problems. Eliza Allen, aged 20 years, of Wheal Anna Francis was only able to earn half her normal wages due to breathlessness and weakness.[31] Anna Wasley, also 20 years old, working at the Cakes and Ale Mine, complained she had been suffering shortness of breath, on exertion, for about twelve months. Sally Fall, 19 years old, working at the Gwennap Mines, described various symptoms, including shortness of breath, since over-straining herself some ten months previously.[29] Christina Pascoe, 17 years old, 'fell into a decline', her breath getting very short, when she worked outside as a spalling maid at Consolidated Mines. She was subsequently moved to work inside at the cobbing sheds.[17]

During the 19th century, the proportion of deaths from consumption was very high in the population as a whole, but was higher in the mining communities than elsewhere. It was not generally accepted, in 1842 at least, that this condition was either aggravated by, or brought on by work on the dressing floor. In the *1842 Commission Report*, Barham sits on the fence on this issue:

'There is reason to believe that consumption is more frequent than in the non-mining districts. Whether it is more frequent among those members of miners families who are engaged in surface labour at the mines …remain (sic) in doubt..' [32]

Pepper, however, in 1862, has something stronger to say about the prevalence and seriousness of consumption among balmaidens:

'It is unnecessary to add, that 'consumption' here is scarcely less fatal with these young women than with the underground workmen.' [33]

Barham commented on 'acute conditions', which could suddenly carry balmaidens off, but he did not specify what they were. George Henwood makes a somewhat bleak (but probably exaggerated) statement on this matter:

'These poor girls (balmaidens) remain from the early age we have mentioned, until they either get married off to some of the miners, or die of consumption, which carries off hundreds annually.' [34]

Retrospectively, we would recognise active or passive smoking as a further danger to the balmaidens' health. Commentators report on the prevalence of smoking, especially among those who worked underground, but it was by no means confined to them alone. Celia Fiennes, when travelling through St. Austell in 1699 wrote:

'I was much pleased with my supper, but not the custom of the country, which is a universal smoking, men, women and children have all their pipes of tobacco in their mouths and so sit round the fire smoking.' [35]

There is no evidence that there was smoking on the dressing floor while the girls and women were working, but they would be almost certainly exposed to the effects of tobacco either directly, or indirectly in the home, or when socialising.

There are few reports of balmaidens with major problems of the circulatory system, but minor problems were probably common. For instance, Muriel Sara records that balmaidens commonly suffered badly from chillblains[36], and Minnie Andrews described the terrible pain in her hands due to exposure to cold water at the frames.[37]

Digestive problems

Due to the extreme poverty experienced in Cornwall from the end of the 18th century almost to the end of the 19th, most mining families survived on very limited and poor quality food. When, in 1841, the mining agent at Trethellan Copper Mine reported that more than half the boys and girls brought 'fish and potatoes', or 'stew with a small amount of meat in it' for their dinner and that in most cases they 'had as much as they could eat', one of his colleagues had a different view. He described how some of the girls were ashamed of their meagre repast and hid away to eat it. This same colleague also believed that some of the girls fainted for lack of food.[38]

In times of hardship when wheat prices were high, the only available cereals were barley or pillas, often grown by the miners themselves. The 'hoggan', made from barley, became the staple diet. These were often the only food brought to the mine by the balmaidens. Digestive problems were rife particularly in older girls and women, and much of this was put down, either to the prevalence of barley bread in the diet, or poor food preparation.[39] Barham also suggested that many suffered in this way due to resorting to stimulants such as teas in order to give them the energy to continue their demanding work which, without food, would cause further digestive problems.[16] He also comments on the uncomfortable and rushed circumstances under which food was often eaten at the mine, as being a contributory factor.[40]

In relatively good financial times the indigestible hoggan or fuggan was replaced with the pasty. Even on this more digestible and balanced diet, the balmaidens did not always receive enough sustenance to support their very hard, prolonged labour. In 1841, Grace Bowden, 17 years old, and Martha Williams, 11 years old, would bring a pasty each for their dinner at Trethellan Mine. However, they had often eaten some of it by mid-morning, usually secretly, in order to allay their hunger pangs, leaving precious little to sustain them for the rest of the day.[41]

In addition to digestive problems caused by diet and lack of food, working in dusty conditions, especially with lead ore or near arsenic fumes, could also affect the digestive system. Bowel complaints had been common at Wheal Vor when arsenic fumes were discharged right into the mine centre. The lack of facilities for balmaidens to wash their hands before eating, and wearing contaminated clothing, also aggravated these sorts of complaints.[42]

Seventeen year-old Fanny Francis, working at United Mines suffered from dyspepsia, and Jane Sandow[43], working at Wheal Gorland, suffered from gastrodynia.[25] Elizabeth Curnow (24 years old), a cobber at Consolidated Mines, described how, about twice a year, she lost all her strength and her appetite. She generally found that the harder she worked, the less appetite she had. She had only been able to work at the mine for two days during the previous two months because of this ill health.[17]

'Women's problems'

Problems of this nature were rarely discussed in polite Victorian Society, so there is a shroud of secrecy around the issue. However the Commissioners of the *1842 Report* saw fit to break silence and the mine surgeon at Wheal Vor reported that 'Females suffer from amenorrhea and dysmenorrhea when they labour' [44] and the mine agent at the same mine said 'amenorrhea and chorosis (sic) are very frequent, and are commonly severe and sometimes fatal.' [45]

This total suppression of periods, or their irregularity, and the associated anaemia may either have been due to severe malnutrition, or to exposure to harmful toxins, such as the mundic waters, at the mines. The agent at Wheal Vor ascribed these symptoms to 'the exposure of the young women to the stream of warm water, especially in framing.' [45]

These serious conditions were probably not unique to Wheal Vor, but remained largely unreported. They would have immediate consequences on the general health of these young women in the prime of their lives. Not only would their reproductive health be affected in the short term, but possibly in the long term as well. Even more tragically, it seemed that there was an unseen army of girls whose premature deaths were just passed over unnoticed in the already high mortality rates in the mining parishes. However, these deaths from anaemia and related illnesses, if brought on by exposure to toxic discharges, should have been entirely preventable by modifications in the way the balmaidens performed their tasks.

Problems with sight and hearing

Although there is no direct documented evidence of these sorts of problems arising from ore dressing, balmaidens who were spalling, cobbing, or bucking, must have been in continual danger of damage to the eyes from flying shards. Similarly, those working close to the stamps or crushers, and those in the large bucking or cobbing sheds, must have been exposed to levels of noise which were potentially damaging.

There are indications of the sort of noise levels generated on the dressing floors. At Dolcoath Mine, in the mid-1850s, we are told 'sixty maidens worked in a row in a great cobbing house known as 'The Roarer', roaring and resounding with noise'.[46] At Wheal Kitty in St. Agnes, there was so much noise on the dressing floor, that the mine bell could not be heard above it. It was the responsibility of one of the girls to watch for the bell to ring, and then call 'Bell-ho' to her companions, assuming they could hear her.[47] An indication of the level of noise generated by the stamps is given in this passage from the novel *Deep Down* by Ballantyne:

'Those who have delicate nerves would do well to keep as far as possible from the stamps of a tin mine! They are fearful things these stamps; iron in spirit as well as in body, they go on for ever - night and day.' [48]

A more modern account confirming how noisy the environment was around the ore-dressing machinery comes from one of the women who worked on the picking belt at Geevor during World War Two:

'The washer and crusher were very noisy, and we couldn't hear ourselves speak. We had to lip read and make up our own sign language.' [49]

She also described how, on occasion, small pieces of 'spar' would fly up from the picking belt into their eyes. When this occurred they would have to report to the First Aid post, and have the piece removed. As the women and girls wore no protection over their eyes, this would no doubt be an even more common occurrence in the cobbing and bucking sheds.

Toxicity and poisoning

The women and girls were sometimes dealing with, or working near, highly toxic materials, such as arsenic, lead, and uranium, but there seems to have been little acknowledgement by the mine management of the potentially dangerous nature of these elements. No particular precautions were taken to avoid contamination. Neither are there specific records of individual balmaidens whose ill-health was attributed to toxic exposures.

There is some indication that the 'mundic waters' (waste from the dressing floors, containing copper, iron, and arsenic) made some of those working on the floors quite ill. 21 year-old Jane Jewell was unable to continue to work at Consols Mine, after working there for only two weeks.[50] The agent at Wheal Vor believed that the warm 'mundic water' at the frames may have been responsible for the gynaecological problems of some of the balmaidens at that mine.[45]

The detrimental effect of arsenic fumes on the countryside, and also on individuals seems to have been commonly acknowledged. The chief agent at Wheal Vor described how in former times, the arsenic calciner flue discharged into the centre of the mine when the whole place filled with suffocating fumes and 'bowel complaints were very frequent'.[51] Later, in 1864, symptoms of arsenic poisoning of wounds was recognised and described as 'gatherings and blotches of the skin'.[52] Possibly some of the women and girls interviewed by Barham in 1842 were suffering from this type of contamination, including Fanny Francis who suffered from skin eruptions.[25] However, Barham had not considered working at the arsenic calciners to be dangerous:

'Furnaces employ very few hands, and these are chiefly adults, neither is their exposure to heat or effluvia at all materially detrimental.' [53]

By the time Baring Gould wrote in the late 19th century however, there was an increased awareness of the dangers of arsenic, although the most primitive of precautions were still being taken. Gould writes:

'Arsenic dust has a tendency to produce sore places about the mouth, the ankles and the wrists. More over, if allowed to settle in any of the folds of the flesh it produces a nasty raw.'

'Unhappily, in spite of all precautions, the work at the arsenic mine and manufactory is prejudicial to health. For the last three years, out of every 100 deaths among persons of all ages in the parish of Calstock 26 have been due to diseases of the respiratory organs, but out of every 100 employees at the arsenic works who died or have become disabled, 83 deaths have been due to respiratory diseases.' [54]

At this time Devon Consols, Gawlor, Greenhill, Coombe, and Devon Friendship were producing 350 tons of arsenic per month.

No particular precautions were taken to protect workers at the lead mines and smelters from lead poisoning. The first official investigation and government enquiry into lead poisoning did not take place until the early 1880s, by which time most of the lead mines in Cornwall and on the Devon border had ceased production. Legislation enacted to protect workers in 1886 applied mostly to factory workers. However, even if the dangers were not acknowledged nationally until the 1880s, it was probably common knowledge that lead was toxic among those who worked with it. In 'The Uncommercial Traveller' by Charles Dickens, published in 1869, which contains apparently factual accounts of visits to some of the poverty stricken areas of Britain and Ireland, an elderly Irish woman says of young women who worked at the 'lead mills' in East London:

'Tis lead poisoned she is, sur, and some of them gets lead poisoned soon, some of them gets lead poisoned later, and some, but not many, niver, and 'tis all according to the constitooshun, sur, and some constitushuns is strong, and some is weak; and her constitushun is lead poisoned.' [55]

Nor were lead poisoning cases unusual. A total of 30,000 cases were reported from the lead mines of Utah State between 1875-1900 [56], and many women and girls who worked with lead paints at the Staffordshire Potteries were also affected in this way. From this we might assume, even in the absence of documentary evidence, that lead poisoning was an occupational hazard for the balmaidens at the lead smelters and mines in Cornwall and West Devon. Unfortunately, there is so little information about their work in general, let alone detailed information on health issues. Unlike the tin and copper mines, there were no first hand interviews or examinations of any of the female lead dressers recorded in the 1842 or 1864 Commissions. However, in writing about the health of the lead miners and dressers of the Pennines, where women and girls were not employed after 1840, Burt makes the following observation:

'The failure of all but the largest mines to provide adequate changing, washing and drying facilities before the late 19th century also undoubtedly increased the risks of non-ferrous poisoning from prolonged exposure to contaminated clothing and surface grime. This was a particular problem for workers in lead mines and applied with equal force to both miners and dressers.' [57]

Other parts of the *Royal Commission Report of 1842*, relating to conditions in other mining areas, make very little reference to the dangers of working with lead. At Leadhills Mine in Scotland, the mine surgeon acknowledged that men working at the lead-smelting mills 'suffered a little from colic pains' and recorded three deaths from inflammation of the brain, five from inflammation of the stomach or bowels, one from gout, three from convulsions and one from paralysis, out of a total of one hundred and thirty deaths in a six-year period between 1835 and 1841.[58] Lead poisoning can take two forms - acute and chronic, the acute form sometimes being fatal. Symptoms can include colic and digestive upsets, anaemia, convulsions, paralysis, gout, and blindness. In females the reproductive capacity is particularly vulnerable, including healthy foetal development. In a study in the potteries of North Staffordshire in 1904, women who had worked with lead paints before marriage, and those who had worked with them after marriage, had three and four times more miscarriages respectively than the control group who had not.[59] In an earlier study of a similar group in 1896, of a total of seventy-seven married women, only thirty-six had given birth to live children, whereas there had been twenty-one still births, ninety miscarriages, and fifteen women were childless. Of the one hundred and one children born, forty had died in the early years, with most of these deaths attributed to convulsions.[60] Although it was recognised that workers at the mines were not at such an acute risk of poisoning as those working in the lead smelters or working with lead products, the risk appears to still be significant.

The gynaecological problems experienced by some women at Wheal Vor in the 1840s may have been due to lead exposure:

'A considerable number of women working in lead processes suffer from amenorrhea, and often from periods of menorrhagia and dysmenorrhea, which as a rule, is the more striking symptom.' [61]

By the mid 1880s, lead was understood to be taken into the body by several key routes: by inhalation of dust, absorption through the skin, and ingestion of contaminated food. At the lead smelters and mines in the South West, there was every opportunity for the women and girls to be at risk. Those at smelters would be exposed to the acrid fumes of the furnaces. Those females who were spalling, cobbing or bucking ore, and especially the latter, would be at particular risk of inhaling lead-laden dust, and all would be vulnerable from eating contaminated food, and from absorption through the skin due to splashes of water from the dressing processes, or from contaminated clothing. When mechanical crushers were installed to replace the hand bucking, the dust problem was made even more acute. With the balmaidens having no proper washing facilities, often eating in contaminated areas, and having no means of washing work clothes each day, the risk of poisoning would be cumulative.[62] Even if the effects of lead on the balmaidens were not as severe as on the pottery workers in Staffordshire, it still seems probable that many would have experienced considerable ill health, and a detrimental effect on their ability to conceive and give birth to healthy children.

It seems almost inconceivable from our privileged position of Health and Safety Directives and a Welfare State, that men, women, and children, should ever have taken up occupations with such known risks. Perhaps the curt remarks of the Irishwoman's daughter in East London give us an insight into the desperate choices facing poor families prior to the 20th century:

'The woman's married daughter had by this time come down from her room on the floor above. She herself had been to the lead mills very early that morning to be 'took on', but had not succeeded. She had four children; and her husband a water-side labourer. She knew all about the sufferings of the unfortunate invalid, and all about the lead poisoning, and how the symptoms came on, and how they grew, - having often seen them. The very smell when you stood inside the door of the works was enough to knock you down, she said; yet she was going back again to get 'took on'. What could she do? Better be ulcerated and paralysed for eighteen pence a day, while it lasted, than see the children starve.' [55]

Parasitism

In the 1890s underground miners began to be affected by hookworm, which affected their breathing and caused anaemia, and had probably been contracted from employees returning from abroad. The condition was well known, for instance, in the Sicilian Sulphur Mines. It was spread by the unsanitary conditions underground, and it is believed that this parasite had been around in the Cornish Mines since the 1850s.[63] The symptoms mirrored other miners' complaints, such as miners' consumption or anaemia, so often went undiagnosed. It was first identified in 1894 at Dolcoath, where almost every underground worker was infested. The disease became commonly known as 'Dolcoath Anaemia'. By 1903 it had 'obtained a firm hold in Cornish Mines'.[64] None of the identified cases were fatal. In that year it was eventually diagnosed as ankylostomiasis.

There are no particular reports of the condition being contracted by balmaidens on the dressing floors, but they would certainly be at risk from infection, either from members of their own families working underground, or due to the lack of sanitary arrangements at surface. As with the underground miners, infection among the general community, including the balmaidens, may have gone unnoticed and the symptoms ascribed to something else.

In the *1842 Royal Commission Report*, Barham expresses concern at the risk of malaria for those workers employed at stamps and stream works, especially those situated in warm sheltered valleys on the coast.[53] However, he doesn't report any actual cases, and no mention has been discovered elsewhere.

General physical health

Most of the foregoing information comes to us from a very small sample of balmaidens who were interviewed for the *1842 Commission Report*. The same report also gives a glimpse of the general health of balmaidens at one of the larger mines. A table showing causes of absenteeism at the Charlestown Mines in 1841 demonstrates a range of general ailments.[65] The most frequent reason (17 reports) given for girls not attending work was headaches, but there were also 12 reports of various digestive upsets, and 4 reports of various fevers and colds. Forty-one incidents of absenteeism were reported for the year, in a workforce of 181 girls, totalling just over 800 days. This averages out at about four and a half days per year per person.

The census material is not normally the place to find medical information, however one entry in the census records describes 49 year-old Grace Williams, of Penstrase, as a 'disabled miner' but gives no details of her condition.[66] Many commentators remark on the healthy appearance of the women and children who work above ground at the mine, especially when compared with the appearance of the boys who work underground, or the women and girls who worked in the safety fuse factory. Barham remarked:

'Whatever the average duration of life … it is difficult to find anywhere a class of girls and young women more free from malformation, distortion or infirmity.' [67]

Even in the 1864 Commission, without interviewing or examining any of the female workers, it seems, Kinnaird makes the following similar point about the general apparent healthiness of balmaidens:

'Though breaking ore is laborious, it does not appear to be an injurious occupation, as the women are remarkably healthy.' [20]

However, it was recognised that their healthy appearance may be due to the fact that only those in good health could work, and that at least some may be languishing from serious complaints at home:

'It seems probable that the ruddiness of hue imparted by constant exposure to fresh air, may have given to these boys and girls an appearance of health to a certain extent deceptive. Moreover, as their ailments are, for the most part of rather acute character, they prevent those who are suffering from them from coming to work … but some of these acute disorders prove rapidly fatal and greater numbers pass into incurable structural changes.' [68]

What ill health balmaidens suffered was very often blamed on themselves. For instance, suggestions were made that digestive problems were caused by lack of personal hygiene[69], the crude preparation of food[40], or the wrong diet[16 40], and that a range of other problems may have been brought on by wearing inappropriate clothing.[16]

Women and girls sometimes continued to labour at the mines, regardless of major health problems. This is illustrated by an elderly woman, working at Carn Brea, despite being well over 60 years old. She continued to do very active work even though she was subject to epileptic fits at least twice a week, and had been so afflicted for the forty years she had continued to work on the dressing floors.[70]

Mortality rates

The 1842 Commissioners looked at mortality rates for females in mining and non-mining parishes. As not all the females in the mining parishes were working, or had worked, at the mines, the figures do not necessarily show the direct effect of a mining occupation on longevity. However, the figures show a clear effect of living in the mining parishes compared to rural areas. In the non-mining parishes, of all females who died in a two-year period, 47.5% were under 30 years of age, but in mining parishes it was even higher at 56.6%. Similarly, in non-mining parishes 33.1% of the females who died in that time had survived to over 60 years of age, but in the mining parishes the corresponding figure was only 27.6%.

Infant and child mortality was also higher in the mining parishes. Deaths of children under ten years old accounted for between 36% and 45% of the total in Illogan, Gwennap and Redruth. This compared with 30% to 35% in Mabe, Mylor, St. Mary's, and Penzance.[71] With poor nutrition, and women often working at the mine for a considerable proportion of their pregnancies, it is hardly surprising that their children had a lower survival rate. The following is an account of one balmaiden who continued to work at the mine until the day of her baby's delivery, with a resulting tragic outcome:

'An inquest was held on Monday touching the death of a female infant, the daughter of Elizabeth Boase. It appeared that the woman Boase worked at Wheal Harmony and about three months ago she confesses to being enceinte. Boase confessed to having delivered herself near the hedge in Treleigh Lane (near Redruth) and that while doing so she lost her senses and lay upon the child for a considerable time; when she came to herself, she found the child was still under her, and she took it up in her cloak and apron and carried it home. Boase admitted that the child was born as she was returning from her work.' [72]

Exploitation and abuse at work

This is also a topic barely aired in the Victorian documentation, but we have indications that the women and girls were on occasion exploited or abused, either physically, emotionally or even sexually. Because of the hierarchy on the dressing floors, it would be very easy for the men (dressing floor labourers as well as the captains or agents) to take advantage of the girls or women in all sorts of ways, without them having any real recourse to justice.

At a very simple level, there were opportunities for surface labourers or captains to express some degree of favouritism. This might manifest itself in giving special tasks to a selected balmaiden, or enabling her to do her job more efficiently or effectively. For instance, the men working at the Polpuff Glass Mine during World War One were quite open about the preferential treatment given to some of the young women by the trammers. Favoured individuals, especially those which the trammers 'fancied', would have better quality ore delivered to their part of the picking table. Conversely, those they disliked would be given

Parish	<30 years	30 - 60 years	<60 years
Non-mining parishes			
Mabe, Mylor, St. Mary's, Penzance	47.5%	19.4%	33.1%
Mining parishes			
Illogan, Gwennap, Redruth	56.6%	15.8%	27.6%

Table 3. Percentage of total female deaths by age, 1838 - 1840.

CEC 1842 table 3

the worst. This would immediately affect the length of the working day for each woman or girl, as they were on task work and could not leave until they had filled a given number of boxes with ore.[73]

A daughter of a balmaiden at Devon Consols described how, in the mid-19th century, the women and girls were paid by the number of trays of washed, spalled, rock they cobbed and sorted in a day. These trays were supplied by men and boys from the washing tables. There was opportunity for men to supply poor quality ore to them, as they were paid by the number of trays they packed, not by the ore content. There were often altercations between the men and the women over this issue.[74]

At another level, women and girls were sometimes bullied and subjected to verbal abuse. Minnie Andrews, the 'last balmaiden', gave an insight into this world, when she described her work at one of the tin stream works. She told of how the manager would not tolerate any distractions:

'You wouldn't look your head off from what you was doing, the old fool would have a stick aimed at ee, or something thrown at ee. Oh, he's some demon, he was, an old thing, he was. He'd thraw a stick at ee.' [37]

Sexual exploitation and abuse was not unheard of either. The story of Patty Tremellin, with her three illegitimate pregnancies, resulting from liaisons established through her work at the mine, hints at this darker side of mine work. She comments:

'Those mines are bad places for boys and girls, for there is nothing but sin to be heard or witnessed all the day long, when the agents are out of the way.' [75]

Implicit here is that all may have been sweetness and light when the mine captains, inspectors, and visitors came around, but in her experience, when just left to the supervision of the surface captain, conversation could become rather unsavoury. She clearly states that her problems were associated with the influences of working at the mine, and at least once (possibly twice, as the text is not clear) she served time in Bodmin Jail for refusing to divulge the name of the father of her illegitimate child. [7][76]

Another 'young bal girl' (unnamed) was brought before the Truro County Court in June of 1868, charged with the theft of some drapery goods from a shop. In the course of the hearing, it transpired that she had an illegitimate child, and had no financial provision, and that the father was one of the agents at the mine where she worked. The judge indicated that he would like to see the person responsible for this before him, and also any others who abused their employees in this way. Within a week or two of these remarks, Mary Harvey accused Samuel Scaddon, the surface captain at Wheal Vor where she worked, of raping her. The case went to the summer assizes where the judge decreed that a rape charge 'was easy to make and difficult to refute'. He instructed the jury to be guided by the demeanour of the girl. He made much of the point that, although she admitted that Scaddon had taken liberties before, she had not made any previous complaint. Not unsurprisingly for the time, the case was thrown out.[77]

A newspaper report of 1897 describes a court case involving a balmaiden from Dolcoath who had also given birth to an illegitimate child, the father being a miner. The man had promised to marry her, but days before the birth he had fled to America, and stayed there for over a year. The man, in his defence, argued that the balmaiden, being 10 years older, should have 'known better' than to fall pregnant. The judge found in favour of the woman, and ordered the miner to pay weekly maintenance.[78]

In the *1842 Employment Commission Report* there is only one account of a sexual attack on a balmaiden, and this was by a group of male workers, and is possibly the most serious recorded:

'In the Central District ... a party of thirty miners are said to have taken a woman violently into the fields and to have subjected her to all the outrage which licentious brutality could suggest.'[79]

No further details are given as to the outcome of the case, or the consequences for this poor woman.

Mental health and traumatic stress

There is very little information about the mental health of balmaidens. Patty Tremellin became suicidal at the time of her second pregnancy[7], and there is this very sad account of a deserted balmaiden who became so depressed that she tried to take not just her own life, but the lives of her children as well:

'Many times I have gone to the wash tray without breakfast, and my two dear children have had to stay until I came home without any food in the house. I have cried myself to sleep many a night. One night I lost heart, so I took my children to a water shaft at Bassett Mines, with the intention of drowning them and myself; but the captain of the mine saw me just in time.' [80]

The outcome of this particular story was encouraging, because, although her husband never returned, the woman received a one pound charitable donation from the mine where her husband was working in Australia, which enabled her to continue to provide for her family.

As well as experiencing desertions, or the stress of living apart when husbands migrated to find work, balmaidens were not strangers to death, either sudden or lingering. Most mining families would know what it was to lose a loved one through a tragic accident at the mine. All mining families would also have watched someone die a lingering death from miners' consumption or a related disease. Bereavements of this kind were so common that questions as to how these women and children faced their daily mine work after such losses were never asked. There is no indication that any support was given to these girls or young women to help them cope with the trauma and memories of what they had seen or felt.

Serious accidents on the dressing floors were not very common, but when they occurred they would usually be witnessed by a good number of people. Invariably among the witnesses were the balmaidens, and very often they were the key witnesses when inquests were being held.

One cold January morning in 1830, Jane Goyne had gone with her cousin Elizabeth to get warm in the boiler house at United Hills Mine. On arrival, the engine man had asked Elizabeth to fetch a pitcher of water for him, but Jane had offered to go instead. She had only been out of the building about thirty seconds when the engine house boiler exploded. She ran for cover and was unhurt. Of the eleven she left in the engine house, nine died, including her cousin, and the other two were seriously injured. Jane then had to give evidence at her cousin's inquest at the counthouse the following day.[81][82]

At Ding Dong Mine in July 1873, Alice Stephens tried to avert the death of her friend, Eliza Hall, when she had jumped on the crown gear wheel. She had urgently called her to come down from the machinery, but Eliza refused, and was crushed. Alice, subsequently, was the key witness when she gave evidence at the inquest.[83]

Annie Olds, one of the ore dressers at Botallack Mine, also witnessed a fatal accident in October 1893. Annie was walking home with 9 year-old Mary Dale, who had just come from school with her younger brother, when Mary ran up on the roof of the arsenic flues. Annie immediately called her off, but Mary ran up on them again. When Mary dropped out of sight Annie assumed she had run to the blacksmith's shop to shelter from the rain. Mary was not missed until the evening, and her body not found until the following day. As she had run over the roof of the arsenic flue it had given way; she had fallen in and suffocated. Annie was the last to see Mary alive so was also called to give evidence at the inquest.[84]

There is no indication that these young women were given any support, either in preparation for giving evidence, or in dealing with the subsequent effects of what they had seen. They would just be expected to continue 'as normal' at their place of work.

Accidents at work

Surface workers at the mines in Cornwall and West Devon were not exposed to so many dangers as those working underground, so the number of accidents in which women and girls were involved seems comparatively few, and the accidents, on the whole, tended to be less serious. However, caution should be exercised in assessing the level of this risk. In 1842 Barham states that:

'A great number of accidents, though for the most part slight, occur in almost every mine. No record exists by which the proportion can be ascertained in which such accidents befall children and young people.' [85]

Having stated that no records of minor injuries were kept, so there was no way of knowing the extent of the problem, he then goes on to assume, rather patronisingly, that:

'The surface operations in these mines are very free from occasions of accident and such as do occur are for the most part slight, arising from strains or falls, or casual blows with tools.' [85]

Balmaidens on the spalling floor of Pednandrea Mine, Redruth, 1858. This picture shows the hazardous nature of their working environment.

Courtesy of Paddy Bradley

One wonders if those who actually suffered these minor injuries thought them so trivial? In his lack of reporting any serious injuries he also overlooked his own collected evidence of some ten reported deaths on the dressing floors in the previous two years[86], and also a longer history of a few, but regular, serious injuries and deaths involving balmaidens and boys over the years.

The most common injuries would be due to minor falls, wrenching of muscles and joints, and cuts and bruises from the various crushing implements. These seem to have remained unrecorded and, no doubt, were considered part of the job. Interestingly, there was an ancient Celtic belief, in Cornwall, that binding an implement which had caused an injury would help to heal the wound itself. Apparently, it was not uncommon for miners to be seen carrying a heavily bandaged pick into the mine, so presumably the sight of a balmaiden using a bandaged shovel or hammer would not be a rare sight either.

However, serious accidents did happen from time to time. The most serious dangers on the dressing floors were the moving parts of the various engines and machinery, or from moving wagons. Along with the occasional exploding boiler, these were the causes of the worst accidents. Unlike their counterparts in the iron mines of Shropshire or the collieries of Lancashire, women and older girls in Cornwall and Devon were not employed as 'landers' at the head of the shaft, and so unlike in these other regions, there are no reports of females falling down the shaft in the course of their work.

Machinery and equipment

Probably the most frequent cause of serious injury and death for the girls and women at the mines was accidents involving machinery. The great engines, crushers, and stamps were generally not made very safe, probably with only cursory arrangements for blocking off the dangerous moving parts. All workers would be warned to keep well clear, and told of the terrible dangers, because, once drawn into them, their was very little hope of surviving terrible crushing injuries.

Although injuries involving these large pieces of machinery were usually fatal, some were lucky. At Wheal Agar, Redruth, on 16th April 1888 16 year-old Rebecca Bottrell moved away from her usual place of work on the dressing floor to talk to one of the boys, when her dress caught in the gears of one of the dipper wheels. The mining accident report recorded that she was 'severely bruised'[87], whereas the local newspaper stated that she was 'seriously crushed'.[88] In 1892 at Dolcoath Mine, 23 year-old Annie Martin (a spaller) inadvertently leant up against the engine pillar of the stone crusher. Her hand was crushed in the crankshaft.[87]

One the earliest reported fatalities was in 1827, and involved a girl of just 17 years of age. The victim was Jane Buzza who lived in Kenwyn (although the newspaper recorded that she was from Gwennap):

'On Thursday last, a young woman by the name of Buzza, of Gwennap, about 17 years of age, met an untimely death in consequence of retiring to a stamp shed, in Poldice Mine, at the hour of refreshment; when by going too near the axle by which the stamps are set in motion, her clothes were caught by one of the caps, and she was drawn in between the stamps and the wall and crushed to death.' [89]

A letter from the land agent at Fowey Consols, to William Rashleigh, tells of a very serious and possibly fatal accident at Fowey Consols which happened just weeks after the publication of the *1842 Commission Report*. It reads:

'A poor girl got her clothes entangled in the wheels of the separating machine, which revolves at a rapid rate; she was instantly drawn between the cogs and whirled around at a frightful rate till both her legs were so mangled as to pass between the wheels without any further impression being made upon them. She was carried home and a surgeon was quickly on the spot. She still survives although little hope remains of her recovery. Her parents reside in St. Blazey Parish.' [90]

The first female to be recorded as injured at Levant Stamps was 'a very young girl', Grace Trembath. On 13th January 1845 she was at work at the stamps and became entangled in the machinery and dreadfully injured.[91][92]

At South Caradon Mine in February 1862, 17 year-old Jane Husband was late arriving at the mine one morning. Instead of going straight to the tool shed to collect what she needed for her work, she hid in the jigging house to avoid being seen by the surface captain. Somehow, her dress became entangled with the coupling of the jigging machine and she was crushed to death.[93]

On 7th July 1873, 16 year-old Eliza Jane Hall jumped up on the crown gear wheel of the winding engine at Ding Dong Mine during her dinner break. Her clothes were caught in the gearing and her leg was crushed between the wheel and pinion. Although the engine driver stopped the engine as soon as he heard her screams, she died a few hours later from her injuries.[94][87]

At Wheal Agar, in May 1888, an unnamed 18 year-old girl was also seriously crushed when her clothes caught in the machinery on the dressing floor.[95]

Reports of boys or men being caught up in machinery and receiving serious injury are rare, probably because the clothing worn by the men on the dressing floor was far more suitable and safe. The girls and women seem to be particularly vulnerable, in part due to the voluminous nature of their skirts or their loose shawls, which could so easily catch in the machinery, without the wearer even noticing. Unfortunately, the women and girls in Cornwall never wore trousers like their counterpart 'pit-brow girls' in the Lancashire collieries. This would presumably have been much safer.

The moving parts of the stationary machinery and engines on the mine surface were not the only dangers. Sometimes the women and girls were at risk from the moving wagons. One such accident occurred at Botallack Mine in January 1872. In early January at eight o'clock in the morning, a wagon was caught up by a gust of wind and started down the very steep incline of the tramway. It damaged railings and woodwork on its way down, but only stopped when it crashed into a shed at the bottom. Unfortunately, this was a shed in which girls were working, presumably cobbing or bucking, and three of them were injured. One, who was not named, received a cut over one eye. Another, whose surname was Ladner received a very badly bruised leg. The third, Sarah Ann Downing, was seriously injured. She suffered a compound fracture her left leg, her kneecap was cut in two, and she had a deep cut over her right eye.[96] However, as the women and girls were not usually involved in moving wagons in the same way as they were in some of the northern collieries, there are no known accounts of fatalities where they were crushed between the waggons themselves, as were their northern counterparts.

Falls, subsidence and floods

One of the main causes of death underground was from falls from ladders or levels, but serious falls at surface were rare. One such serious fall did happen about 1841 at United Mines, when Fanny Francis, 17 years old, was barrowing. She suffered fits as a consequence.[25]

Elizabeth (Betsy) Noy, who was a 58 year-old widow, must have been one of the older tin dressers working at Morvah Consols in St. Just. On 1st August 1874 she had gone to the engine room to dry her clothes. Whilst there, she had a dizzy turn and fell to the next floor. She struck her head on the machinery below and fractured her skull, and died the following day from her injuries.[97]

One of the other most common causes of death for underground workers was from drowning, either during flash floods, or when huge bodies of water were suddenly released when old workings were breached. At surface, in a conventional deep mine, drowning was rarely a danger, unless a worker fell unconscious into one of the many areas of shallow water. However, those working at tin streams or sea tinning could be at risk from sudden floods or storms. For instance, in St. Agnes in 1812, a balmaiden working at one of the tin-streams tried to rescue her hat from a swollen stream. She fell in and was carried downstream for half a mile. Luckily she survived, but was very shaken, cut and bruised.[98]

Another major danger below surface was subsidence. On 24th August 1858 there was a sudden rock fall at the Porkellis Moor Mine in which seven underground workers were killed. This also caused a massive subsidence on the dressing floor. It was probably caused by the falling-in of extensive slime pits, where the underground workings had come too close to the surface. It happened while the girls were working, and without notice. Some of the frames fell in entirely, and others were damaged. All the women and girls who were at the frames and slime pits managed to jump clear, and amazingly, none were injured.[99]

Boiler house explosions

Early on Wednesday 3rd February 1830, a bitterly cold morning, several workers at the United Hills Mine at Porthtowan took shelter in the boiler house. Within a few minutes the boiler exploded. Of the eleven people there, all were severely burnt and scalded, and nine died, either instantly or within a few hours. Among them was 20 year-old Elizabeth Goyne, from Mount Hawke, St. Agnes. Elizabeth was buried 5th February 1830 at St. Agnes Parish Church.[100][82] One of the newspapers described the terrible accident:

'All the deceased were dreadfully burnt and bruised, so much so, that their persons could scarcely be recognised; some were so scorched, that the skin of their hands fell off, and when picked up, was not unlike dry leather gloves.' [101]

A similar accident happened at Boiling Well Mine in Gwithian on 10th February 1858. It was also a wet and cold morning, so several men, women and children had gathered in the boiler house to dry themselves before beginning work at 7 a.m. The boiler exploded while they were there, and the engine driver was killed instantly. Two women, Mary Webster (aged 30) and Alice Jones (aged 16) died within hours from their injuries, another man died a few days later. Six were badly scalded or burned, but survived. A broadsheet printed at the time gives a graphic description of both Mary and Alice's plight and suffering.[102] (Mary's husband had been killed in a mine not long before and she left orphaned children).[103][104]

'Inconsequential losses' and 'invisible' accidents

Significantly, none of the accidents recorded here appear to have generated any compensation. Historically, in common law, an employer was liable for the results not only of his or her own negligence, but also for that of his or her employees when acting within the scope of their employment. However, from 1837, it was deemed that an employer was no longer liable for an employee causing damage to another employee. In practice this meant that the adventurers could find ways of avoiding liability for damages in almost all cases of accidents at the mines.[105] Official reports regularly implied, in the way they were worded, that the blame lay with the victim, and this is true of most reported mine accidents of the early and mid-19th century, not just applying to injuries or fatalities to females. For example, Eliza Hall died because 'in spite of warnings from other girls' she 'persisted in jumping onto crown wheel of the whim and riding round'. Annie Martin had her 'hand crushed by crank of engine driving the stone breaker, she having thoughtlessly leaned up against the engine pillar', and Jane Buzza died 'by going too near the axle by which the stamps are set in motion'. There was no acknowledgement that the mine adventurers had any responsibility to ensure employees could not have access to dangerous moving parts of machinery.

The mining companies were not liable for employees safety until 1879, and even then to a very limited degree.[106] For instance, in December 1896, when 8 year-old Ada Harris died from falling into an unfenced arsenic flue at East Pool, as she was not an employee, the company did not have to pay any compensation.[87] Children were expected to behave with adult concepts of responsibility and danger, and youngsters who forgot the warnings and played on or near moving machinery and were injured, were viewed with very little sympathy.

A cavalier attitude to life and limb is indicated by the casual way in which accidents involving women or girls were reported, or sometimes not reported at all. Women, when injured, or even killed, were not always given the dignity of identification in public reports assuming they found their way into reports in the first place. In contrast, men and boys are named almost without exception. Only two of the seven deaths mentioned in this chapter (which should have been reported) seem to have come to the notice of the Inspector of Mines. The accidents to Mary Webster and Alice Jones (1858), Jane Husband (1862), Sarah Ann Downing (1872), and the unnamed girl at Wheal Agar (1888) do not appear in the Inspector's records.

Under-reporting of accidents was general. In the *1842 Report* there is a summary of seventy five fatal accidents which had occurred in mines in Cornwall and West Devon between 1839 and 1841, and ten of these fatalities related to surface workers. Five were killed in a boiler explosion at Consols, three died when they were entangled in machinery at Tresavean, Fowey Consols and Balleswidden, and two were involved in unspecified accidents at Restormel and East Polberro Consols. It is probable that a considerable proportion of these fatalities were female, and yet, other than being a statistic in this table, we have no further information about these terrible accidents or who was involved.[86]

Barham believed that the fatality figures for 1839 to 1841 were under-reported by about twenty-five percent, so, even discounting the five fatalities due to a boiler explosion as atypical, this suggests about thirty fatalities on the dressing floor per decade, or three hundred per century. If this figure is anywhere near accurate, it illustrates the severity of the under-reporting of serious accidents. After considerable research, only eleven serious or fatal accidents involving females have been identified so far, covering a period of fifty years. This reflects a similar under-reporting of mining accidents in the Llanelli area, where a colliery agent, in 1841, recalled 'about 24 fatal accidents at one works' in a period of 25 years, whereas 'published sources between 1816 and 1841 give no indication that so many fatalities could have occurred in a single colliery.'[107]

Making mines safer

In 1842, as a result of his findings, Barham made strong recommendations to the government, which would have significantly improved the working environment for the balmaidens.[108] These changes included:

1. No child under nine to work at the mines.
2. No child under thirteen years old to work more than eight hours per day.
3. 'Hoggans' to be discouraged; a place for employees to warm food and prepare a hot drink to be made available; a minimum of 45 minutes for dinner time.
4. A place to be provided to change and dry wet shoes and stockings.
5. More holidays provided and more task work available.
6. Mine management to sponsor evening classes for their young employees and day schools for the miners' younger children, with an appropriate deduction made in miners' pay.

These recommendations, if put into practice, would have improved the educational opportunities, and health and safety for all balmaidens working at the metalliferous mines in Cornwall and West Devon. In the event, none of these recommendations were implemented, and the legislation enacted as a result of this report was applied only to the collieries. It was to be another thirty years or more before similar recommendations would bring significant improvements to the circumstances of the balmaidens of Cornwall and Devon in 1872. It was to be more than thirty-five years, in 1879 and following, before mine managers were made more liable for the safety of their workers, and, even then, only in a partial way. By the time more appropriate levels of protection were achieved for employees, women and girls were no longer being employed at these mines.

The Bal-Maiden

Often, in the ruins, she intrudes:
emerges from the background of the mine,
like someone from the past I overlooked,
the black cloth of her bodice shawled with cloud,
a figure with no character, whose face
is framed within a shadow, non-descript,
some old neglected value, unknown depth
that draws me to the moorland. Even now
I see her in the charked light of the shaft
surrounded by the headgear of the whim
still aiming at the weak spot of the stone,
the wound-chart of her sweating flare-scarred arm
still shattering its thirty tons a week,
to feed the valley stampers. Battering on,
half-covered by the rockdust of the floors
eternally returning with the same
mechanical precision, as each blow
re-echoes through the granite, where the gangs
still drill away the boreholes in the wall
and tamp away the sticks of gelignite
to blast away the veinstone from the lode.

John Gurney
Courtesy of Peterloo Poets

Chapter 10

MINE CLOSURES: THE END OF THE
ROAD OR A NEW LIFE?

In order to understand the enormous changes that confronted balmaidens when the mines closed or became mechanised, it is necessary to appreciate the comparative economic and social freedom that their mine work provided. Working at the mines gave balmaidens a degree of independence and sense of personal identity that was denied many other working class women of their time. As with many manual jobs, the work was hard, dirty, poorly paid and often done at the expense of their health and education. Despite all this, there were advantages to this type of labour over the other alternatives available to them, such as working as farm labourers or domestic servants.[1] It seems that mine work was generally better paid and not quite as seasonal as farm work. In the novel *Norah Lang, the Mine Girl*, after the mine closed and Norah lost her job as an ore dresser, she considered going to hoe turnips as a very inferior job.[2] In common with domestic service, the farm-labouring hours were invariably longer than those at the mine, resulting in much less free time. Both of these occupations usually entailed 'living in' which brought the double disadvantage of less freedom and almost non-existent wages, once board and lodging had been deducted from the pay.

Another advantage of mine work was the companionship and bonding that occurred between the women and girls as they worked together. A particular type of team relationship developed on the dressing floors, where many different tasks had to be co-ordinated to ensure smooth flow of the processes. Girls and women were often called off one task to another, to assist girls already working there, if a bottleneck was building up at one of the stages in the operation. The girls, therefore, needed to be adaptable in what they were able to do, as well as flexible about who they could work with. The almost collegiate nature of the balmaidens relationships was expressed in the way in which they gathered together to travel to and from work, more often than not forming their own spontaneous choirs, and singing complex harmonies on the way.

In the earlier years balmaidens were also able to have some control over their own lives in the commonly accepted practice of 'keeping company'. Young people would sometimes establish sexual relationships without marrying in the first instance, choosing to remain with their own families. This arrangement would be considered an unofficial betrothal.[3] In this way they could both continue to contribute to the economy of their own family whilst, hopefully, being able to save towards their own future home. They would usually then marry when a child was on the way, and when the balmaiden could no longer work at the mine, due to her condition. While still living at home, in the slightly better economic times, older balmaidens contributed more to the family budget than they actually cost the household, as well as being able to save for their own home. In this situation both the families and the couples benefited. Conversely, in hard times, the system would not work well, as the balmaiden would not have enough to pay her way and save any money.

Long before a balmaiden started saving for her own home and family, she would have been acutely aware of the way in which her few shillings a week bolstered the family economy. In a mining family consisting of seven people, in the Gwennap area in 1841, two sisters contributed to the family income by working at the mine. The eldest, 21 years old, contributed about one sixth of the family income, thus subsidising the other members, and the youngest, just 12 years old, contributed two shillings.[4] In good times, a balmaiden's earnings, however meagre, might enable small luxuries, such as sending a sibling to school, or paying for a visit from a doctor. In hard times it could mean the difference between hunger and having enough food, and between being cold or having fuel on the fire. Either way, the balmaiden would normally feel that her work and earnings had played a significant part in the economy of her own family over the years, and she would also expect to make a considerable contribution to her own marital home, before her earning days ended with the arrival of the first children.

From this it is possible to picture young women who were part of a very distinct working group within their communities, tightly bonded, and having some sort of financial independence, even if their hard earned money was used entirely to support the family's basic needs. They would also be marked out as a group by virtue of their patterns of spare time, and those not courting would band together for jaunts to the Saturday markets, or the special seasonal fairs. This psychological sense of financial independence, along with social freedom in terms of free time, seems to have led to a real sense of self-worth. This was often indicated by the various ways in which balmaidens stated their individuality, mostly through what they chose to wear, both at the mine and elsewhere.

Each balmaiden, therefore, must have had to make considerable psychological adjustment if her employment suddenly and unexpectedly ended. With wide-scale closures of mines happening repeatedly in the history of Cornwall many a dream must have been shattered. Each would have to find her own way through the dramatic change in roles, and startling reduction in independence.

The beginning of the end

This process became a stark and final reality for whole communities of women and girls when the mines began to close *en masse* from about 1867. It has been estimated that between 1861 and 1900 over 26% of Cornish women between the ages of 15 and 24 emigrated overseas, and over 35% migrated to other counties in the UK. Many of these must have been balmaidens. It was only then, when the numbers of people affected was so vast, with poverty and hunger driving people to desperation, that the needs of these women in their changing roles were actually publicly acknowledged and addressed. Particular charities and schemes were set up during these difficult years, for instance in 1867, 1876 and 1879, to try and meet some of their needs.

As the tasks for which the women and girls were responsible became mechanised or the mines began to close, what options were there for these women and girls who lost their jobs? The simplest solution might be for the family unit to absorb the financial shock and rely entirely on the male breadwinners. However, invariably the men were also being thrown out of work. There was rarely any slack with which to re-adjust the family budgets. Finding home-based alternative occupations for the women and girls, such as dressmaking or food production, was occasionally an option, but with whole communities having reduced incomes, there was very little money for purchasing these extra goods or services. Often the trades and home-based industries within the community also went out of business.

A few statistics illustrate the sudden reduction in employment in the mines of Cornwall from 1867 onwards. In a matter of months the number of females employed at Botallack had been reduced by 40%. One hundred and forty-four children had been put out of work in Chacewater, and between 300 and 400 children had lost their jobs at Dolcoath.[5] In some families it had been the children who were the only breadwinners, and even work for them was at a premium. In March 1867, ninety mines were wound up at the Stannary Courts. In an eighteen month period during 1866 and 1867 Balleswidden, Carn Brea, Wendron Consols, Great Wheal Busy, South Wheal Tolgus Mines, Wheal Reeth, and United Mines all closed, along with many other smaller mines, and a total of 11,400 were thrown out of work.[6]

At the same time as these dramatic job losses, the prices of basic commodities had increased so that the buying power of a miner's meagre wages had been reduced to one half. As a result, whole mining communities were becoming destitute. Extreme hardship had been caused not only by high corn prices, but by the scarcity and high price of cotton due to the American Civil War. This meant that mining families were not only unable to buy bread, but unable to afford replacement bedding or clothing. The vicar of Sithney and Breage wrote in April 1867:

'The clothing of the miners is nearly worn out, and sad to relate, many of them have had no under linen for sometime. Although the want of clothing is great, still the craving of hunger seems to throw this want into the background. The average gettings of the majority of the miners for the last twelve months has been from twenty five to thirty shillings per month. Many cases have come before us where families have been without bread for some days, and they have had to subsist on a bare supply of barley bread and boiled turnips.' [7]

A County Distress Fund was set up in 1867, with smaller district committees responsible for administration in different areas. In December 1867 reports to the District Fund indicated widespread deprivation. Across the mining parishes over seven hundred families were in receipt of help from the fund - most earning less than two shillings per head per week, the amount considered necessary to buy flour for one person.[8] In the Helston district, at this time, it was estimated that one third of the mining population, over a thousand families, were in need of clothing. In the east of the county, when local magistrates visited cottages in the Tywardreath area, they found that forty families did not possess a single blanket, while forty others had scarcely any bedding at all.[9] Miners were going underground with no breakfast and only a slice of barley bread for 'croust'. It was reported that some balmaidens in the Truro area went to work two days in a row having had only fried turnips to eat.[8]

The most immediate relief was given in the form of food, blankets and clothing, with the County Distress Fund giving grants to District Sub-Committees for clothing and bedding, and for setting up soup kitchens. For instance, soup kitchens were set up in Tywardreath in January 1868.[10] History was to repeat itself from 1876 to 1879, and again from about 1893 when 3,500 surface workers alone lost their jobs over a period of seven years, and the conditions in the mining parishes were described as 'positively appalling'. In 1876 a Miners' Relief Fund was set up by Rev. H. J. A. Fothergill, the curate of Sithney, one of the parishes worst affected at that time. In the same year kitchens were set up at Blowing House Hill at Wrestling Green, to provide soup, at 1d per quart, three days a week for destitute china clay workers. In 1879 the County Distress Fund aimed to provide clothing and bedding, and 'aid in sickness' to those who were most destitute.[11]

In addition to supplying emergency provisions, more permanent solutions were sought. Particular attention was paid to find alternative employment, and an assortment of schemes were devised for young balmaidens who had lost their jobs. Various local initiatives were taken, like this one by a local mine manager:

'Capt. N. Climo, formerly manager of Camborne Vean, has taken a plot of ground a little below Penponds viaduct to erect some machinery for untinning slimes, a quantity of which he has purchased on Camborne Vean old sett. This will give employment to many little ones resident in Baripper and Gwinnear, who now have to travel three or four miles to Dolcoath and adjacent mines.' [12]

Some migration to find work at other mines within the South West was still possible, up until about 1876. Workers could sometimes find work at the china clay pits or at the copper mines in the Tamar valley, which were both still expanding in terms of production in the early 1870s. However, these local initiatives and transfers within the mining industry were destined to be only be a temporary measure, as virtually all mines and pits would be either closed, or fairly highly mechanised, by the beginning of the 20th century.

The workhouse

The ultimate fear was to end up in an institution, and for some, the fear of the workhouse became a reality. By 1891, a significant proportion of the inmates of the local workhouses, and at the County Lunatic Asylum in Bodmin, were ex-miners. Tin dressers Rosina Colenso, Margaret Eustice and Elizabeth Thomas, who were all over 60 years old, and 73 year-old Belina Morkam, became resident at Helston Union Workhouse.[13] However, it was not just the older women who were unable to support themselves and found themselves there. Twenty-four year-old 'mine girl' Phillipa Reynolds was described as a pauper and was resident in Falmouth Workhouse in 1891.[14] In the same year, widowed 24 year-old Mary Thomas was in Kenidjack Workhouse, with her three children aged 10, 8 and 8 months, her mother-in-law (also widowed), and two sisters-in-law.[14] There were also four females residing at Bodmin Asylum described as 'mine girls' or 'tin mine dressers', one of whom was blind. They were only recorded by their initials, and three were over 55 years old.[15]

In 1891, the parish which had the largest number of ex-balmaidens in the workhouse was Illogan with twenty-three 'former tin mine labourers' recorded in the census, also noted just by their initials. With the exception of one widow, all of these women were single. Their ages ranged from 16 to 70 years old, with over half between 20 and 45. They were all resident on their own, independent of other members of their family.[16]

Making maids out of balmaids

One alternative for the redundant mine women and girls was to find local employment in the service industry. There was a huge increase in the number of people employed as domestic servants during the latter part of the nineteenth century, and most of them were girls and women. Much of this increase of available work appears to be among the ranks of artisans and tradespeople who, in wanting to emulate the upper classes, found that inexperienced servants could be hired relatively cheaply via charitable institutions, prisons, or direct from the workhouse:

'Artisan and trades people were the usual customers at the workhouses and the charitable institutions; when they went away empty handed it was more likely to be because of a shortage of supply, not because of the price.' [17]

With precious few jobs available in the mining industry, this expanding market of domestic service seemed to be one of the most obvious outlets for the surplus female workforce in Cornwall. Projects and schemes were set up across the mining parishes to find domestic work for ex-balmaidens, such as happened in the parish of St. Day during 1878:

'The recent reductions of surface hands at many of the mines have compelled numbers of the bal girls to try domestic service; though clumsy at first, they are generally painstaking and honest.' [18]

A similar scheme, for placing the young women in service, was adopted in Redruth:

'The distress in the neighbourhood of Redruth is caused in a great measure by a number of girls and boys being thrown out of employment by a curtailment of operations at the various tin streams. An effort is being made to provide clothing for the girls, and to place them in families to be trained as domestic servants.' [19]

One of the balmaidens who found work in service within the county was Marah Goninan. In 1881, at the age of 13, she was working as a tin stream labourer, near Connor Downs, with her older sister Catherine. By 1891 she was working as a servant on a farm in the parish of Crowan.[20][21] With limited opportunities of finding domestic work within the county, schemes were also developed for finding work outside Cornwall. For instance in 1867, a hotelier from Oldham had written to the County Distress Fund suggesting that girls from the mines could be sent north where there was a shortage of domestic servants,

Marah Goninan, who had previously been a balmaiden, in service in Cornwall in 1891.
Courtesy of John Saunders

and a training scheme was suggested in order to prepare them for this type of work.[8] In 1896 balmaidens from Redruth were also being placed in domestic service outside the county. The difficulties faced by balmaidens in trying to adapt to a very different living and working environment are captured in the following two newspaper extracts. The first is a conversation reported between two ex-balmaidens, one who continued in service, and one who left after a few weeks:

'I put some working men in the drawing room and called them 'Sir', and, when they told me I had made a mistake, left a gentleman who called standing on the doorstep, telling him to wait there, for Master was engaged, and then forgot to mention a word about it when master was disengaged. Another day, I asked the missus what I should take up the soup in as I couldn't see any basins, and she said in the soup plates; so out I goes and takes up the soup in the vegetable dishes.' [22]

The second is from a report made to one of the District Relief Funds:

'The Redruth Ladies' Committee had applications from all over the county and outside the county for general servants, many asking for respectable girls, and stating they were quite prepared to teach them. They had been able to send away three women. The Rev. H. Oxland said that they had sent some women away from Illogan; but up to that morning six of them had returned. One, a woman of 28, for whom a situation in a good family in Fowey was found, came to him as pale as a ghost, and said that she was sorry to say she had 'taken fear' and could not go, adding that she had never been in a train, and was afraid for her life.' [23]

It seems that some women managed to make the transition from balmaiden to servant, and then were happy with their new life:

'Some few, who from time to time have done so and who have fortunately got into places where pains have been taken to instruct them in their duties, would now on no account exchange their present position for mine work: on the contrary, they affirm they are much more comfortable indoors, out of the wet and cold. … Mine girls when they settle in service, are generally trustworthy and honest; but they are fond of liberty and require plenty of patience to make them good servants. At times they are inclined to be uncouth, and steadily resist any fancied infringement of their right; but this is often more than made up by their other sterling qualities. [22]

When the various schemes were set up to encourage balmaidens to take up employment as domestic servants, certain geographic areas appear to have been targeted. When Deacon analysed the *1891 Census* looking for Cornish-born females, he found an amazing 17,757 in Devon, 10,005 in London and Middlesex, and 4,439 in Lancashire, many of whom were in service. Of the 17,500 found in Devon, the greater proportion were in domestic service in the Plymouth area.[24]

It is highly probable that a proportion of these women and girls had been balmaidens, and had taken these posts when they were thrown out of work as the mines closed. Mary Hannah Reynolds may well have been one of these. When she was 13 years old, in the *1861 Census*, she was recorded as working at the mine. At the time she was living at Polwheveral, near Constantine, and was probably working at Wheal Vivian Copper Mine. By 1864, when Mary Hannah was 16 years old, the mine closed. The next record of Mary shows that she was living in Croydon at the time of her marriage in 1873, where her family believe she had been working as a domestic servant. Although it is not known how or when she came to Croydon, she may well have been one of the many balmaidens encouraged to go into service in London.

Although many balmaidens remained as servants and made new lives in their adopted homes, there were some who found this impossible, and returned to Cornwall. Mary Hannah Reynolds was one of those. By 1881 she had returned home to Constantine, but she was deserted by her husband, and raised her two sons on her own. She experienced great poverty and hardship, living in a 'one up, one down' cottage with no water or other services, until her death in 1935 at the age of 86 years. During her years in service there had been no opportunity to make provision for her own future.[25]

'Better the nor' than oversea'

Whether by their own initiative, moving with their families, or being placed by a charitable scheme, by far the more common outcome of the closure of the mines for balmaidens was migration out of the South West altogether. Large numbers moved either within this country or went abroad. In some mining parishes, up to three-quarters of their young people moved within a period of about twenty years, leaving the villages and towns they left behind almost like ghost towns.

Many of the redundant mine workers and their families felt that if they had to move, they would rather stay in this country than go abroad. A common saying among them was 'better the nor' than oversea'. Even in the 18th and 19th centuries, whenever there were desperate food shortages or major mine closures, there had been various waves of internal migration out of Cornwall, to the various other mines in Britain. In the early days, migration had been mostly to the metalliferous mines, where the skills learnt at the Cornish mines were most transferable. For instance, considerable numbers of Cornish miners went to the lead and silver mines in mid Wales in the 1830s and 1840s, and took not just their mining skills, but their methods as well. Cornish mining communities sprung up at places like Llywernog and Cwmystwyth in Cardiganshire (now Ceredigion), and Llanfyrnach in Pembrokeshire. As was the Cornish practice, women and girls were employed on the dressing floors at these mines, but it is not clear how many, if any, of these females were Cornish balmaidens.[26][27]

By the time of the mass exodus from the mines in Cornwall from 1867, mining jobs (mostly in the collieries, but some at iron mines) were being offered in many different places in Britain, as well as Ireland. Advertisements offering opportunities at the mines in other parts of the UK were often placed in Cornish newspapers, or displayed on flyers or billboards in the main towns such as Redruth and Truro. Sometimes agents from these companies would travel to Cornwall and hold public meetings to attract would-be employees. This was especially true of the coal mines, and, for the first time, Cornish miners started to work in appreciable numbers in the collieries of the North and Wales, as well as in the 'hard-rock' (metalliferous) mines. These advertisements appeared in the *West Briton* in 1865 and 1866:

'About a dozen miners wanted for Ironstone Mining at Grosmont, Yorkshire. Constant work.'[28]

'During the last fortnight, Messrs. Brown and Howatson, from Glasgow, representing the coal and iron masters of that city, have been engaging miners to proceed to Scotland, and already 300 have contracted. The liberal terms offered viz. 4s a day, certain for 12 months, and free transit, have proved attractive.'[29]

Some miners and their families travelled north to work in the iron mines of Shropshire or Furness. Others found work, often strike-breaking, in the coalfields of South Wales, Staffordshire, Lanarkshire, Co. Durham, Northumberland, Yorkshire and Lancashire. Some settled well, but others were not happy, as a South Wales coal company manager reported from Cardiff:

'The miners we had from St. Just and St. Ives are doing well; a number from that neighbourhood have come on their own account. I do not think we shall have any further trouble getting men from your county. I am sorry to say the Calstock men do not like the work. They complain of the dust, and of too much wind in the pit.' [30]

Many of the mining areas to which the Cornish miners went also had a tradition of women working at surface. In Shropshire women and girls were employed seasonally to pick out haematite from the heaps of weathered ore-stuff. In Lancashire, for example at Wigan, St. Helens and Burnley, young women pushed full coal wagons around the floors from the pit-head to the screens. In Lancashire and Yorkshire they also picked out rubbish after the coal had been graded at the screen. In the Staffordshire collieries they even landed the kibbles as they arrived at surface.

In these mines and collieries, it seems wives and children of local miners were probably given first priority over the Cornish, for any available jobs. So far, there is no record of Cornish balmaidens working at these tasks. For those families who had been strike-breaking, it would be unlikely that the local women would welcome the Cornish balmaidens at the bank, pit-head, or screens, to work with them. With increasing middle-class abhorrence at women and girls working at mines at this time, and increasing mechanisation of the jobs which the remaining women did, there was little hope that these migrant balmaidens would find work on the dressing floors or picking belts again. So as balmaidens made plans to move, whether with their families, their husbands, or independently, they knew that their economic role was going to change, and they would need to look for jobs outside the mining industry.

The early 1870s were a time of great expansion of the textile industry in Yorkshire and Lancashire. Advertisements were regularly placed in newspapers in Cornwall for workers for the newly opened cotton and woollen mills. Here was the opportunity for secure employment, and many jumped at the chance:

'Since 1868, between Chacewater, Gwennap and Redruth 2,750 persons have removed their homes in Cornwall to the North of England. In Burnley alone, there are about eight new factories about to be opened, each of these will absorb about 800. At Bacup there are two more factories waiting for hands. At Skipton, Oldham and others places Cornish hands are in great request, at from 8s to 25s per week. It is evident that for young women and children to work at the mines for 4d and 6d per day is simply a waste of time and opportunity of doing better. One family, for instance, reports having been half starved in Cornwall upon 48s per month at the stamps, burning houses and night duty at the arsenic works, where in Burnley they now obtain from 50 to 55s per week, work regular hours, and are always sheltered from the wet and cold.' [31]

In September 1872, agents from the cotton mills visited Lostwithiel, encouraging people to take up this type of work. Seventy people left Lostwithiel by train that month to take up the offer:

'There is great advantage in the north for people who have large families, as the children earn several pence per day, and are sent to school certain times in the week.' [32]

Although most, but not all, of the jobs available at the mills in Lancashire and Yorkshire were for girls and women, but there were other jobs outside this industry available for the men. Some work was offered at the Yorkshire and Lancashire coal mines, but also Cornish miners were highly valued for their skills in cutting tunnels for the ever-expanding railway network. In the 1870s there were many tunnels being built through the Pennines, including the famous tunnel under Whernside. Once again, advertisements appeared in the Cornish press:

'Midland Railway; Settle to Carlisle Contract No. 1 Blaemoor Tunnel. Wanted, now and in the course of a few months, upwards of 500 miners for the above tunnel, in gritstone and limestone. The works are dry and there is good air. Ample accommodation close to the works in healthily situated huts. Applications for huts and for further particulars, apply to John Ashwell, Contractor, Ingleton.' [33]

With work available in these areas for both men and women, Cornish families would still have the opportunity of a multiple wage, and ex-balmaidens would still be able to earn their own keep. The connection between the Cornish men working on the railway and Cornish women working in the mills can be seen in several census entries for Skipton in 1881. Twenty year-old Mary Lord, born in St. Just, had married a railway mason and was working as a cotton weaver. Whether she was an ex-balmaiden we do not know.[34] Ellen Rule had been working at the mines in Camborne in 1871, probably at Condurrow, at the age of 14, but by the age of 23 she was a thread polisher in Skipton, where she was lodging with railway workers.[35][36] Whether she had travelled with her family from Cornwall to take up work at the mills, or whether she had made the journey on her own we do not know, but she, too, had made use of this Cornish connection with the Yorkshire railway navvies.

These balmaidens who went to work at the cotton mills found themselves employed in slightly more comfortable circumstances than at the mine. However, they were still faced with all the inherent dangers of working long hours in a very noisy and dusty atmosphere. Also they still had to be very careful to avoid injury from the largely unprotected machinery with which they worked. How many balmaidens from Cornwall took up this sort of work is unknown.

To far away places

From about 1840 onwards, travellers returning from their journeys, and miners writing home, told wonderful stories of fortunes to be won in far-off places. As copper and gold was discovered in Australia, advertisements placed in local newspapers encouraged emigration, and very cheap passages were offered to people with skills relevant to mining. In the 1840s a company was formed in London to work a seam of lead on land called Glen Osmond, belonging to Osmond Gilles, in South Australia. A Captain Pascoe set out from Cornwall with ten miners and their families to work the lead mine in Cornish fashion. On arrival the girls in the party, who were 10 or 11 years old, were employed to wash and sort the ore.[37] However, this custom of employing females at the mines did not continue long in South Australia.

Because of the predominance of single men in these early mining settlements, men were encouraged not just to take their families, but also to take unmarried sisters or female relatives. There was a great need of women to undertake various domestic tasks, so single women also travelled. A significant number of unaccompanied girls and women must also have migrated. Twenty were recorded in 1837, but this number was to increase over the years. In addition to the 'Labour Office' in the port of Adelaide, a special hostel was opened for 'single unprotected women'.[38] How many of these were ex-balmaidens is unknown, as previous occupations of the women were not often recorded. Only eight women who applied for assisted passage to New South Wales, between 1837 and 1877, were described as mineworkers.[39] The earliest recorded balmaidens to travel out to Australia were Jane and Suckey Fletcher, both from Wheal Burton, who emigrated to Australia in 1839. Whether they travelled with other family members or to meet boyfriends who were already there, we do not know.[40]

Later, as more gold, silver, and copper was discovered around the world, there became a wide range of destinations - North and South America, Italy, Sardinia, and South Africa for instance - to work both in the mine fields and also to 'open up' the land to agriculture and settlement. Many Cornish left during the 1850s, not always out of necessity but due to the attraction of the 'Gold Rush', and many a balmaiden must have been lured away too. Further waves of migration were generally from necessity, especially in 1867, 1876-9, and again on the mid 1890s. The following advertisements for New Zealand and Nova Scotia are typical of what would appear each week in the Cornish press:

'Assisted passages: a few miners having grown-up daughters, farm labourers, single females, miners able to do farm work as well, carpenters, shepherds, smiths, masons and others, may obtain assisted passages to New Zealand by applying to Mr. W. Wade, Redruth. NB. Emigrants paying their own passage to new Zealand will be taken for £15, and to New York by steam for £5.5s.' [41]

'Miners, mechanics, and labourers to work on railroads, at the coal mines and at the gold mines, will find constant employment at high wages. A great demand for female servants. For further particulars, apply John S. De Wolf and Co., 1 Tower Chambers, Liverpool, emigration agents for Nova Scotia.' [42]

Although passenger lists rarely indicate the status or occupation of women and girls, it is commonly understood that the majority of wives or girlfriends travelling out to places such as Moonta and Wallaroo were ex-balmaidens.[43] How many single unattached balmaidens travelled with their brothers or cousins in search of adventure is hard to tell. However, many ex-balmaidens married in order to travel with their partners, often at short notice, when decisions were made quickly to take up jobs overseas. Twenty year-old Mary Ann Hooper, an ore dresser living at Illogan Highway married John Teague (also written Tyack), a miner, on 16th July 1854. By 24th October 1854 they had arrived in South Australia, and made their way, in the first instance to Moonta. Similarly, 17 year-old Ann Snell, a copper ore dresser in Gunnislake in 1851,[44] married William Sleeman, a miner from Callington, in May 1854 and they emigrated to the Buningyong very soon afterwards.[45]

First settlements in the mining areas were generally tents and hurriedly made shelters, as seen in the 1855 picture of Ballarat. Once considerable amounts of ore were found, permanent mining towns were established, with the usual array of community facilities. Few females went out with their menfolk to these early mining camps, but there were exceptions. Mary Hallock Foote, the artist and novelist, and the wife of a mining engineer, discovered that at New Almaden Quicksilver Mine in California in 1876 there were two quite separate mining camps, one for the Cornish, and one for the Mexican miners. They were both squalid affairs, turning into dust bowls in the dry season, and with no sanitation. Despite the desperate conditions, many of the Cornish miners had their wives with them.[46]

Ballarat, Australia, in 1855, showing the gold miners' settlement.

Most women and girls emigrated to established ore fields, where settled mining communities were built, with some of the luxuries of modern living such as schools, stores, medical services, churches and chapels. Once there, they met an entirely different economic framework from the mining communities of Cornwall.

On arrival, ex-balmaidens would find that they were not needed for ore dressing. In some cases, as with gold, which is found in almost pure form, there was little dressing to be done. Where ore dressing was required, it was increasingly done by machinery. Alternatively, where ore needed hand-dressing there was usually no shortage of indigenous labour. For instance, in California in 1849, some miners were employing fifty or sixty American Indians at their gold diggings.[47]

There seemed, also, to be an expectation that in their new, and hopefully more prosperous, life, women and girls would be saved the indignity of working at the mine. This type of manual labour was generally considered undesirable.[38] In some of the colonies it was even made illegal for women to take up employment at the mines (e.g. in Queensland).[48] Occasionally it seems they would be needed, and would help with the mining processes in an emergency, but the general expectation was that this would only be a temporary measure. The only known report of children being employed was at Glen Osmond Mine in South Australia, in the very early days, where it was reported that 'a number of boys and girls were busy washing and cleaning ore'.[49]

In the early years in the mining camps and settlements there was a dramatic gender imbalance, and a chronic shortage of people with the skills to attend to the domestic life. Any unmarried woman in the mining camps and settlements would not only be eagerly sought after to provide domestic comfort and succour for the single miner, but would soon also be prevailed upon either to open a boarding house or a store, or to cook, wash, mend, sew, or nurse the sick, for the wider mining community. Likewise, any woman with a basic education would be encouraged to teach. Consequently, the female's prime contribution to the economy of the mining family lay, not in the mining skills she may have brought, but in her domestic, caring and teaching skills, such as they were. Having been used to their own financial independence, here was the new economic opportunity. When Zanjani writes about the role of women in the American mining communities she remarks:

'Since gold rush days, running boarding houses had been a leading occupation for entrepreneurial mining camp women, both married and single. They provided a service much appreciated by the miners and prospectors tired of their own cooking, their own housekeeping, and their own company. A woman who arrives in a new mining camp was likely to be importuned to open a boarding house or at least to cook meals. Like most working women of the period, the boarding house keeper laboured long and hard - one woman recalled that her day's work began when she prepared breakfast at seven and continued without respite until well into the evening.' [50]

When Ruth Hopkins investigated the roles taken by Cornish women in Victoria, Australia, she found that they included running small stores, dressmaking, or running boarding houses or hotels.[51]

When silver was first found at Caribou, Pennsylvania in1869, 60% of the initial mining population came from Cornwall. New arrivals stayed with friends and relatives, or at the boarding houses run by Cornish women. These boarding-house women in Caribou often lent money to other miners, especially to enable them to bring their families to join them.[52] In the novel *A Miner's Right*, set on the other side of the world in the Yatala goldfields of Australia the famous 'Mrs. Mangrove' fulfils the same sort of role from her general store:

'Mrs. Mangrove laughed at our undiggerlike despondency when we came up one Saturday night and vowed we would not take some beef and flour having no money. "Bother the paying", said the buxom cheery woman, "we shall get our money sometime or other. You shall and must take your rations till times mend."' [53]

Although the balmaidens role had changed dramatically, their skills from the dressing floors were still useful. They could play their part when it came to the heavy manual labour involved in the construction of buildings or clearing land, as this comment from South Australia illustrates:

'Wives usually gave a hand, and some of them could use a shovel as skilfully as a man. Usually these were balmaidens who had worked as ore-dressers at mines in Cornwall.' [54]

It is very difficult to trace individual balmaidens from their work at their mines in Cornwall, into their new lives overseas. One of the few whom it has been possible to follow is Lavinia Rowe (née Terrill). When she married James Rowe of Camborne in 1845 she was described as a 'miner' indicating she was a balmaiden, probably at Dolcoath, where her husband worked. By 1859 James's four brothers were already working a gold claim, called 'Mosquito' near Fryer's Creek, in Victoria, Australia. Because of James's mining skills, they requested him to go out and join them. As a result, Lavinia travelled out to Australia with her husband and their eight children, sailing from Liverpool to Melbourne on the 'Black Eagle'. They went directly to the Fryer's Town mine, near Castlemaine.

The mine was relatively successful and the brothers eventually became mine owners, known as 'Rowe Bros.'. By the late 1880s, however, the goldrush was in decline and the government was making land selection blocks available in areas near the river Murray. The Rowe family decided this would be the best future for them, so three of their children applied for adjacent blocks. They moved to Yalca in 1876, where they were required to build houses, and then clear the allotted acres and bring them into cultivation within certain time limits. Sadly James was already in decline from 'miner's pthisis' and was never to enjoy this new home. He died in 1879, aged 58 years, whilst still in Fryer's Town. The widowed Lavinia joined her three children, initially working under hard and primitive conditions to clear the land. They built up a prosperous farm, calling it Pendarvis, and it continued in the family until 1908. It was here that Lavinia spent her final years. She died unexpectedly in 1895, at the age of 71, whilst away from home, visiting a married daughter in South Australia. She never returned to Cornwall, and her body was taken back to Fryer's Town, so that she could be buried with her husband. A fine headstone still marks the grave.[55]

Another Lavinia who had been a balmaiden, and who also made a new life in Australia, was Lavinia Magor from Salem in the parish of Kenwyn. She was born in 1836, and had been an ore dresser at the time of her marriage to John Symons, a miner working at Wheal Busy, on 12th May 1855 at Kenwyn Church. It is highly probable that Lavinia was also working at Wheal Busy, and this is how John and she met. Their first son John was born in 1856, and they sailed on the 'Marion' for South Australia, arriving in 1857. John Snr. took up work at the copper mines in Burra, and then later moved to Moonta. They had nine more children, and their eldest, John, was to become Mayor of Moonta in 1890.[56]

Mary Bennetts Rowe was believed also to be a balmaiden, and went to make a new life overseas, her destination being South Africa. Born in 1876 in St. Just, as a young girl

Mary Bennetts Harry (nee Rowe) and her family, in St. Just in 1914. Their eldest son was serving in the First World War at the time, and his photo was added to complete the family portrait. Mary's husband died three years later.

Courtesy of Harry Trembath

she had lived with her family on Trewellard Hill, and probably worked as a tin dresser at Carnyorth Mine, just outside St. Just. Her 'young man', William Thomas Harry, had left for South Africa to work in the gold mines on the Rand, probably in the 1890s, when many mines were closing on the St. Just area. He became an underground mine captain. Mary subsequently travelled out to South Africa to marry William in 1895. Tragically, as happened all too frequently, her husband's health was seriously damaged by the very sharp dust from the mining drills, and they had to return to Cornwall. Mary travelled back first, and then William followed. He took up work at Wheal Cock, and Levant, then finally worked a tin stream on Carnyorth Moor. During this time Mary had seven children. The eldest, William, was to become a well-known mining engineer, and another son, Raymond, wrote the book *Mine under the Sea*, featuring himself as Jack Penhale. Mary's husband William died in 1917, when she was 41 years old. She continued to live in Carnyorth Terrace, St. Just and died in 1967, aged 91. She is buried in Pendeen Cemetery.[57]

Many a balmaiden's dream of making a new life or finding a fortune on the gold, silver or copper fields overseas came to nothing, due to failing ventures, sickness, accident or even death. Some returned home very quickly, due to homesickness, failing health, or having lost their partner. Even for those migrants who were able to stay in their new country of abode, there was rarely the opportunity to remain in one place for long. The vagaries of mining enterprise often meant that mines were quickly worked out, or became uneconomic. Better returns were often promised elsewhere, and so families would be on the move. Mary Ann Teague (née Hooper), who had emigrated with her husband to Moonta in 1854, only stayed there for a short while, during which time their first child was born. Soon afterwards they made a long wagon trek across Victoria, with her brother-in-law and his family, to Campbell's Creek, Castlemaine, where they eventually settled for good. While there, she gave birth to another ten children. Sadly Mary Ann died in 1872, at the early age of 38 years.[58]

The independent spirit of the balmaiden also lived on, even when fortunes let them down thousands of miles from their native Cornwall. While some women returned home on the premature death of a partner, others made the best of it on the other side of the world. As with their sisters at home in Cornwall, they resorted to the well-tried economic expedients for the independent widow; laundering, dressmaking, midwifery or taking in lodgers. At Moonta Mine, for instance, widows of miners were provided with a basic 'laundry kit' consisting of a mangle and a sort of industrial iron, a long wooden container filled with stone. With this basic equipment they would charge other miners a few pennies for their laundry (for example, two pence per six items passed through the mangle), and therefore support themselves and any family they had. They were expected to return the laundry equipment when it was no longer needed, for instance, when their children were old enough to support themselves and their mother.[59][60]

Despite the prevailing attitude against women working at the mines in the late 19th and early 20th centuries, there are now stories emerging of women who actually involved themselves in mine prospecting and mine management in the New World and elsewhere. Sally Zanjani, in her book *A Mine of Her Own - Women Prospectors in the American West 1850 - 1950*, tells the story of over one hundred women who were involved in mining in the USA, some in conjunction with other employments, and others where prospecting became their total world. Similarly, in *Pioneer Women in New Zealand*, Sarah Ell records the story of 'Little Biddy of Buller' (Bridget Goodwin 1813-1899) who was part of a three-person gold prospecting team in Buller in the mid-19th century.[61] Although none of these stories have a proven Cornish balmaiden connection, one can only surmise, that among the thousands of balmaidens who emigrated from Cornwall and West Devon, there must have been a few who tried their hand at mining and prospecting in their own right. We can glimpse a little of what their lives may have been like from the biography of Ellen Jack. Ellen was not Cornish, but was born in Nottinghamshire in 1842. She had married an American sea captain, but embarked on a career as a gold prospector and miner around 1870, after she was widowed. She almost perished in the snows on her long journey over the Rockies, and she slept on a sofa in the office of the only hotel in Gunnison, when she first arrived. For a few weeks she rented a 'cot' in another woman's tent. Then she saved up to buy her own housing lot and tent. She lived in the tent with only a bed and several crates for furniture until she eventually found enough gold to pay for building a log cabin. She then set up the tent as a paying bathhouse for the other miners.[62]

A few stories have emerged of Cornish women being involved in mining enterprise overseas. Mary Buzza was mining full time at Red Streak, Creswick and another enterprising Cornish woman, Mary Porlock, brought mining machinery with her on board ship from Cornwall. She sold this machinery on arrival and then entered into a partnership to supply machinery to the mines in Ballarat. Similarly, at Bendigo, a Mrs. Leggo and her sister-in-law, Mrs. Rowe, dug briefly for gold with one of their husbands, and were quite successful. They buried the gold under the floor of their tent and then sat on top of it to keep it safe, making plans at how they would spend it.[63]

One Cornish balmaiden who was almost as adventurous as Ellen Jack was Sidwell Kruge. She had travelled out to Australia with her family as a young woman. She met and married a son of a Norwegian sea captain, and together they became 'hawkers' (travelling sales people), supplying basic requisites to miners in the outback of New South Wales and Victoria. Eventually they opened a remote wayside trading post and hotel. At this time, Sidwell was shown ore samples and was the first person who identified them as being rich in copper. This was how copper came to be discovered at Cobar. Her story is told more fully in the final chapter.

Early etching of balmaidens cobbing ore. The woman in the background is cobbing two-handed.
From Cyrrus Redding's History of Cornwall

Balmaidens at Mitchell's Shaft Skips, East Pool Mine, c 1904.
Courtesy of Paddy Bradley

Chapter 11

MYTH AND REALITY

No exact figures are available for the total numbers of girls and women who worked at the mines in Cornwall and West Devon from 1720 to 1920. Conservative estimates are that somewhere between fifty and sixty thousand females may have worked at the mines over this period of just over two hundred years.

Of this huge army, we have precious few personal details at all. Almost no personal writings or diaries survive, and only a handful of photographs, drawings and independent records. It is rare to find a record of the personal feelings or reflections of these women and girls - they seem to be almost entirely lost. The nearest to personal reflections that we have are records of interviews with a handful of girls and one woman for the 1842 Royal Commission, the retrospective glance at the life of Patty Tremellin, probably based on the short journal she wrote, and a total of about twenty-four interviews recorded of women who worked in the mines of Troon and Camborne (c.1880-1900), at Polpuff Glass Mine (WW1) and at Geevor (WW2).

On the other hand, we do have records of how observers perceived them, mostly from the pen of wealthy and privileged travellers, mine inspectors, managers, surgeons, clergy, schoolteachers, and contemporary writers or artists.

The myths

Outsiders writing about the mining communities could be over-sentimental, patronising or unrealistic about either the general subservience or well-being of the mining community, as shown in this *West Briton* report of a festival in Wendron:

'From the church a procession formed, comprising agents and persons employed at the mine, with their families, and, preceded by the Porkellis Band, they marched to the account house, where tables were laid and nearly 700 persons sat down. A happier party can scarcely be imagined - there sat the miner with his goodly wife and healthy children - the fine muscular sumpman - the intelligent tributer, and the bold, tutwork man, with many a fair 'bal girl', and those who constitute the stamps pair - and all looked grateful and pleased, and even the babe seemed to enjoy the festival by crowing in its mother's arms.' [1]

Some writers who tried to describe the mining communities fell into the age-old trap of needing to discern the 'deserving' from the 'undeserving' poor. This resulted in judgements about lifestyle, and how people chose to spend their earnings, meagre though they might be. Generally condemned is the perceived over-consumption of alcohol and tobacco, and the lack of money spent on good food. Consistently the women and balmaidens come in for criticism for their 'squandering' of hard-earned money on their appearance. In 1841, one of the clergy in Camborne remarked:

'The young women are more expensive in their dress than desirable', and he has heard of 'clubs among them for the purpose of procuring more showy articles of dress than they could individually afford to purchase, lots being cast to determine whose property they should be.' [2]

Similarly a writer in the *West Briton* in 1849 observed:

'The miners as a class, sacrifice to a great extent their domestic comforts to their inordinate love of dress. This failing has long characterised them, but within the last few years it has greatly increased. ... To see the miners, both men and women, at church on Sunday, or enjoying themselves at a fair at Redruth, one would not suppose that there was much distress of any kind among them. Most of the men are attired in fine broad cloth, whilst women parade their finery. But many ... emerge from holes and dens more resembling pig-sties than human abodes.' [3]

Such judgements continued until comparatively recently. This 20th century author, writing about the late 1860s, still observed their budgeting priorities with a critical eye:

'The mining population of Cornwall had never been noted for its thrift or abstinence. Pay-day, feast and famine had customarily alternated with regularity throughout their working lives and now, in spite of, or perhaps because of the privations during the 60's and 70's, this improvident way of life was maintained. Money that would have been better directed towards the feeding of large families continued to find its way into beer-shop and brothel or into the dextrous pocket of Johnny-come-fortnightly. The Sabbath silk dresses and fine black coats of bal-maidens and their mates caught the eye of many a visitor otherwise appalled by conditions which, in this period of economic decline, revived the county's old name of 'West Barbary'. [4]

Also prevailing in the writing and reporting of the mid-19th century onwards was the idea that the proper, and safe, place for girls and women was in the home doing, or learning, their 'wifely' and 'motherly' duties. Here are George Henwood's views:

'Their being so long from home, renders them wholly unfit to perform and attend to those domestic duties which should constitute the comfort and charm of every home, particularly that of the working man.' [5]

Others lament the lack of domestic skill:

'In alluding to domestic economy, we may observe how desirable it is that the wives and daughters of miners should be better acquainted with culinary and other domestic affairs. Being employed from their girlhood the entire day at the mine, little time or opportunity remains for them to acquire knowledge of matters of so much importance to the health and happiness of those with whom they become connected.' [6]

'Very slight knowledge of culinary work possessed by the young women leads to a coarse preparation of food.' [7]

One of the clergy writes in the same vein, but also judges them to be too much 'out and about' rather than in their rightful place:

'I have visited at least a thousand houses of miners at St. Agnes and here (St. Just) and I find the

Cartoon sketch entitled 'The Three Graces' by George Seymour Jnr. c. 1870.
Courtesy of the Mining Journal

females taken from the mines very deficient in skill in domestic work. Unable to make or mend they are not much inclined to stay at home.' [8]

At the time of the 1841 mine inspections, and later in the 1850s when Leifchild and Henwood were describing life at the mines, Victorian Britain had been shocked by the revelation that women and girls were working at the mines, and, of course, in the north of England, Scotland and Wales had actually been working down the mines. The dismay was not so much to do with the hard and demeaning labour - long hard hours of agricultural and factory labour were still the norm - as with the supposed 'moral degradation' of females working in such close proximity to boys and men.[9][10][11]

They were horrified that the two sexes should even mix, let alone that the girls might be exposed, as they perceived it, to rough language and habits. Even worse, in the north, where women and girls were working underground, the boys or men worked with the minimum of clothes, or occasionally none. The girls and women sometimes laboured 'semi-naked' as well. This was viewed as the most horrific scandal, and a terrible corruption of the female mind.

Although women and girls had not been known to go down the mines in the South West, the concern for their 'moral welfare' was still strongly expressed. Henwood, for instance, comments in the late 1850s:

'Whilst at their work, and under the supervision of the master dresser, all goes tolerably well, save coarse joking, and that continual association we so much complain of; at meal times, and on going to and from their work, it is almost impossible to prevent that conversation and rude behaviour we so much wish to see prevented ... The indiscriminate association, in their employment, of the sexes naturally begets a want of modesty and delicacy, so important in the formation of character.' [12]

Despite their concern for the moral exploitation of balmaidens by their association with the opposite sex at the mine, some of the same 19th century writers then go to great lengths to feature the girls as unrealistically naive and innocent. Just as they are often portrayed as untouched by the physical grime and dirt of the mine, they are sometimes seen as untainted by the perceived 'moral' grime and dirt of their working environment. We are continually treated to romanticised pictures of balmaidens at their tasks. Lucy Fitzgerald, travelling in Cornwall in 1825, described balmaidens in this way when writing to her relative, Lady Sophia Fitzgerald:

'The little girls washing and picking out the best parts, the bigger ones beating it with hammers all the time, thirty nine in a row, was a very pretty thing. They were, all singing hymns which sounded so beautiful, and they looked so blooming and healthy from being so much in the air.' [13]

One suspects that other Victorian visitors to the mines either viewed the dressing floors from a distance, passed relatively cleanly-dressed maids on the way to and from work, were only introduced to balmaidens who had been sent to wash and change, or just over-sentimentalised the picture:

'They give quite a picturesque aspect to the Cornish mining scene, and although they have to handle stones, wheel barrows, manage machinery and work among vessels and streams of water they usually present a very clean and neat appearance. Their boots are nearly always blackened and polished, their large sun bonnets and short print dresses are seldom either soiled or torn, and altogether they afford such an example of tidiness as is well worthy of imitation, even by some whose employment is of a domestic nature.' [14]

In the same decade Leifchild describes them in much the same way:

'How happy and healthy they look compared to children in coal pits and colliery work! There they sit, doing all manner of mining mysteries, and delighting in them too. Hark! The whole set are singing a hymn, and singing it in parts too! How well the girls take their parts!' [15]

He was not the only one to compare the balmaidens' work favourably with other possible employments open to girls and women. In the *1842 Report* Barham described work at the mines as more healthy for girls than working at the local fuse works[16], and the following was written about balmaidens working at East Pool as late as 1889:

'The spalling of the ore was done mainly by women, for whom the breaking of stones sounds a rough employment. But it does not seem so to look at it. It was a blithe company that wielded the long-handled hammers and cracked the dull red rock into fragments whose fractured surface revealed the lustrous metal within. The women looked gay under the bright sunshine in their

picturesque hoods, aprons, and gloves, all white, and some wore nosegays. They laughed, sang, and chatted merrily. There was none of the un-intermittent, machine like drudgery of the factory nor its close atmosphere.' [17]

Repeatedly portrayed is the picture of the obedient balmaiden, born into a life of poverty and hard work, but knowing her place in society. She is the one who loyally plays out her role as reliable and honest labourer, and faithful, loving wife and mother. Leifchild, to illustrate this, records the words of the hymn that he reports balmaidens used to sing. These are two of the verses[18]:

> *'O Lord! We mining children raise*
> *A grateful song to Thee;*
> *Thou wilt accept the feeblest praise*
> *From all that bend the knee'.*
>
> *'O give us grace to do thy will,*
> *What ere that will may be,*
> *To labour daily, praising still,*
> *Loving and serving Thee!'*

When the Rev. John Buller wrote about balmaidens in 1842, just at the time that the *Royal Commission Report* was made public, he too mythologised the balmaiden into either the one who struggled under terrible burdens of poverty and responsibility, or was vain and self-indulgent:

'Under the sheds of these mines the stranger may observe many females, toiling like slaves, from morn to night, to gain a hard-earned pittance. One, with the virtuous object of ministering to the wants of an aged and worn-out parent: others, not infrequently to gratify their vanity, and display their goodly figure in a costly dress on the approaching holiday.' [19]

Victorian novelists also portrayed pictures of purity and innocence:

'At night they (balmaidens) returned in little companies, singing very sweetly as they passed homeward through the lighted streets. On Sundays, or when choirs and Sunday Schools had their outings, they went gaily dressed'. [20]

Hand in hand with this subservient obedient image of the balmaiden is the picture that they were virginal and sexually naive. Dr. Lanyon, a mine surgeon, described balmaidens in this way in 1838:

'In chastity, it may be said, they (balmaidens) are not excelled by any, not withstanding the constant intercourse which daily takes place in their work, among the sexes, we may aver, that the mine girl is as much to be admired for her virtue.' [21]

The mythology of the balmaiden, then, is complex and contradictory. A saying, still current in Cornwall, certainly reflects some of this:

'Balmaidens were famous for the whiteness of their aprons and the foulness of their language.'

The reality

How strange that no one noticed the contradictions in the public myths of the working balmaidens. On the one hand they were tainted and corrupted by an unsuitable working environment and lack of training for domestic life, on the other hand demure, sweet, obedient, hardworking and pure. Sharron Schwartz summarised this when she described 19th century commentators as seeking to 'trivialize, moralize, criticize, condemn, champion or romanticize' them.[22]

In the first instance, the dressing floors were not the clean and tidy places readers of some Victorian descriptions might be led to believe. However, despite the dirty working environment, it seems that balmaidens on the whole had enough pride to dislike being seen looking dirty and unkempt. They often refused to have their pictures taken, or covered their faces. Most pictures that survive from the 1860s and 1870s indicate that they have not been photographed while actually working. They have invariably changed into their clean aprons, and seem to have had a wash and brush up. Hence, despite the grime, visitors were often surprised at how neat and clean the girls looked, as was this visitor to Morwellham Quay in 1841:

'The dress of the women, of whom a great number are employed on the different works here, was when we visited, mostly white; and, although some of their occupations are of a nature in which we could hardly expect much neatness, they all appeared quite clean, their light dresses frequently contrasting strongly with their sombre employments.' [23]

The female author of the article in the *Ladies Journal* of 1872 was very taken with their neat and clean appearance too, but somewhat oblivious to the impracticalities and dangers of their bulky costume:

'She wears a clean print dress, cut very short, stout shoes well covering the feet, a white canvas apron with bib or stomacher, and canvas sleeves to protect her arms. On her head is perched a sensible sun bonnet ... always kept scrupulously clean ... Round her ankles, to save them from the inadvertent blows from the ore when swept from the table, the Balmaiden swathes strips of flannel, which she mostly removes when work is done. There cannot on the whole be a more practical costume ... On washing her hands and throwing off the coarse apron ... the Balmaiden is as neat and clean as if she never handled copper ore or hammer.' [24]

Contemporary photos and drawings show that, although there was a basic dress for balmaidens, the women and girls found all sorts of creative ways of expressing their individuality, despite a limited budget. (This was much to the despair of Victorian commentators, who felt their money should be spent elsewhere.) For instance, unusual collars, bows, and other decorations were added to blouses and dresses, especially around the neckline. Flowers and bows were added to straw bonnets, and simple but attractive jewellery was sometimes worn. When Princess Victoria visited Botallack Mine in July 1865 we are told the balmaidens were dressed in their best attire and 'Johnny Fortnight took care, by supplying the poor mine girls with the latest fashions'.[25] Shortly after, she also visited Devon Great Consols, where she was so taken by the dress of the balmaidens that she asked if she could take one of their ribbons! She, at least, did not feel that their dress was frivolous.

Reading between the lines, however, are the signs of a rebellious nature and wildness, independence and ability, courage and determination, and, most importantly, individual personality. For instance, not all the balmaidens' music was sweet and reverent hymns! It is generally believed that much traditional Cornish music was lost when Methodist conservatism outlawed it and replaced it with the hymns of John and Charles Wesley. Folk songs and working chants, which may have told us much about the balmaidens way of life and their attitudes, have not generally survived. However, here is a sample of one of their songs that has. It must have been the 19th century equivalent of teenage pop music[26]:

I can buddy[27] and I can rock[28],
And I can walk like a man.
I can lobby[29] and skaky[30],
And please the Old Jan[31]

Despite the Victorian anxiety about the roughness and coarseness of the balmaidens' occupation, there is very little evidence of them generally being unruly. However, one small newspaper report indicated that at least some were well able to look after their own interests. In February 1819, a ship was wrecked off the north coast of Cornwall, not far from Padstow. It seems that news had spread around the neighbourhood that plunder from the shipwreck had been secreted in the sand dunes of St. Minver. A group of local young women went searching and discovered a large box of figs. Just as they discovered this prize a group of balmaidens came along on their way home from Pentire Glaze Mine, which was about a mile away. It is not clear whether the balmaidens were the ones that had hidden the figs in the first place and therefore considered themselves the rightful owners, or whether they just felt that with their superior strength or numbers they could claim them for themselves. Whatever the situation, a major scrap ensued, which lasted over two hours, and resulted in minor injuries and torn clothes. Eventually, the balmaidens won, and presumably carried off their prize.[32] These were certainly not weak and feeble young girls if they could sustain a two-hour fight after a day's labour at the mine. In another account a balmaiden picked up her 'boss' and 'thraw'd'n in the kieve' (large barrel for separating tin stuff).[33] We do not know what had transpired to cause her to act in this way, but she was obviously well able to look after herself.

Sometimes a more objective view of the demeanour and behaviour of the balmaidens can be found coming from the pen of the mining professionals of the 19th century, especially with regards to their home lives. In 1841, the agent at Wheal Vor comments that there was some swearing by the women and girls on the dressing floor, but that they were generally well behaved and honest. Some commentators thought there had been improved behaviour and industriousness throughout the mining communities during the 19th century, which they accorded to the increasing influence of the non-conformist churches, especially Methodism. Closely connected with the expansion of Methodism, they believed that membership of Temperance and Abstinence Societies had significantly improved the quality of life for many mining families. The Collector of the Poor Rate in Redruth reported that:

'I have noticed a decided improvement in the living of the mining lasses with these last thirty years.' [34]

Several reporters to the 1842 Commission also had a different view on the domestic competence of balmaidens. One mine agent reported:

'The young women employed in the mines make generally very careful, cleanly wives when they get steady husbands'. [34]

Barham himself, then concluded that balmaidens made able household managers:

'Their hearts are in their homes and they are for the most part tender mothers and industrious wives. Indeed the laborious occupations to which they have been inured make household duties appear comparatively light'. [35]

A decade later, in 1851, John Taylor makes the following observation about the abilities of balmaidens, not just in managing the domestic aspect of the home, but in having a very sound economic instinct:

'I may observe that they are strong and healthy, active, well-formed girls, and make for the most part, very good wives, generally contriving to hold the reigns of power in their own hands, ruling their husbands and finances with a good deal of tact and discretion: for be it known, that the whole earnings or gettings are generally entrusted to the wife's care; and, like a good Chancellor of the Exchequer, she lays out the surplus to the best possible advantage.' [36]

Looking at marriage and baptismal registers, and alternative reports, we are also given a very different picture of the sexual standards of the balmaidens. Most girls continued working at the mines until their marriage, usually, between about the ages of 18 and 22, but with some marrying as early as 17. They invariably married into other mining families, and often within the extended family, sometimes cousins.

Amid the prevailing myths, of either sexual innocence or complete corruption among balmaidens, one lone voice in the *1842 Report* mentions the ancient Cornish custom of 'keeping company'. This was an arrangement by which a young couple entered into a sexual relationship prior to marriage, but with the understanding that the relationship was binding and that marriage would ensue. There is mention of this as early as 1810, when Joseph Farington visited Cornwall:

'The men and women marry at a very early age, and generally signs of connexion make it necessary for the credit of the female. But when this sign does appear the men are very faithful; and (when) a marriage has been solemnised there is no after reproach.' [37]

Sabine Baring Gould made the same observation:

'The Cornish woman will sometimes have a baby before she is legally married, it is only an old custom of the county, though less deeply rooted than the corresponding custom in Wales.' [38]

Similarly, in the 1820s and 1830s Patty Tremellin speaks of:

'Keeping myself from all company, until I went to work at the mine, when I gave myself to company again.' [39]

How this system of betrothal worked, and the way in which had fairly general acceptance in Cornwall is made clear in this article in the *Morning Chronicle* in 1849:

'It really seems, in many places, to be taken as a matter of course that a young woman will be found with child before she is married. Indeed, I have reason to believe that in an immense number of cases young people come to a distinct understanding with each other to cohabit illicitly until the woman becomes pregnant, the man promising to 'make an honest woman of her' as soon as that takes place. This they find more convenient than marrying at once, in as much as the girl

may be of service for herself, and the man elsewhere employed all the time… living better on their separate earnings than they could do in a house of their own.' [40]

This custom of 'keeping company' led the agent at Charlestown in 1841 to observe that although pregnancy before marriage was not unusual, illegitimacy and single parenthood was rare, as most couples subsequently married before the birth of their first child. Marriage and baptismal registers bear this out as a fairly common practice throughout Cornwall. The surface captain at Levant Mine remarked:

'More, I think, of those who have been married from this mine, have proved to have been in the family way when married than not.' [35]

It does seem, though, that with the influence of Methodism, in its various forms, in Cornwall in the 19th century, an alternative moral climate developed, where it was considered that sex outside of the marriage bond was unthinkable. Those of active Methodist persuasion and more mature years would be members of a class meeting and probably also an 'in-band' class, where their everyday behaviour was open to close scrutiny. Not only would other members observe them, and feel free to comment on their behaviour, but each member was expected to use the 'in-band' meeting as a confidential confessional. The story that Patty Tremellin tells illustrates these conflicts very well. It seems she engaged in a sexual liaison with the usual expectations of marriage, became pregnant, and was then deserted. In the case of at least one pregnancy she felt the need to keep the identification of the father secret,

Balmaidens at Dolcoath Mine, c. 1890. Some of the women had not wanted to be photographed and have only allowed it after partially covering their faces.

Courtesy of the Cornwall Centre Collection

even though it resulted in her going to jail. Later, looking back from her new Methodist perspective, she saw her behaviour as shameful, and believed she had committed the most grievous of sins, not just once but three times. It would be easy to make assumptions about two moral codes operating side by side, one for the churched and one for the unchurched. Parish registers, however, show that this is probably too simplistic an interpretation.

In the 19th century then, it seems that balmaidens were not necessarily sexually naive, but nor were they necessarily promiscuous. The traditional economic expedient was for some betrothed couples to indulge in sexual relationships, but to continue, for a while, to live separately in the parental home. This custom meant that some balmaidens were sexually experienced at marriage, but probably having had a stable and monogamous relationship prior to matrimony. As in the case of Patty, pregnancy did not always result in marriage, but a newspaper reporter in 1893 had this to say about balmaidens who were single mothers:

'Personally I know of many cases of mine girls who have illegitimate children; and except they lack husbands, they live irreproachable lives.' [41]

Despite the common custom of 'keeping company' and the possible risk of abandonment, very few balmaidens seem to have been left to raise children on their own. In the *1861 Census*, out of about 5,500 females working at the mines, only 17 were recorded as single parents. Twelve of these were in the workhouse. One was in Bodmin Jail, with her child, for unpaid debt. Six were seeking to support themselves, and their child, by working at the mine. Some illegitimate children, of course, may have just been 'absorbed' into the extended family and passed off as siblings or cousins.

Glimpses of how balmaidens were viewed by society in general can be gained from contemporary literature. In the novel *Norah Lang, the Mine Girl* by Salome Hocking, we are given the impression that mine girls were generally 'looked down on' by the rest of society. When Norah applied to work at the mine in order to earn money to support herself and her family we are told:

'It was a hard struggle for Norah to decide to work at a mine, for though only a miner's daughter, she had always been greatly respected in the village in which they lived, and envied by not a few; and she knew that being a mine girl she should fall in the estimation of a certain class of people.' [42]

The same book sets about challenging these judgements as unfair, suggesting that mine girls could rise above this social stigma. Norah rails against an accusation that she has ambitions above her station:

'Why should I not keep down to my own level? Norah Lang, the mine girl, has no right to expect to be treated like a gentleman farmer's daughter. I have no right to learn music or read poetry. I had better keep to household, and knitting stockings!' [43]

More concrete indications of this social stigma come from census material, which invariably shows that while the sons of mine agents or professional people often worked at the mine, the daughters certainly did not. There were exceptions to this, where women or girls worked in an administrative capacity. For instance, Gussie Retallack, the daughter of the mine manager at Polpuff Glass Mine, was the tally checker. Occasionally women, such as Hettie Julian, a surface captain's daughter who worked in the clay pits during World War One, actually took over jobs previously done by men.[44]

Frontispiece picture from the novel *Norah Lang, the Mine Girl*
by Salome Hocking.

The idea that being a balmaiden was slightly socially unacceptable seems still present in the communal memory in Cornwall today. Most present-day descendants of balmaidens express great pride in their forebears and what they achieved, but this pride is sometimes tempered with a little doubt. 'It was nothing to be ashamed of, was it?' is a comment frequently heard, as if answering an expected criticism before it is made. There is still a concern that some families may feel it demeaning to be shown to have balmaiden ancestors. One correspondent wrote:

'I can remember my grandmother telling me how her parents used to impress on her how important it was not to take a job in the mines, and how it would be better to take a job in service, because the balmaidens were reputed to be 'fast'.' [45]

And what did balmaidens think of their life and work? Because of the lack of first-hand records it is hard to know. What glimpses we have are, not surprisingly, contradictory. At the very beginning of the industrial employment era, it seems that women and girls chose to take up new employment opportunities at the mines rather than go into service, and some even gave up their jobs as domestic servants to go there. In 1736, the Rev. William Borlase of Ludgvan laments that his household was:

'Under the great necessity for a servant, no woman to be hired here in this parish for friendship nor money, being employed about copper.' [46]

The allure of work at the mine is also depicted in the novel *Tales of a Tin Mine* by Silas Hocking. Lucy Penarth who works as a barmaid in her father's kiddlywink (tavern) announces:

'That she would no longer serve drink at his bar, and that she would go to the mine as other girls did, and earn her living.' [47]

Certainly in the *1842 Commission Report*, the general consensus appears to be that the young people who worked at the mines generally did so in good spirits:

'The air of the children and young persons employed at the surface is cheerful and alert, and a disposition to make the most of the intervals of labour in sports of various kinds is generally evinced. Even when labour is excessively prolonged, it is rare to perceive any external sign that the flow of spirits has dried up.' [48]

Of the girls and women interviewed, two had taken up work at the mine in preference to their previous employments, one from straw bonnet making and the other from domestic service. The former had to leave her job due to ill health, but found mine work was better. The latter preferred the relative freedom of working at the mine, compared to working as a live-in servant.[49][50] During the late 19th century, when various schemes were set up to place out-of-work balmaidens into service, many found it was not for them:

'Everything was so strange to me, it seemed to me I was a regular gawk: I couldn't understand half they meant for me to do. I made awful mistakes. … After that (thinks I) I'd better start[51] for I shall never get on. And I did start.' [52]

When John Tonkin interviewed the women who had worked at Polpuff Glass Mine during the First World War, he found that, with the exception of one person, they all looked back with some sort of pride and affection for their time there, even though it had been gruelling and hard. Sixty years on they still had amazing memories of each other, indicating the close friendships which developed between these working women.[44]

Not all the balmaidens enjoyed their work, had good memories, or preferred it to other employment. Patty Tremellin saw her work as a balmaiden as the cause of her misfortunes, and called the mines a 'devilish place'. She subsequently advised young girls not to go there.[40] When a visitor to Dolcoath in 1893 asked some spalling girls how much they earned they refused to tell him. He also described an occasion when the girls refused to pose for a photograph, and, under duress, only posed in such a way that their features were not visible. These actions, he concluded, were because the women had a 'rooted dislike for their calling'.[42] For some, the opportunity to find alternative employment was embraced with great relief:

'Some few, who from time to time have done so and who have fortunately got into places where pains have been taken to instruct them in their duties, would now on no account exchange their present position for mine work: on the contrary, they affirm they are much more comfortable indoors, out of the wet and cold, but all they can say on the matter will not induce some of their companions to follow their example.' [52]

Traditionally the balmaidens had been looked on as very feminine, possibly fragile creatures. The real balmaidens behind the myths were capable, hardworking and down to earth. They had to be (and generally were) physically and mentally tough. A visitor to Dolcoath in 1893 made the following observations about the spalling girls there:

'Only exceptionally strong girls and women can do this work, and so dexterous do they become that they can usually do more work than men who may be occasionally employed with them.' [42]

It was nothing to them to be carrying weights, adopting postures, or performing repetitive actions, which would be banned under current Health and Safety regulations, and which would be totally beyond the capability of many people today. Those that survived the vigorous demands of the work, must have had remarkable strength and resilience. Reiding, on visiting Carn Brea in 1881, was amazed at the strength of an elderly woman he saw filling a waggon with copper ore. He likened her ability to 'the willing vigor of a young man' and 'much more activity than the average navvy'.[53] It was little wonder that these women made good prospective partners for those who would try their chance at pioneering in new lands. One commentator described balmaidens as 'strong like men'.[54]

When there were accidents at the mines the women and girls, where appropriate, would be involved in rescue operations alongside the men, using their physical strength. In August 1899, men at Wheal Basset Mine were trapped behind a fall of thousands of tons of rock at the mouth of one of the tunnels. From a contemporary newspaper report it seems that the balmaidens were involved in the rescue over several days. Although details are not recorded, the balmaidens almost certainly helped barrow away the spoil as it was brought to surface, probably working shifts, day and night. These actions caught the attention of national newspaper reporters:

'It is not generally known beyond the boundaries of Cornwall that hundreds of peculiarly dressed, but attractive and clean looking girls are daily engaged in breaking the stones of ore which are brought to surface. Many of them are as strong as men, as indeed they need to be to work the livelong day in a big shed open in the front and at the sides, subject to exposure and the strain of continuous labour in a stooping posture... No milk-and-water misses these, as you would think if you saw how they relish their potato pasties for dinner or their 'figgy hoggan'.' [55]

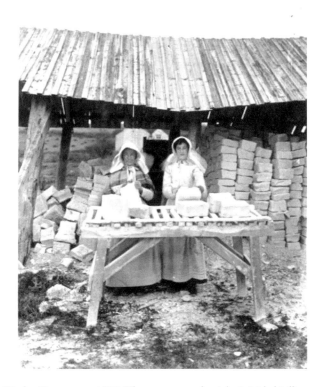

Carloggas Clay Works, Nanpean, c. 1905. The woman on the right is Mabel Lillicrap, the daughter of the mine captain. She dressed in her grandmother's clothing to replace a woman who refused to have her photograph taken. The balmaiden on the left is Cassandra Snell.

Courtesy of Wheal Martyn

181

As well as their general physical strength, it seems that balmaidens, on the whole, did not lack intelligence either. As early as 1825 John Taylor, one of the leading mining entrepreneurs in Cornwall, remarked on the innate ability of the average Cornish miner:

'Education is much sort after among miners, and that its benefits are improved as much as the means will admit, and even far beyond what would have been expected from the new opportunities at present afforded them. Miners in general are a superior class of men, and, in the deep mines particularly, the constant exercise of judgment and thought which is necessary, produces a proportionate degree of intelligence.' [56]

It was within this context, where mining families often strove to improve their lot by education, that so many balmaidens were raised. The story of William Murrish in the *Miner of Perranzabuloe* illustrates the great care with which adults attempted to improve not just their reading and writing skills, but their general knowledge as well. Those who could, avidly read any scrap of printed material they could find, and they just as eagerly shared their new-found skills with the children and young people around them. This hunger for knowledge among balmaidens is illustrated by their attendance at Sunday School up to the upper age limit of 18 years old. We also catch some of that desire to learn from Reiding's account of balmaidens at the Carn Brea Cooper Mine in 1881:

'At the mill we found large numbers of young girls, … all neatly clothed and intelligent, even pert in manner. They can all write, and the literature much sort after and devoured in spare time - penny instalments after work.' [57]

It seems that balmaidens rarely became rich unless by a fortunate marriage. Because of such low levels of pay compared to the cost of living, balmaidens were never in a position to make a real living, let alone a fortune, from their work. Those that remained single and had to support themselves, and those who had to support ailing or disabled relatives, were in real difficulty. Many found themselves in debt, like Patty Tremellin who ended up in debtors' prison.[58] Amazingly only two balmaidens are recorded in Bodmin Jail for non-payment of debt in 1861. They were identified by initials only – 21 year-old 'C. H.' and 18 year-old 'E. J. H', who also had a 10 month-old daughter with her.[59]

Many watched a widowed parent also struggle to provide for the family. The mother of Mary Jane Nicholls collected shellfish.[60] Ellen Nicholls's 76 year-old mother broke roadstone[61], and Jane and Eliza Craze's mother sold 'small things'.[62] It seems that the chance of marriage was significantly reduced for those balmaidens who had to support parents or siblings. Older spinster balmaidens with widowed mothers or invalid siblings were common, whereas unmarried men with these responsibilities were rare. Quite often in these struggling families several, if not all, of the daughters remained single, such as Amelia, Ann and Mary Bennetts[63], and Hannah, Jane and Mary Williams supporting their 60 and 77 year-old mothers respectively, in 1861.[64] For many, it seems that the death of their father meant the end of their hopes for marriage, and the requirement to become the main breadwinners in the family.

In reality then, the balmaidens did not fit the mythical images easily. As a group they were neither sweet, innocent and ineffective nor brazen and brash. Summarising the innate abilities of balmaidens, in terms of strength, courage, wit and intelligence, Hamilton Jenkin describes them as:

'… forming a class of workwomen to themselves. A class as a whole, shrewd, honest, respectable

and hardworking. Though sometimes rough in speech and generally plain spoken enough in repartee, as anyone who addressed them disrespectfully soon found, their work brought no demoralization of character.' [65]

Skills, leadership, responsibility and stereotypes

It was usually assumed that the women and girls were working at the mines as a 'temporary measure', and that their jobs were at very least a useful money-earner between going to school and getting married. At most, it was seen to be a vital short-term addition to the family budget. As a result there was no proper structure for progression, increased responsibility, and earning capacity, as there was for the boys and men, other than a simple increment of wages depending on age. The mine or works management did not offer any, and the women and girls, and their families, did not expect any. The boys could graduate from the dressing floor, if they remained healthy and were industrious, until they eventually became fully-fledged miners. From then, they had the opportunity of becoming tributers or specialised artisans like engine drivers, blacksmiths, or carpenters. If they were lucky they could possibly become mine captains, agents, or even owners. The girls and women could only graduate from washing and picking to cobbing, bucking or barrowing, and then marriage.

Despite the lack of structure and opportunity, the balmaidens often showed the ability to organise themselves. In several known instances they took industrial action in protest at working conditions or pay. The earliest record is of balmaidens on strike in 1806 at Wheal Friendship.[66] They also went out on strike at Devon Great Consols in 1850, Wheal Basset in 1871, Dolcoath and Ding Dong Mine in 1872, and West Seaton in 1877.

However, they were invariably the losers in these confrontations, and were either replaced by other workers, or forced to accept increased hours or reduced pay.[67 68 69 70 71] A rare exception to this, was when 170 boys and girls (all under the age of 18) walked out at Phoenix United Mine in August 1882. A mine inspector had discovered that the young people were working too many hours on Saturday afternoons, thereby contravening the *Employment Acts*. The management subsequently reduced the Saturday working hours, expecting them to work the extra hours during the week for the same pay. As the mine had always closed early on pay day, every four weeks, the young people were effectively being asked to work two and a half hours more in the pay day week than previously, for the same pay. The young people lost two days pay while out on strike, but, before they returned to work, the management had to offer payment for the extra hours.[72]

Apart from their informal mobilisation into action groups, there was probably an informal, or sometimes formal, working hierarchy among women and girls. For instance, in 1836 Kittey Grigg and Ann Brook seem to have had some seniority over other women and girls carrying clay out onto to the moors for drying at Goonvean Clay Pits.[73] They were either the sub-contractors who were paid for the work that was done by the group, who they effectively employed, or they were the leaders of a group of women or girls who presented themselves for employment, and they were the women who received payment on behalf of the whole group. Much later, in 1918, Mary Higgins was responsible for the women and girls at Polpuff Mine, as the 'shift boss'. At the same mine, 18 year-old Gussie Retallack (daughter of the surface captain) was the tally checker.[44] At some mines, one senior woman was appointed by the surface captain to oversee the very complex task of the re-sorting and redistribution of ores ready for sampling.[74] As this was a particularly complicated task this person must have been multi-skilled, and also an accepted appointee from the point of view of the labour force.

Evidence to the 1842 Employment Commission indicates women and girls of mixed ages sometimes working at similar tasks.[75] This may indicate a senior woman or girl responsible for smaller working groups, for instance, to oversee the very young girls or boys at each picking table. There were also women or girls who were singled out for making preparations in the dinner sheds for 'croust'. The Commissioners in 1864 noted these arrangements at North Roskear Mine, where there were six separate dining sheds for the surface workers:

'Half an hour before the bell rings for the hands to leave work, one of the girls for each house goes in, prepares the fire, boils the kettle, makes the tea, puts the pasties in the oven etc, so that when the bell rings and the dressers go in, they can sit down to a warm meal at once.' [76]

Two decades later Minnie Andrews was given similar responsibilities in the dining shed at Tincroft Betty Adit:

'I used to go in the dinner-house and cook, not cook, used to get their food ready and the hot and things; used to put their pasties and things in the oven and warm them again and they come in twelve o'clock and get the tea, get their tea ready, and then I used to tell them when it was turn for them to bring their tea. Now I used to say 'You must bring your tea, whose turn is it? You ought know, I ain't got no tea here', so they bring their tea, like that, and they'd have a good cup of tea and then we used to go on like that.' [77]

Although the stereotype of women's and girls' tasks at the mine were strictly limited to the dressing floor or the counthouse, there were a substantial number of girls and women who broke the mould. Some became waggoners, transporting ore or clay from the mines and pits to the nearest ports or railways for export, as with Ann Key and Nancy Phillips (probably at Wheal Prosper)[45] and Grace Briney who drove wagons from Redruth to Portreath. Grace Briney, it seems, had never been a balmaiden as such. She began work at the mines as a driver for the horses at the whim, she then went on to landing kibbles, a highly dangerous job requiring great strength, and usually the unique preserve of the stronger men.[78]

In very exceptional cases it seems that women achieved and sustained major management roles, against the norm and expectation of their time. Lydia Taylor was manager of Wheal Lovell Mine from at least 1840-5, and may also have been involved in the management of Wheal Towan. Across the county, in the clay mining areas, Phillipa Lovering, Rebecca Martin, and Sara Michell, were among several women who became clay merchants on the death of their husbands.[44] They were not 'sleeping partners' but took a full and active interest in their businesses, and were quite capable of forming new policies, and taking steps to expand their empires.

The tasks which were allocated to the balmaidens on the dressing floors at the mines in the 18th and for the first half of the 19th century were many and varied. In the course of her working life the 'average' balmaiden would have learnt to pick and sort ore, and probably carried out a variety of dressing processes which required not only strength, but dexterity, care, and an eye for detail. Sorting, and separating the 'values' from the waste at all stages of the process required considerable skill, but most especially at buddling and racking.

The women and girls frequently moved from one mine to another for work, which would invariably involve learning slightly different techniques, and sometimes moving between tin, lead or copper mines, and facing entirely new types of work. Some would be processing more than one mineral at a time, such as Ann Paull of Silverwell, Jane Beryman of Kirley, and Grace Rogers of Truck's Lodge, all of whom were dressing tin and copper. This was despite a common understanding that the skills were not transferable:

'The one class of dressers are quite incapable of performing the work of the other; 'Tin men are not copperers' as the Cornish miners say.' [79]

Often the tasks that required the most skill were mechanised first, and gradually the balmaidens were taken away from the complex tasks to the simpler ones, so becoming more and more de-skilled. In their final years it seems that the balmaidens were restricted to the physical spalling of ore, filling buddles, which the men emptied, overseeing racking frames which were almost totally automated, or barrowing ore. The communal memory generally seems to associate the balmaidens' work with these comparatively simple but physically demanding and repetitive actions.

Changes in the way in which these women and girls were described subtly reflected this change in perception. For instance in the *1841 and 1851 Census* records, the balmaidens were often referred to as 'dressing ore', or 'ore dressers', with the adult male workers on the dressing floors described as 'surface labourers'. In the *1861 Census*, a change in language is noticeable, with 'mine woman', 'mine girl' or 'mine labourer' becoming more common. By 1891, the nomenclature had reversed, so that the females were generally described as 'mine labourers', and the men as 'ore dressers'. The memory of a multi-skilled, talented, and experienced workforce of girls and women seems to have been superseded by these later images of unrelenting non-skilled physical labour, resulting in a rather sad under-valuing of the abilities and achievements of the earlier balmaidens.

The Bal-Maidens

They worked here on the south side of the moor,
cramped up around an anvil like a womb,
spalling at the dull blood-coloured ore
with hessian hands, and fragments of a song

of love's predestination, as the storms
poured over head and arms, and down their backs
that ran with the Atlantic.
I watched them in their landscape ringed with wheels,

old Doric chimneys, stacks, wind-pillaged flues,
that smoke away that dark primordial curse
of time's old smouldering wedding with the world,
with life tied like a shim-ass to the bal's

slow consuming circle.
They autograph the moorland graveyards now,
laid up among their infants weak as gruel
that hung once from their thin work-emptied breasts

with scarce the strength to bid against the stone
one passing proposition;
yet stand here in this sepia photograph
erect within their countryside of pain,

a rough and callous beauty in their forms,
rag-handkerchiefs tied up above the soul's
fierce sunlight:
vanning the abstract heaps of wind-cracked spoil.

John Gurney (*Cornish Review* 21, Summer 1972)

Chapter 12

BALMAIDENS - THE REAL PEOPLE

LYDIA TAYLOR: Mine manager

Mrs. Lydia Taylor is the only known 19th century female manager of a tin mine, in Cornwall. She was manager at Wheal Lovell Tin Mine, Wendron, during at least 1840-1845. It was situated on what is now the Manhay Estate, east of Crahan Farm.[1][2] Her co-adventurer was Christopher Wallis, but he does not appear to have taken an active part in managing the mine. This was possibly Christopher Wallis Popham, who was owner of Tresarno Mine nearby, and grandson and heir of Christopher Wallis, a Helston solicitor. Wheal Lovell appears to have been an amalgamation of Commellack, Mengearne and Treguntis Mines.

Very little is known about Lydia, other than that she had a son William Cowper, indicating that she had probably been married twice. She had been responsible for setting up the mine at Wheal Lovell and lived in the counthouse there, where she was involved with the day to day management. During this time she employed Captain William Kite as purser, and the following as agents: Captain J. Crease (1840), Captain Hannibal Perry (1841-44) and Captain Richard Kendall (1844-45). There was also a clerk and storekeeper. On this particular mine, tin was found in pockets or chimneys, and the three most productive lodes were Quoin (Coin) Work, Middle Work and North Lode. Cape's and Goblet Lode were also being worked in about 1842. Lydia's Shaft, in the main part of the mine, was named after Mrs. Taylor.

There is little information about the overall production of the mine. Lydia sold £4,402 worth of black tin in 1841. Subsequent mines in the area, in 1871, took their tin to be stamped at Glebe, Wood or Treloquithack Stamps, a few miles down the valley. It may be that this was the case, also, with Wheal Lovell. There were two accidents recorded at Wheal Lovell in December 1842, one of which was a fatality.[3] In 1843 she sold just over 130 tons of tin-stuff at auction, indicating that the ore was not being dressed before sale.

In April 1844 Lydia negotiated to buy one of Wheal Montague's engines. Treleaven described her as 'Cornwall's only woman mine manager', and records how she sent some of her men, with Mr. West, her engineer, to move the engine. Treleaven did not allow them to proceed, as he knew nothing of the arrangement nor whether any payment had been made. Eventually, in May 1844, William Kite, the purser for Wheal Lovell, removed the engine after John Williams Jnr. of Burncoose had stood surety for the £455.[4] This was probably the engine for the new work on the west part of the sett, where they subsequently failed to find sufficient amounts of tin.

After considerable investment in this failed venture, the mine ran into difficulties. There were cases brought against Captain Kite by James Cliff, a tributer working on Coin Lode, and Hannibal Perry, one of the agents, to the Vice-Wardens Court in Bodmin in August 1844, for non-payment of wages.[5] In the second case at least, the court ruled against the mine, and ordered the outstanding £36 12s to be paid by 1st October.[6] On 19th October 1844 Lydia mortgaged Wheal Lovell to John Williams Jnr. and brothers, along with another mine at Porthtowan, St. Agnes.[7] Operations at Wheal Lovell appear to have stopped about this time and the mine was eventually sold to William Carne of Falmouth, for £7,000. In 1870, at East Wheal Lovell, a later mine in the same area, it was found that, instead of the expected good tin lode running through the sett, they were in fact mining a vertical cylinder of tin which ran for only seventy fathoms.[8] As this was often the pattern of the tin deposits in the area, it may well have been that Lydia experienced the same sort of situation at Wheal Lovell, so that the return on this limited deposit of tin did not cover their expenditure.

As records have only been found for Wheal Lovell from 1840-45, it is not known when Lydia Taylor first took over the management of the mine. It could be that she inherited the mine on the death of her second husband. She also had interests in a mine at Porth Towan, probably South Towan Mine, where her son was an absentee manager. From about 1840, he was serving in the army in Canada. Although Christopher Wallis mostly acted on behalf of William Cowper, Lydia would deal with some of the administration in his absence.[9] [10]

GRACE BRINEY: Kibble lander and waggoner

Grace (or Gracey) Briney is the only known woman kibble lander in Cornwall or West Devon. She worked at one of the mines in the Redruth area in the latter part of the 18th Century, and the early part of the 19th. Kibble landing was generally considered too hard and dangerous for women, and involved landing the large iron bucket full of ore-stuff, as it came to surface from the levels below. This work was usually done by a man standing on a landing platform, using an iron hook to haul in the kibble. It required strength, coordination, and great care, to avoid the kibble swinging back over the shaft and taking the lander with it. In 1886 the task that she carried out was described as follows:

'Landing the kibble when it came to the surface … was a somewhat difficult task, and a very comfortless and exposed one, without shelter from wind and rain. It was accomplished by seizing the mouth of the kibble with an iron pot hook, and drawing it off the mouth of the shaft on to a landing stage. Difficult and dangerous though it was for a man to accomplish, in one instance, and I think the only one known, a woman attended to this duty.' [11]

Grace's real name was Grace Huchens (Hichens or Hitchins), and she was born in 1778 in Gwennap. It seems that she had been raised in the workhouse, and at a very young age was sent as a pauper to work at one of the copper mines in Redruth. She was apprenticed to Capt. A. Treneer, and her job was to drive the horse at the whim which raised the kibble from underground.[12] From an early age she would have watched how to land the kibble, and her ability to control the whim horse at that moment would also have been crucial.

As a young girl she became pregnant, but nothing is known of the circumstances, or what happened to the child. Subsequently she is described as having a change of personality, and from then on usually wore a mixture of what was considered masculine and feminine attire. It may be at this time that she became a kibble lander. However, as a young woman she was renowned for her ability to wrestle, fight, run, and do heavy work. She was obviously a colourful and well-known figure throughout West Cornwall, and there are several surviving descriptions of her. Generally her outer clothing was consistent with that worn by the male surface labourers at the mine, and as kibble lander she would have been considered, presumably, part of the male surface labouring team:

'Her dress consisted of a man's high hat, known among her fellow workers as a 'long sliver', 'bell topper', and more recently 'Par stack'; a blue clawed hammer coat (so called from the shape of its tails) having a thick, deep collar and brass buttons; under this a blue frock with white spots, and very thick, nailed boots.' [11]

'Her feet were encased in coarse blue worsted stocking and thick rough boots, a short skirt with woollen or printed apron, a man's jacket and a man's hat completed her attire, while she generally carried in her hand a good cart whip.' [13]

'She dressed in the very unfeminine costume of a blue cloth coat with gilt buttons, a high hat, petticoats, stockings, and shoes - a style of dress from which she never departed for the last 35 years.' [14]

She obviously had bought her own horse and cart, and was later employed as a waggoner, transporting tin or copper from the mines in Redruth for shipping from Devoran or Portreath. Her odd attire would contribute to her safety in journeying with her cart up and down the county.[13] For many years she lived in the east end of Redruth at East Turnpike Hill in a single room, and on pay day was a regular drinker at the local miners' pub the 'Pick and Gadd Inn', in Treskerby. It was the Treskerby mines for whom she worked.[14] She also sold fish at the weekly market in Redruth.

Grace Briney, aged about 75 years.
©Royal Cornwall Museum

In her latter years she continued selling fish, as well as dealing in mazzards (cherries) and other fruit. Passmore Edwards recalled that as a child he used to carry strawberries, which his father had grown, to sell to Gracey at her stall in Redruth market.[15] She bought cherries from the Bere Alston area in season and, it seems, sold them throughout the west of Cornwall. As a trader she must have been a formidable woman:

'Rugged, but not altogether unpleasing, with a rough voice, she ruled those who came in contact with a rod of iron. Her journeyings as a wholesale purveyor of fruit took her from the Tamar to Penzance, especially in the cherry or mazzard season. Indeed, her influence with the proprietors of the mazzard gardens seemed unlimited. Only in the towns she approved of could mazzards be had, and again in towns in which the retail dealers had offended her, she retaliated by keeping mazzards from the districts.' [15]

After an accident when she was 75 years old, she walked with the aid of crutches, and was dependant, in part, on parish relief. However, even just a few weeks before she died she had travelled fifty miles to St. Dominic, near the Devon border, to buy cherries for the Redruth Mazzard Fair. She died in Redruth on 18th October 1869, aged 91 years, and was buried at Redruth Parish Church on 21st October 1869.[16]

REBECCA MARTIN: 'Clay Baron'

Rebecca was born in St. Austell in 1799 and married John Martin, who was heavily involved in the development of the major clay works in the St. Austell area from about 1835. Together, they lived in Blowing House, St. Austell. John died in 1844, and Rebecca took over the responsibility for the running of their various businesses. It seems that she inherited considerable holdings in the Cornwall China Stone and Clay Co. which failed in 1848,[17] but, at the same time, she was one of the five independent producers who together controlled over one third of the china clay output in Cornwall.

In 1849 she seems to have been the prime mover in pushing for an agreement between producers to regulate china clay prices, and to put an end to the practice of allowing purchasers to accumulate enormous debts.[18] Steam engines were introduced relatively late into the clay works, from 1837, so, as Rebecca was selling an old steam engine at Little Treviscoe in 1851, her works had presumably been among the first to install this technology.

By 1852, Rebecca appears to have been in partnership with John Lovering when Carnclaze Tin Mine was taken over, with a view to exploiting the mine for china clay. In the final month of entries in the cost book for the tin mining enterprise (January 1852), she received a payment of £7 7s 6d (three months at 52s 6d per month).[19]

In 1858, she was managing at least six works: Carvear, Screeda, Lansallson, Huel Virgin, Mellangoose, Little Trevose, and possibly North Gunbarrow as well. The clay produced from these works in that year totalled 6,900 tons, and it was used for paper and bleaching as well as pottery.[20] In 1862, she also took over the lease for Lee Moor Clay, Brick and Tile Works, along with seventeen houses, two associated tin-stream works and a railway. This lease was to run for three terms of twenty-one years. Interestingly, in the *1861 census*, Rebecca is recorded as being blind, so presumably these later transactions must have been carried out despite considerable disability.[21]

Although she had three sons, William Langdon, Thomas and Edward, all of whom were involved in the clay business, it seems that during her lifetime she held the control of the family ventures. She died in 1863, at the age of 64, only one year after taking out the extended lease on Lee Moor.

Rebecca was described in this way:

'She was a lady of great determination and, in spite of her small size, was more than a match for her sons or any other clay producers. Her reputation for forthrightness did not enhance her popularity amongst her rivals, but they respected her nevertheless because she was honest and fair in her dealings with them.' [22]

What businessman or businesswoman could want for a better epitaph?

PATTY TREMELLIN: A hard, short life

Of all the stories in this chapter, this is possibly the most poignant. A tiny book, no more than three inches by one and a half, published in 1841, tells the retrospective story of Patty, who died in 1837 at the age of 33. The book is called *Patty Tremellin: the Life of a Cornish Mine Girl Written by Herself*. At first glance it appears to be written as a fictitious 'improving novel', to be an inspiration and warning to other young women, sometimes in the first person, sometimes in the third. However, the book carries much irrelevant detail, and has a distinct lack of flow and structure, indicating that it was probably based on real life, rather than being a constructed novel. Subsequent research of parish registers of Redruth, St. Mewan, St. Ewe and St. Austell supports the general framework of the story, and almost certainly identifies the central character as Patty (Patience, also known as Martha) Tremellin (Tremellyn, Tremelline or Tremelling). It seems that the book was written after her death, based on a journal she began to write during her illness, and on conversations she had with the author of the book. We do not know who the author was, but it may possibly be the minister who had been pastor to Patty in her final years.

Patty states that she was born in Redruth in 1804, a daughter of a mining family. Her parents were almost certainly Francis and Martha Tremelling, and her baptism was recorded at St. Uny Parish Church on 18th March 1804. We are told in the book that when she was 2 years old she was taken to Penzance, to be looked after by an aunt. Her aunt and uncle ran a shop in the town, and were probably childless. Unlike her own parents, they were able to afford to send Patty to school. Patty firstly went to a school where she did 'reading and sewing', then went on to the 'writing school', which she attended until she was 8 years old. She then was taken out of school to help her uncle in his shop, but was sent to evening classes instead. By this time she had presumably acquired the reading and writing skills which she was to use to good effect in later years.

Suddenly, when she was about 9 years old, the happiness and stability that she had known in Penzance was shattered. The aunt, whom Patty thought of as 'mother', became seriously ill. Over the next few years she was shuffled between her own family, who had moved to the St. Austell area by 1812, her invalid aunt in Penzance, and yet another aunt. Eventually the beloved aunt in Penzance died, and Patty went back to her parents again, to look after her ever-increasing number of siblings. Her mother sometimes went out to work at the mine, but was often too ill to go. When she was ill Patty nursed her as well. When she was 16 years old Patty also went to work at the mine, but still had to carry out the household chores at home. We are not told where Patty and her family worked, but it was at some distance, adding about an hour's travelling time each way to the working day. Patty described their family circumstances in this way:

'My father's wages at that time were small, my mother very ill, our family large, and corn dear, so that both my father and mother had to go to work without meat. Many days we had nothing

but boiled greens to make use of. I had three miles to go to work every morning, and all the work of the house to do after my return at night, as my poor mother was laid up of cancer.' [23]

Worse was yet to come, when they were all thrown out of work because the mine closed. Patty went to Truro to find work, and started going to 'the dancing rooms' until ten or eleven o'clock at night, probably, with other girls from the mine:

'I became deeply attached to a young man … who had often promised marriage. Soon after he deserted me, and I was left to bewail my condition and lament my fall. When near my confinement my father ordered me to leave his house; but I got a place to go, with a very sober woman, about half a mile from our house.' [24]

Patty subsequently had three illegitimate babies. After the birth of her first child, her health began to decline. She was obviously suffering from a progressively degenerative disease which caused haemorrhaging, and her death certificate confirms that she was suffering from tuberculosis. Despite being the mother of young children, and her declining health, she was twice committed to Bodmin Jail. The exact sequence of these events are not clear from the book, but is partly supported by formal records. It seems, when Patty was about 24 years old, she gave birth to her first child. This first child may have been Richard Bray Tremellen who was baptised at St. Austell Parish Church on 6th June 1830, and recorded as the son of Patience Tremellen. After the birth Patty went back home, where she was bedridden for nine months. When she was eventually 'better', she went back to work at the mines. She then reports:

'Three years and six months from this time I fell into the same gross sin again.' [25]

During this second pregnancy Patty became suicidal, and even went to the mine shaft with the intentions of throwing herself down it:

'I was struck with trembling whilst standing on the brink of the shaft, and I seemed to be on the verge of hell.' [26]

It was at this time that a balmaiden friend, who was a Methodist, began to help and support her. When her second confinement was near Patty went to live with two elderly people nearby, doing a little sewing to support herself. William John was probably born in the summer of 1831, when Patty was 27 years old, but he was not baptised until 1834. She put the child out to nurse so that she could go back to work at the mines to support them both. She then fell into debt, possibly to the wet nurse, when she became ill again and could not work. As a result she was committed to Bodmin Jail. On release she returned home to her family in St. Austell.

'After my return home I kept myself from all company until I went to work at the mine, when I gave myself to company again. The third time I brought myself to shame.' [27]

Patty's third child, John Francis, was baptised on 29th April 1832 at St. Ewe Parish Church, where he was recorded as 'bastard child of Martha Tremelling (servant)'. She was once again committed to jail, this time for refusing to divulge the name of the father of her child. An entry in the Bodmin Quarter Sessions of 1833 reads:

'2nd July: Martha Tremellen, St. Ewe. For refusing to name father. To remain in custody.' [28]

She was very ill in jail and suffered a major haemorrhage, so obtaining early release on health grounds. During this time, she had more and more contact with the Methodist community, and her faith began to deepen. It seems that it was after her return from jail the second time that she began to write the journal, which is quoted in the book. However, after release from jail, in November 1833, she was again ill. She was never to regain her health. On 30th September 1834 her middle child William was baptised at St. Ewe Parish Church, at the age of 'almost three years old', where he is described as 'bastard of Martha Tremelline, servant'.

Patty was bedridden from 1835, but began instructing the young children of the neighbourhood in reading and needlework, and in her faith. Her bedroom was her schoolroom. In this way, presumably she was also able to support herself, rather than enter the workhouse. Eventually she died on 10th October 1837, aged 33 years. An entry in the St. Austell Parish Church burial register simply reads:

'12th October 1837: Martha Tremellen aged 33 of Wrestling Downs, bed lier for 3 years.'

Her death is among the first recorded with the General Register Office for England and Wales, as the legal requirement had only been made a few weeks before. Her death certificate, issued on the 4th November, in the sub-district of St. Austell, reads:

'October 10: Martha Tremellen 33 years spinster'

The cause of death is described as consumption, and Patty's mother, Martha, was the informant who had been present, as the book describes, at her death.

It seems that Patty took little pleasure from her years of working as a balmaiden, and looked back the mine as an 'evil place'. She considered that it was this working environment that had been the corrupting influence in her life, encouraging her to the dance floors. Some of her final words recorded in the book, to her young sister, were:

'I ... beg of you, not to give your mind to dress, it is a very great snare; and to avoid the dancing room, it is often the first step to the ruin of young women.' [29]

'Those mines are bad places for boys and girls, for there is nothing but sin to be heard or witnesses all the day long, when the agents are out of the way.' [23]

It was, however, her friends from that same mining environment that had supported her, and encouraged her in her darkest moments. It was balmaiden friends, one in particular, who had shared their faith with her, so that Patty was able to 'shine' in those last difficult years of her life.

MARTHA BUCKINGHAM: Copper ore picker

Martha Buckingham, who was born in 1827, was one of the ore dressers who gave evidence to the 1842 Royal Commission on the Employment of Women and Children at the Mines. Hers was the most detailed interview recorded, and gives considerable insight into her life, both at home and at work.

She was interviewed in May 1841 at the Consolidated Mines, by the mine surgeon, Dr. Charles Barham, author of the report. At that time, Martha was just 14 years old. She had been working at the Consolidated Mines in Gwennap, for about four years, working mostly at the picking table, but occasionally she was called on to barrow, riddle, or spall. Of all the tasks she did, she found barrowing the hardest job of all, and sometimes had to do it all day (presumably at sampling). She said that it gave her back pain. At Consolidated Mines ore picking was normally done under a shed with a roof but no sides. In winter this afforded virtually no shelter from the wind and rain, and Martha's feet were often cold and wet. She only had one pair of shoes, and, having no dry shoes to change into, she reported that she sometimes caught cold.

Martha lived at Bissoe Bridge, which was about three miles walk from the mine. She normally got up at about 4 a.m. and prepared her own breakfast, and would leave home at 5.30 a.m. to start work at 7 a.m. In the evening she would finish work at 5.30 p.m. and arrive home about 7 p.m. When she arrived home, she would have supper, and then go to bed between 9.30 and 10 p.m., giving her about six and a half hours sleep. However, for a week or fortnight in every month (at sampling) she would start work an hour earlier at 6 a.m. and not finish until 8 p.m. She admitted how tired she was at these times, with a fourteen hour working day, and about six hours sleep. When sampling was over they were allowed one whole day at home to recover, but they were not paid overtime for this extra work. Martha said that work was usually available continuously during the winter months, but due to water shortages it was not always available during the summer months.

At Consolidated Mine the balmaidens were allowed an hour for dinner. Martha would take a pasty or hoggan, which could be warmed in the dry when the weather was cold. The girls ate together in the dinner shed. They did not have a mid-morning break, but by 9 or 10 a.m. they were usually already hungry, and would often take a bite or two of their pasties while still working, and when the surface captain wasn't looking.

Martha was one of seven children, and her mother was widowed. Many years previously, her father had gone to Scotland to work, leaving the family in Cornwall. He had been sending money to support his family, but, unfortunately he died there when she was 6 years old. Her older brothers and sisters went to work at the mine to support the family, and, in due time, she was sent to the mine to work as well. She had one younger sibling not yet working. One of her brothers, who normally worked at Poldice Mine, about five miles away, was chronically ill. She attended the local Methodist Sunday School, and was learning to read and spell. This family appears to be the family of Delia Buckingham of Bissow as described in the *1841 Census*, although Martha and her 30 year-old sister Mary were not described as working at the mine, whereas her brothers were. The youngest child of the family was only 2 years old at this time.[30]

When interviewed by Charles Barham for the 1842 Commission, Martha described having 'overheated her blood' from carrying too much at the mine, and that she was continuing to 'break out'. The mine surgeon reported that she was generally healthy despite a 'cough and papulous eruption'.[31]

THOMASINE PILL: 'Better the North'

Thomasine Pill was born in Cocks, a small hamlet in the parish of Perranzabuloe, in 1837, and was the third daughter of copper miner, Robert Pill. Although she had a few years in school, by the time she was 14 years old she had followed her older sisters to work at the mine. They were probably working at the Perran St. George Copper Mine out on Cligga Head, which employed about 500 people in the 1850s.[32] All of her brothers who were over the age of 7 years were also working as ore dressers at surface, or below ground with their father. Thomasine continued to work at the mine until her marriage at the age of 19, to John Bawden, who was also a miner.

After marriage, as was the norm, it seems she did not work at the mine again. She had eleven children, ten of whom survived into adulthood, and all of whom went to the local lead mines to work as soon as they were old enough. In 1875, however, when the mines closed in the parish, Thomasine's husband, John, and some of her sons found work in the Durham coalfields. This was probably offered to them by visiting agents from the northern coalfields, who were looking for non-union Cornish miners to strike-break. They were offering reasonable wages, a one-year contract, accommodation, and free travel to miners and their families. The starving Cornish miners would not be happy with this situation but the common saying was 'Better the North than Oversea', which was the only other option to find work. So Thomasine and the family up-rooted, with the exception of the eldest daughter who went into service locally, and moved to Sunniside in Weardale. It seems that Thomasine was pregnant when they made this move, as her last child was born there, soon after. Despite the annual contracts the Cornish miners were in fact free to go after only six months. Understandable animosity from the local miners often forced the Cornish on, and in a short time it seems that Thomasine and her family had moved again.

They moved to the Furness area of Lancashire, where Thomasine already had relatives working. Her widowed mother had travelled there with Thomasine's brother and family some years before. Thomasine's husband, John, and their sons, found work at the iron mines at Stank, just outside Barrow in Furness, and they moved into one of the new terraced houses, built especially for the miners, at Roose. This community was known as 'Little Cornwall', and some descendants of those Cornish miners still live there today. Thomasine's husband, John, died very suddenly in March 1883, when Thomasine was only 46 years old, after they had been in Roose for seven years. Thomasine's elder children had left home, or were about to marry, by this time, but she had three children of school age still at home. She resorted to the tried and tested means of supporting herself and her family, relied on by countless generations of miners' widows before her - she rented out a room, and she took in other people's laundry. This first expedient may have had more long-term consequences than she envisaged, as two of her three daughters still at home married lodgers.

Meanwhile, history was to repeat itself, and by 1888 the mines at Stank closed, so the Cornish miners once again had to move on to find work. Although most of her sons left, Thomasine, at the age of 51, did not go with them this time. She stayed in Roose with two of her married daughters, whose husbands had been offered work in the Vickers Shipyards. Thomasine ended her days in Roose, dying in November 1906, at the age of 69 years. She is buried in the windswept cemetery in Barrow, overlooking the Irish Sea, a long way from her Cornish home.[33]

LORETTA COON: A brave young woman

Loretta was born in August 1857 at Kilhalland, Tywardreath, and was the daughter of John and Elizabeth Coon. In 1861, while Loretta (Lauretta) was still at home, her father and two sisters were recorded as working at a copper mine, and were almost certainly employed at Fowey Consuls. Sometime before 1871, the family had moved from Kilhalland to St. Cleer. This was probably because of the closure of Fowey Consuls in 1867. They went to live in the mining community of Common Moor, St. Cleer, where Loretta and her brother, who was four years her senior, both followed their father to the mines. Sadly, by 1871 their father had died, and Loretta, at 15 years old, was dressing copper ore, and her brother was mining underground. Most of the other young women living at Common Moor were also balmaidens, including 17 year-old Mary Truscott, and Ann and Christiana Goldsworthy, who were 25 and 34 years old respectively. This little group of women probably made their way to and from the mine together. Perhaps Loretta and Mary would have been particular friends, being of a similar age. Loretta almost certainly continued to work at the mine until her marriage in 1874, and it is there that she probably met her future husband.

Loretta was married at St. Cleer Church in August 1874, nine days before her eighteenth birthday, according to her birth certificate, although she was recorded as being fully 18 years old in the marriage register. She married 21 year-old Thomas James Wilton, who was an ex-miner. He was already probably blind at the time of his marriage, and he was working at the local village shop in St. Cleer. Although the exact circumstances of him losing his sight are unknown, it is thought that he had been blinded in a mine accident, probably by a delayed or accidental explosion.

It is not known whether Loretta and Thomas had been courting before the accident which blinded him, or if their courtship developed afterwards. Either way, Loretta married him before her eighteenth birthday, her widowed mother presumably giving parental consent, as she was a minor.

Loretta subsequently helped Thomas to run the general shop in St. Cleer. They also had fourteen children, although four of the girls tragically died before their second birthdays, and one of the boys at 12 years old. The surviving sons helped Loretta and Thomas with a local coal round in the village. Loretta died in 1926, aged 69, and was buried in the churchyard at St. Cleer. Her husband, Thomas, died only a few months later and is buried with her.[34]

Loretta and Thomas Wilton outside their home in Common Moor, c. 1910.
Courtesy of Edna Collins

THE OLD WOMAN AT CARN: Work or the workhouse

When American, William Reiding, and his friends, visited a copper mine in Carn Brea in 1881 they encountered an elderly woman loading wagons with ore stuff ready to be taken to the copper crusher. William was so startled by her that he wrote a graphic description of her appearance:

'Picking our way through the purplish mud and stones below Karn, we discovered a little old woman labouring over a pile of unmilled copper ore. We had to look twice before we could assume ourselves of her sex: not only was her dress perplexing, but there was an unreality and weirdness in her person. She was very small, almost dwarfish, with bent shoulders and wrinkled hands and face, her skin had the texture of parchment, and was curiously mottled blue, her hair was thin and wiry.' [35]

She was wearing petticoats which ended above the ankle, and which were stained purple with the hue of the copper. Her legs were covered in woollen wraps, and she was wearing substantial shoes. They watched as she loaded the wagon with ore, using her Cornish shovel, and they noticed the ease and strength with which she moved despite her age:

'She seemed very old, but her eyes had a shrewd and penetrating quickness, and her movements were utterly without decreptitude. Indeed, she applied herself to her work with the willing vigor of a strong young man. Shovelful after shovelful was thrown in with an easy muscular swing, and with much more activity than the average "navvy" ever exhibits.' [35]

They engaged her in conversation about her age, and the heavy nature of her work. She replied:

'Deed, sir, I don't know how old I am, but I've been at it this forty years. I'm not young any longer, that's sure. … No use being tired; when you are tired, there's the workhouse for you.' [36]

When they asked her if she had a husband, she explained that she had never married, and that since being pushed down stairs by her employer at the age of 24, when she was in domestic service, she had suffered regular fits:

'No, sir; nobody would ever have me, nobody would have me or go with me, as I was always subject to fits – terrible they are. I still have them once or twice a week sometimes.' [36]

Eventually, when she had almost filled the wagon, two other younger balmaidens joined her to help. Then, together with two of the surface labourers, the three women pushed the wagon to the crushers. One of the party visiting with Reiding was an artist, and apparently drew a picture of the scene. By her own admission this woman must have been at least 64 years old.

ELIZABETH ASHTON: Assayist and smelter

The story of Elizabeth Ashton is a remarkable one, and features our only woman not born in Cornwall. We do not know Elizabeth's maiden name but she was born in Aylesbury in either 1845 or 1846. Unusually, in her early twenties she trained as a chemist, probably in London, and this must have been where she met her husband-to-be, Edward Ashton, who was also a trained chemist.

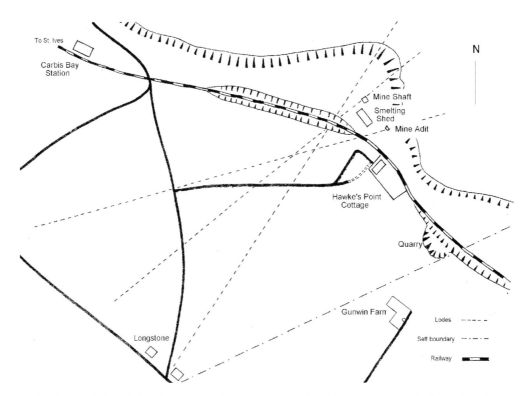

Sketch map of Carrick Gladden showing the position of Hawkes Point Cottage and Hawkes Point mine.

It is not known exactly when Elizabeth and Edward were married, but, after completing his training in 1866 Edward, together with his brother Nicholas, moved from London to St. Ives. They opened chemist's shops in Hayle and St. Just and both included a photography studio. It seems Elizabeth remained in London in 1867 until their daughter Minnie was born, but she then followed her husband down to Cornwall. By 1871 the three had also opened a shop in St. Ives. They were to run this shop for many years, whereas the first two shops had closed by 1880.

In July 1883, Nicholas Ashton, Elizabeth's brother in law, leased the derelict Wheal Fanny Adela Mine at Carrick Gladden, between Carbis Bay and Lelant, calling it by its original name, Hawkes Point Mine.[37] This mine had been closed since about 1871, but had previously been mined for tin, copper, lead and nickel-silver. The building of the St. Ives Railway had resulted in the excavation of a cutting at Hawkes Point, and this revealed some of the old copper lodes. Under the supervision of a Mr. Barry Lord, the Ashtons re-opened the mine.[38] Originally nineteen men were employed, and some quantities of copper and cobalt were extracted. There were high hopes in the St. Ives area at the time, that the revival of this mine would provide much needed employment in the area, but this was not to be. Hamilton Jenkin was uncertain of the exact location of this mine, but believed the workings ran under the headland at Carrack Gladden, adjoining the railway.[39] A surviving sketch map shows Big Ben Tin, Cobalt and Copper and Ashton's Caunter Lodes.[40] To what extent the Ashtons expected to make a commercial venture out of the mine, and how much they intended it just to supply essential elements for their pharmacy and photography business, is not clear. The detailed outcome of this early venture is unknown, but it seems that no great fortune was made by anyone. An ex-miner from Hawkes Point Mine remarked:

'There was too much of everything and too little of anything ever to make a keenly bal.' [39]

198

However, during the subsequent fifteen to twenty years the three Ashtons continued to run the mine themselves, extracting cobalt, nickel and peacock copper, presumably for use in their chemist and photography business. Together they dressed, assayed and refined these ores in a small smelting house on top of the cliffs at Hawkes Point, where they were frequently observed working at their furnace all through the night.[37] The ores were separated and the copper dressed in the normal way. The mixed cobalt and nickel ore was probably left in the open air for up to a year so that the cobalt component would oxidise. When this process was complete, the weathered ore would be sieved and crushed to a powder, ready to be burnt in the furnace. After a light roasting, nickel could be run off. Further roasting then reduced the oxidised cobalt to pure cobalt.[41]

During these years of work at the mine and smelter, Elizabeth also carried out most of the dispensing at their chemist shop opposite the Market House in St. Ives, and latterly ran a 'picnic site', known as Grannie Ashton's Tea Gardens, from their cottage on Hawkes Point. She was described 'quite as good a chemist as her husband' and that 'she had knowledge of most things'. She was also well-known for her healing powers, ascribing them to the 'magnetic' qualities of her hands. It is said that a magnet could be deflected when near her, but bearing in mind her years of working with cobalt, which has ferromagnetic properties, this may not be such an unreasonable suggestion. She first started offering massage in about 1875, and, even in her old age, many people still went to 'Little Granny Ashton' in the hopes of finding relief from a whole range of ailments of the muscles and joints. She could also dowse for water, and is said to have found water locally where mining engineers and geologists had failed.[42]

About 1905, when she was about 60 years old, it seems that Elizabeth grew tired of the amount of time and energy that the three were investing in the mine, and the consequent dressing and smelting of the ores, and so she took matters into her own hands. Reputedly, she went down to the workings on her own one evening, and pulled out some of the pit props, causing the roof to fall in, effectively closing the mine.[39]

Both Elizabeth and her husband, Edward, survived into their nineties, with Elizabeth outliving her husband by just twelve months. She died in May 1934, and was buried in Lelant churchyard. There was a very large attendance at her Requiem Mass at the local Catholic Church. She had long since become quite a local personality. [40]

SIDWELL KRUGE: The discovery of the Cobar copper field

Sidwell is thought to be the daughter of Ephraim Woolcock (or Willcocks and other variants) who was a miner in Illogan, and Bessie Willoughby. Little is known about the family, but Sidwell was born in Illogan about 1834, and worked as a balmaiden at one of the many copper mines in the area. The family emigrated to Australia in 1848 or 1849, at first going to Burra and then settling in Armagh, near Clare. In Armagh, Sidwell helped look after the children of her married sister, Emily. During this time she met Henry Kruge, the son of a Norwegian seacaptain, and they were married on 19th June 1858 at St. Barnabas Church in Clare, when they were both 24 years old.

The two of them then embarked on the nomadic life of 'hawking', basically running a mobile general store from their bullock-drawn wagon, travelling the river valleys of Victoria, South Australia, and New South Wales. At some time in the 1860s they chose a point halfway between the River Murray and Bourke to settle, calling it Gilgunnia. As Henry was skilled in the carpentry and the smithing trades it was an ideal spot to open trading post, smithy and workshop, and subsequently a hotel which they named the 'Gilgunnia'. In due course a small settlement grew up around them, and they opened a post office in their store, with Henry becoming the postmaster.

Meanwhile, they had also acquired the lease of 600 acres of land and had started to keep livestock. In 1869 there was a severe drought, and the Kruges had to travel with their livestock nearer the Murray River, to Priory Station, in order to find water. Here they met up with three well-diggers, Charles Campbell, and Thomas Hartman, both Danes, and George Gibb from Scotland. Whilst being cut off by floods in the area, some aborigines had helped these three young men find their way through and had led them to their Kubbur waterhole, an old aboriginal sacred place. While camping there they noticed the unusual blue-green rock in the sides of the water hole. Not knowing what it was, as they were only familiar with gold ore, they took a sample. When they met Sidwell and Henry at Priory Station, they showed them the ore which they had not been able to identify. Despite her relatively tender years as a balmaiden in Cornwall, Sidwell immediately recognised the ore as a form of copper carbonate. They all returned to Gilgunnia, where Henry heated the ore in a crucible to smelt it and poured the molten metal into a sandy groove in the ground. They were able to confirm Sidwell's identification of the ore. The three young men then departed for Bourke, to register a mining claim for the Kubbur area. This was the beginning of what was to become one of the largest copper mining areas in Australia, known as Cobar.

Henry and Sidwell did not become involved in the opening up of the mines as such, but continued to run their store and hotel at Gilgunnia. A nephew took over the store and Post Office in 1886, leaving Sidwell and Henry to run the hotel, but Henry died suddenly, two years later. Sidwell remarried in 1889, her second husband being James William Dean, also a hawker. Subsequently there were problems with the management of the Post Office, and James left Gilgunnia about 1893. Sidwell continued running the hotel until 1908, probably with assistance from her nephew and his wife. She then sold the hotel and land, and went to live with her niece in Cobar. She died on 17th April 1913, and was buried in the Methodist section of Cobar Cemetery.

Sidwell and Henry Kruge, c. 1885, and the headstone marking Sidwell's grave in Cobar.
Courtesy of John Symons

As a mark of Sidwell's involvement in the discovery of copper at Cobar, the adventurers of the Cobar Copper Company presented her with a gold brooch with word 'Regards' set in diamonds. The date of this presentation is unknown, but was probably after 1885, when the Cobar Copper Company was making good profits. The Stele monument was erected in Cobar in 1969 to commemorate the part Campbell, Hartman and Gibb played in the founding of both the mining industry and the township, but no mention is made on it of Sidwell and Henry Kruge. Today, however, there is a commemorative display, telling their story, in the Great Cobar Heritage Centre.[43 44] Henry and Sidwell are honoured as the founders of the township of Gilgunnia.

HETTIE JULIAN AND THE DAVIS SISTERS: Work at the monitors

During the First World War some women took over the tasks of men in the 'clay bottoms' of the clay pits. By this time, all the pits were very deep, and at most works the clay was removed by the hydraulic method. This involved men loosening the sides of the clay pits by explosives, and then the broken clay matrix being washed out of the clay pit sides by directing water through narrow hose nozzles at pressure. The hoses were usually held on a wooden frame, and directed by an operator by means of a lever arrangement. These hoses became known as 'monitors' due to their lizard-like appearance. The liquid clay 'wash' was channelled into gullies and eventually pumped up from the quarry to the separating and settling tanks.

It was this task of handling the hoses which was done by the women. During the course of their shift, the women would need to keep moving the jet of water over the 'washing face' in order to obtain an even sample and to 'advance' the face safely. At regular periods, the position of the hoses and frames would need to be moved in order to work on another part of the face of the clay.

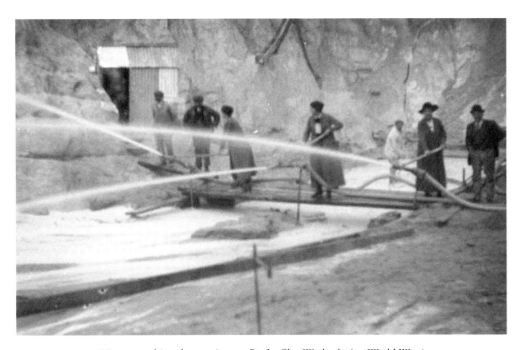

Women working the monitors at Rocks Clay Works during World War 1.
Two of these are Mary and Jane Davis.

Courtesy of Wheal Martyn

Mary and Jane Davis at Rocks Clay Works,
World War 1.
Courtesy of Wheal Martyn

Three of the women who carried out this work were May and Jane Davis, and Hettie Julian. The Davis sisters worked at Rocks Clay Works under Captain Fred Pinch. They were two of four women working in pairs on six-hour shifts. Although they were expected to work in all weathers, apparently they were given slightly favoured treatment, compared to the men, by the captain, and were told 'when ice forms on your oilers (oilskins), you can leave the bottoms for a warm up'. The photo on page 201 shows three of these women standing on a wooden platform, forming a bridge over the liquid clay, operating the monitors.

Hettie Julian was the daughter of Captain Jack Julian (also known as Capt. Guts) of Bluebarrow Clay Works. She was selected specifically to work at Bluebarrow, when they were short handed during World War One, because the family lived in a house on site, and so no special provision needed to be made for a female employee. Like the Davis sisters, she too worked 'on the hose' in those wartime years. Her father was in his mid-sixties at the time, and, if there was a problem with the pumps at the pit overnight, she would go to sort it out, so that her father was not disturbed. This involved going out into the vast clay pit with a lantern, whatever the weather, and climbing down into the pump shaft. Once there, and having secured her lighting, she had to use an enormous spanner to undo sixteen two-inch nuts on the air-seal door. Having loosened the nuts she then had to swing the 300-pound steel door open, by its chain. She then needed to remove any obstructions very quickly from the valve below, as, once this air-seal was broken, the shaft would rapidly fill with water. She then had to do this all in reverse and find her way back home safely.[45]

PHYLLIS THOMAS: On the picking belt

'During the Second World War seven of us worked on the picking belt at Geevor Tin Mine, while the men were away. We were all single, except for one who was a widow. Our job was to remove as much of the waste from the tin-bearing ore as possible, before it went to the crushers. We all lived in the village of Pendeen. When we started we had no real training; we were just shown what to do by the supervisor.

'The hooter sounded at Geevor at 8 o'clock to start work; at 12 o'clock for dinner time, at 1 o'clock to be back at work, and at 5 o'clock to finish for the day. It also sounded at the New Year and any other special occasion. Our normal working day, then, was eight hours, but we had to work late if the plant broke down. We worked a full day Monday to Friday, and then Saturday mornings as well.

'The seven of us who worked on the picking belt all changed places every hour so that we all took it in turns at the different jobs, including lifting off the large granite stones. Some were very big and could not go down the chute, so they were thrown on the floor to be broken up by the foreman. If a stone got jammed in the washer chute we had to run around shutting down the plant, and then start it all up again when it was clear. The ore-stuff had first come through the washer, so we always had our fingers in water. The other smaller pieces of granite which we picked out were put on another conveyor belt, to be disposed of. The ore was carried to another house where it was delivered down chute into waiting trucks. This was then on to the crushers.

'Sometimes we had to work until 11 p.m. if there had been a breakdown, so that all the tin was gone from the main bunkers for the night-shift men to have room in their bin. We had plenty of other jobs to go to while the fitter was mending the machinery. One was to clean the tin sacks. This was done on the tin floors, and we used to beat the bags on an iron stand and then pick off the pieces of string. Another job was to get in the bunker and clear out all the tin that had been left in the corners and shovel it through the square holes out to the shaking tables.

'The washer and crusher were very noisy, and we couldn't hear ourselves speak. We used to lip read and made up our own sign language. The working conditions were also very dirty. However, we worked undercover, in sheds, so that we were able to work despite weather conditions. Sometimes small pieces of spar would fly up into our eyes, and we would have to go to the first aid post to have it taken out.

'There was a canteen at Weatherhead, and we used to have pasties from there, which we ordered early, if we didn't go home for lunch. Sometimes we brought our own lunch. We had our own little tearoom and took it in turns making tea. We took our tea breaks two at a time. We were paid weekly.

Phyllis Lockett (nee Thomas) at the picking belt at
Geevor Mine in 2003.
Courtesy of Phyllis Lockett

'We wore our own clothes and shoes to work, and some of us brought clogs, as they lasted longer.

'Although working on the picking belt was hard work, we all got on well and we all enjoyed ourselves.' [46]

MRS. MINNIE ANDREWS: The last balmaiden?

Minnie Andrews was born in Camborne in 1874. She was interviewed by a journalist from the *Cornishman* newspaper in April 1967, and a few weeks later by Justin Brooke. It was believed she was one of the last surviving balmaidens, if not the last, in Cornwall, who had worked on the traditional dressing floors. She was then in her early nineties, and when asked about her days at the mines, she could still give a very clear account of her experiences.

She was born in a house adjacent to the Square in Beacon, on the outskirts of Camborne. She was probably the daughter of William Symonds Harris, a tin miner from Marazion, and Mary Ann, who was born in Crowan. She had at least one brother, Robert, and a sister, Bessie. Even before she began work, she was familiar with work at the mine, as, from the age of 5, she used to carry dinner to her father at Carn Camborne, just over the road from her home. He subsequently suffered ill-health, and when Minnie was about 9 years old he became too ill to carry on mining. It was then that she was sent to join other girls from the village already working on the dressing floors at Wheal Frances. She remembered having to leave home very early to walk across the moors to start work at 7 a.m. She recalled that they were allowed twenty minutes for crowst and half an hour for dinner.[47]

She first worked at the racking frames, and remembered how difficult it was. She had to learn how to keep the channels of the frame unblocked. She worked long hours and described how desperately cold and painful her hands became:

'I was turt (taught) to the frames and cleaning the holes and getting the water to run, and taking out gravels out from the holes; it did choke up the holes, you know, they things. Oh, I worked awful hours, mister, because I been dying with the cold, my hands, no wonder they go dead, I didn't, they don't go dead, my lor'.' [48]

After learning to rack, she sometimes had to fill the buddles. These she filled twice a day, while the young men would empty them out when the ores had separated out. At first she was earning fourteen shillings per month. By the time she was 18 years old she was earning eighteen shillings per month, but that year the mine closed, and she had to find alternative employment. She went to work at Betty Adit, Tincroft.

She worked at several different mines over the years, depending on the availability of work, and the wages offered. She said that the girls and women would often move to work at another mine if the rates offered were better. Wages also increased with age, but the most she ever earned was twenty-two shillings per month. She commented several times that she often worked harder than the men, presumably meaning the surface labourers, who actually earned much more.

At some stage Minnie worked picking copper at Carn Camborne, where her father had worked. While there, she worked with an elderly lady, possibly a widow, called Anna Sincock. Their task was to remove the 'deads', leaving the better ore in the strip ready for washing and dressing. Over time, she also worked at Dolcoath, as well as at several tin streams, including Old's and Rodda's. She did not like working at Dick Old's, as he was so abusive:

'I worked down Dick Hole/Old's streams. And then I worked down to Rodda's streams, down by the adit. That's the only streams I worked. They two. Dick Old. You wouldn't look your head off from what you was doing, the old fool would have a stick aimed at 'ee, or something thrown at 'ee. Oh, he's some demon, he was, an old thing, he was. He'd thraw a stick at 'ee.' [48]

Coming from a very poor family, Minnie only had one hessian work apron, unlike some of the other balmaidens who had one apron to work in, and a better, possibly a cotton or linen one, to wear for best, and to and from work. Instead, she would try and wash her hessian one as white as she could. It seemed to be a matter of pride to look as smart as possible. She also described the hand cloths they used to wear to protect their hands:

'We wore a towser.[49] *I used to come home in the evenings and wash my towser. I never had but one, I was too poor to buy the rest, I tell you true; I never bought but one. I had to wash un every so often, and he was white, he was lovely, he was, he wasn't a white stuff, he's like the hessian bags you do see, and you try wash em' white, come white lovely. And I used to go Monday mornings with a clean towser on, clean hand-clothes; we put hand-clothes on our hands, 'cause we was proud, we didn't want to soil our hands.'* [48]

Minnie wore 'a sun bonnet' (gook) at work, and she described how some women covered their faces with the bottom edges, just leaving the eyes uncovered:

'I had a sun-bonnet. Could be pinned round here (round her neck). When I worked West Frances (there was a woman who) used to pin the bonnet in round, that nobody shouldn't see her face, hardly, or just leave her eyes showing.' [47]

For most of the time as an adult, Minnie worked at Tincroft. Here, as one of the more senior, and obviously more reliable, girls, it was her job to go to the women's shed to get ready for dinner time. She would be responsible for making the tea and warming the pasties and organising the tea rota for about a dozen other women and girls:

'I used to go in the dinner-house and cook, not cook, used to get their food ready and the hot and things; used to put their pasties and things in the oven and warm them again and they come in twelve o'clock and get the tea, get their tea ready, and then I used to tell them when it was turn for them to bring their tea. Now I used to say 'You must bring your tea, whose turn is it?' [48]

She remembered, that when she was about 14, they journeyed to work from Beacon to Tincroft during the blizzards of 1891 by walking over the tops of the hedges. Once there, they still had to work despite the appalling weather conditions. Another story she told was of some of the other girls from Beacon being persuaded to go underground, which was normally considered very unlucky. Minnie refused to go with them. They were caught and the man who took them down was severely reprimanded by the mine captain. [47] When working at Brea Tin Streams, she remembered going to the Brea Inn for 'a quick penny glass of porter' with some of the other women and girls for a treat on pay day, but added 'but I never liked the stuff!' [48]

Eventually Minnie married a miner from Tincroft, and, as was the custom, gave up her work at the mines. She continued to live in the village of Beacon all her life. She raised one son and two daughters, and was widowed for the last seventeen years of her life. Sadly, she died within a year of these two fascinating interviews. Her last days were spent at Barncoose

Hospital, and she was buried at the cemetery in Troon in March 1968.[50]

What a precious record these two interviews are, preserving Minnie's memories of a lost age, giving us insights into the real lives of the balmaidens, the language in which they spoke, and the words and expressions which they used. These stories seem a world away from the rather pristine and sentimental pictures that the Victorian visitor to the mines would give us, and we can begin to glimpse the rough, tough, real world of the balmaiden. The rest we can only surmise.

GLOSSARY

Account house: see counthouse.
Adventurer: shareholder in a cost book mine.
Anker: small barrel.
Attle: waste rock.
Beetal: mallet used for splitting slates.
Beetle: see beetal.
Blende: zinc ore.
Boxes: tables where ore is picked.
Bing ore: lead ore reduced to small hazelnut-sized pieces after 'cobbing'. A term more commonly used in the Pennines.
Bucking: method of breaking cobbed copper or lead ore down to fine granules and powder.
Bucking hammer: short handled hammer with a flat face for bucking ore.
Bucking plate: cast iron anvil on which ores are bucked.
Buddle: rectangular or round apparatus for separating fine ores from waste.
Buddling: one of the sedimentation techniques for separating ore from waste.
Burning house: see calciner.
Calciner: furnace for roasting ore to remove arsenic.
Captain: mine overseer. Origin of word uncertain. In Cornish mines captains sometimes given separate areas of responsibility, e.g. underground captain, surface captain, etc.
Cassiterite: tin oxide.
Casualties: see leavings.
Chimming: see tossing or towsing.
Cobbing: method of breaking medium grade tin, copper or lead ore into small pieces, to separate waste.
Cobbing hammer: short handled hammer with pointed end for cobbing ore.
Core: one shift at the mine (usually three of eight hours each in a day).
Cost book: accounts ledger for mine or clay works.
Counthouse: mine office.
Cover: a reservoir for holding tin slimes.
Crazing mill: mill used in early days of Cornish mining for grinding stamped ore into fine grains. Originally hand powered, then water- or horse-driven.
Crib: midday meal at the mine.
Crib bag: a rough linen drawstring bag used by mine workers for holding a pasty or hoggan for dinner. Usually made out of flour bag material.
Crib house: dinner shed at mine or clay pit.
Croust: mid morning break.
Deads: waste material.

Dillueing: see jigging.

Doles: piles of crushed ore, usually two or three feet high with flat summits, laid out ready for sampling.

Dradge or drage: see dredge.

Drags: settling pits for separating mica and sand from china clay.

Dredge: stony ore of low value, which is then bucked to obtain mineral.

Dresser: see grass captain.

Fire-setting: method by which ore-bearing rock is dislodged from a rock face by building a fire at its base, and then cracking it with cold water. (Pre-explosives era).

Foul tin: tin-stuff or mixed material before dressing.

Frame: see racking frame.

Framing: see racking.

Frue vanner: ore separator used on the tin dressing floors from about 1900.

Fuggan: see hoggan.

Gangue: medium grade copper ore.

Garboldi: see garribaldi.

Garribaldi: bodice worn by bal-maidens.

Gollibolder: dialect word for garribaldi.

Gook: felt or cotton bonnet with wide brim and edge falling over shoulders.

Grass: surface of the mine.

Grass captain: supervisor of dressing floor.

Hanaways: see halvans.

Hennaways: see halvans.

Halvans: poor copper ore-stuff separated after the first washings, and often reprocessed.

Halvings: see halvans.

Hoggan: coarse savoury barley bread, fuggan being the sweet version with raisins.

Huggan: see hoggan.

Hures: copper ore-stuff.

Hutch: a shelter without sides, a water reservoir, or a wooden box for holding tin slimes.

Hutch work: see jigging.

Jigging: sieving fine copper or tin-stuff under water, in order to raise light waste to the top. Initially done by hand, but eventually mechanised.

Karer: a sieve.

Kibble: large iron or steel bucket for bringing ore up from mine.

Kieve: vat or large barrel for washing ore.

Knits: small particles of lead ore.

Kitty bags: leg protectors worn by bucking girls, probably made of tarred hessian.

Knocking: part of the dressing procedure for lead ore where ore is reduced to small pieces, equivalent to cobbing in copper dressing.

Knock-bark: lead ore reduced to pea-sized pieces (equivalent to bucked copper ore).

Jack: zinc ore.

Lappior: old name for boys and girls who worked at the buddles. Pryce suggested it was from the Cornish 'lappior' meaning dancer.

Launder: wooden gully through which water was delivered to machinery and equipment at the mine.

Leavings: poor tin ore left after the first washings, often reprocessed.

Limp: semi-circular flat board used for skimming off waste from sedimented ore in the kieve. Originally made of wood, sometimes shod with iron on the circular edge. Latterly made of iron.

Loobs: tin slime or sludge containing mineral.

Materials man: see grass captain.

Monitor: the high pressure hose pipe used for washing out clay at the clay pits, named after its particular configuration on the wooden support frame.

Mundic: iron pyrites, arsenic or sulphur waste from tin or copper dressing.

Niflin: traditional Cornish meal made from dried cod.

Orthoclase: see potash felspar.

Parcel: a measured heap of ore, dressed and ready for sale.

Peasy: lead-rich sediment obtained from the kieve.

Pillas: barley-like grain that will grow on very poor soils. Commonly grown in Cornwall up to the beginning of the 20th century.

Picking rough: copper hures which after sieving were sent to the picking table to be sorted.

Potash felspar: used as an important constituent of glass.

Prill: piece of solid ore.

Racking: the finest sedimentation technique to separate tin ore from waste using ragging frames.

Racking frame: large rectangular frame, built on the slant which is used to separate very fine tin particles from fine waste, by running water across it.

Recking: see racking.

Ragging: see racking.

Reeders: towers of china clay blocks set out for drying, or the reed hurdles that covered them.

Rill: inner part of dole taken for assay at sampling.

Shaft small: the finest copper hures from the mine which fell through the sieve on riddling and could be sent straight to the bucking table.

Shambles: place where waste from the mine is taken.

Shed: long sideless shelter under which the cobbers or buckers work.

Shode: rock containing tin ore.

Sist: see subsistence.

Slimes: fine mud containing metallic ore.

Smitham: lead ore sediment obtained after its final washings.

Soap rock clay: soapstone.

Spalling: breaking of larger rock pieces from the mine into suitable size for going on to the crushers (tin) or for cobbing (copper).

Spalling hammer: long-handled, blunt-ended hammer for breaking large lumps of rock.

Stamps: ore crushing machines for tin, originally water powered, latterly steam or electrically powered.

Stanking widths: puddling the fine racked tin with the feet, to raise any remaining water to the surface.

Strake: wooden trough in which copper ore is placed for washing and sorting.

Streke: see strake.

Strips: sedimentation areas for collecting the tin-stuff that had passed through the gratings at the tin stamps.

Subsist: see subsistence.

Subsistence: wages paid ahead of time, where need was demonstrated (up to 50% of wages).

Surface captain: see grass captain.

Summer leaving: china clay left to dry over the summer months.

Sun-rising houses: houses built overnight on common land, in order to gain tenancy. A chimney had to be built, and a fire lit, before dawn.

Surface labourer: male manual labourers on the dressing floors who carried out the heaviest tasks such as kibble landing, barrowing and ragging.

Tailings: worthless portions of ore washings.

Terloobing: see tossing.

Ticketing: selling of ore.

Thumblebeans: see thumblebinds.

Thumblebinds: leg protectors, made by twisting straw into ropes, around the thumb.

Tossing: settling fine tin ore in kieves, by knocking the side of the barrel either manually or mechanically, until a solid mass of fine ore had accumulated at the bottom.

Towrag: traditional Cornish meal based on dried cod.

Towzing: see tossing.

Towser: the hessian working apron worn by balmaidens at the mine.

Tozing: see tossing.

Train oil: oil obtained from pilchards, and used for rush lights. Usually stored in large earthenware pots outside the home.

Travelling iron: gouge used in the quarries for marking slates prior to shaping them.

Tribute: typically Cornish system of employment at the mines, where a team accepts work at a given rate for ore raised (and sometimes dressed) from a prescribed area in the mine.

Trunking: part of the tin dressing process, separating slimes ready for framing.

Ulster: best apron for wearing to the mine.

Venturer: see adventurer.

White granite: china stone.

Winter leaving: china clay left to dry over the winter months.

Yard of cardboard: type of balmaidens' head covering worn in some parishes, consisting of a piece of straight cardboard placed on top of head and covered with cotton print and tied under the chin.

FOOTNOTES

Chapter 1

1. WB 5th February 1819 and 16th May 1823.
2. Sara (1970) p. 43.
3. Pryce (1778) p. 136.
4. Inch, A. R. CFHS Jour. 56 (June 1990) p. 9.
5. CRO Poldice Cost Books DDX 475/4.
6. *1891 Census Camborne* 1891/9/27/29.
7. Although it was considered unlucky for women to go underground, it seems that female members of the Royal Family (commencing with Queen Victoria at Polberro Mine in 1846) set a precedent for females visitors going underground, and after that date, there was steady trickle of women visitors who ventured there. This included the wife of underground mine photographer Burrows, who helped him with his equipment when he took the first photos of the mines in the 1890s.
8. Todd (1967) p. 47.
9. Gerrard (2000) p. 23.
10. Beare (1586) p. 1.
11. Phil. Trans. (1678) p. 949.
12. Lewis (1965) p. 189 quoting PRO Exchequer, *Treasury of the Receipt: Council Book of the Duchy of Cornwall 25-39 Edw. III ('White Book of Tenure in Cornwall')*.
13. PRO E101 260/22, 260/33.
14. Lewis (1965) p. 196, (Accts Excheq. K.R., bundle 263, no. 17).
15. Donald (1994) p. 328 ff.
16. Agricola (1556) p. 269.
17. Agricola (1556) p. 293.
18. Ford, Trevor. "15th Century Mining as shown in the Kuttenberger Kanzionale" p. 81ff. in Ford, Trevor; Willies, Lynn. *Mining before Powder*, Peak District Mines Hist. Soc. Bull. Vol. 12 No.3 (1994).
19. Mattingly (2001) p. 97.
20. Childrey, Joshua. *Britannia Baconia* (1660) p. 10 quoted Lewis (1965) p. 1.
21. Raistrick, Arthur; Jennings, Bernard. *A History of Lead Mining in the Pennines* (Davis Books 1983) p. 135.
22. Fiennes quoted Morris (1949) p. 257.
23. Pryce (1778) p. 136.
24. RIC: Calenick Smelter Petty Cash Book 1704.
25. RIC: Calenick Smelter Receipt Book 1704.
26. CRO DDJ 1784.
27. MSS Borlase CRO.

28. Wheal Bassett Cost Book CRO DDX 316/1.
29. Pocock quoted in Chope (1967) p. 191.
30. Berg, Torsten; Berg, Peter (ed.). *R. R. Angerstein's Illustrated Travel Diary, 1753-1755* (Science Museum 2001) p. 120.
31. Carew: BM Add. Mss 29762.
32. Pryce (1778) intro. d.
33. Henwood (1826) p. 145.
34. Hunt (1887) p. 713.
35. MJ 20th February 1858 p. 128.
36. Schwartz (2000) p. 87.
37. *Metalliferous Mines Regulation Act 1872.*
38. PRO PP 1890, XX Cmd. 6060. *Report of the Chief Inspector of Factories and Workshops for the Year Ending 1889.*
39. Calciner operator.
40. Burk (1986) p. 185 quoting *Stannary Court Records Penhalls 1879.*
41. MJ 23rd April 1892 p. 455.
42. MJ 23rd May 1914. p. 493.
43. Troon Women's Institute (1952) p. 12.
44. Schwartz (2000) p. 93.
45. Lemon (1838) p. 70-75.
46. Spargo (1865) p. 38.
47. *1841 Census Kea* 147/0/1/31.
48. Lanyon (1841) p. 117.
49. *1841 Census 150 St. Agnes and Perranzabuloe.*
50. Deacon, Bernard. Talk given to China Clay History Soc. Sept 2002
51. Barton (1989) p. 102.
52. MJ 21st March 1868.
53. Rowe (1993) p. 8.
54. Lemon (1838) p. 57.
55. Leifchild (1855) p. 173.
55. Lemon (1838) p. 73 and Tables XVI and XVII.
56. CEC (1842) p. 42.
57. Watson (1843) p. 3.
58. Barton (1989) p. 240.
59. Williams quoted in Todd (1967) p. 16.
60. Rowe (1989) p. 157.
61. PP111 *General Census of England and Wales (1871)* p. 253.
62. Reiding (1881) p. 811.

Chapter 2

1. Taylor (1814) p. 22.
2. CEC (1842) p. 27.
3. CEC (1842) p. 133.
4. CEC (1842) Evidence No. 93. p. 131.
5. CRO Wheal Agar Cost Book TL96.
6. CEC (1842) Tables 11-16.
7. CEC (1842) Evidence No. 56. p. 115.
8. CEC (1842) p. 43.
9. Schwartz (2000) p. 71.
10. CEC (1842) p. 102.

11. *1841 Census Kenwyn* 147/15/20/59.
12. *1841 Census Breage* 136/10/2/34.
13. *1841 Census Phillack* 1585/8/15/72.
14. *1841 Census St. Just* 1596/4/11/44).
15. CEC (1842) p. 109.
16. Personal correspondence (I J/LM 2002).
17. *1861 Census Illogan* 1582/14/25/104 + Camborne 1583/5/24/137.
18. *1841 Census St. Agnes* 231/12.
19. *1861 Census Phillack* 1585/6/26/32.
20. *1861 Census* 1529/8/6/56.
21. *1861 Census St. Colomb Major* 1544/3/19/60.
22. CEC (1842) Evidence No. 18. p. 105.
23. *1861 Census Redruth* 1580/15/1/101.
24. Bartlett (1994) p. 85.
25. WB 12th February 1858.
26. *1841 Census Crowan* 1841 141/5/1/4 and 6/16/33.
27. PRO PP111 *General Census of England and Wales* (1871) Vol. 111 253ff.
28. *St. Teath Census 1881.*
29. *1891 Census Illogan* 1849/11/1/4.
30. Rideing (1881) pp. 806-810.
31. *1861 Census Kea* 1562/10/1/89.
32. Personal correspondence (JE/LM 2002).
33. *1841 Census St. Agnes* 15/229/8, *1861 Census St. Agnes* 1554/8/4/76.
34. *1841 Census St. Agnes* 7/106/13, *1861 Census St. Agnes* 1555/1/6/6.
35. *Cornishman* 6th April 1967.
36. *Cornishman* 12th November 1893.
37. CMHRS: *Women's Mining Accidents.*
38. Paxton (1984) p. 200.
39. RCG 27th January 1872.
40. Brooke (1967).
41. CEC (1842) Evidence No. 75. p. 124.
42. *1861 Census Camborne* 1584/11/27/87.
43. Bartlett (1994) p.77.
44. Kinnaird (1864).
45. Rowe (1993) p. 8.
46. Wheal Cock Cost Book RIC Mining V.
47. WB 23rd February 1855.
48. RCG 13th August 1870.
49. Barton (1966) p. 94.
50. WB 8th February 1867.
51. Barton (1971) p. 71.
52. Toll (1958) pp. 17-19.
53. Razzelle (1973) p. 29.
54. Henwood 1856 p. 35.
55. WB 2nd July 1847.
56. WB 8th July 1859.
57. Hamilton Jenkin (1951) p. 58.
58. WB 1st July 1814.
59. WB 20th June 1856.
60. PRO E101 260/22, 260/30.
61. RIC Calenick Smelter Petty Cash Book 1704.

62. RIC Calenick Smelter Receipt Book 1704.

63. CRO Pool Adit Cost Book DDJ 1784.

64. Borlase (1759).

65. Noall (1982) p. 6.

66. Henwood (1857) p. 166.

67. CRO Wheal Towan Cost Book TL 96(6).

68. Jenkins (1948) p. 10.

69. Lemon (1838) p. 64.

70. Lewis (1997) p. 70 & 83.

71. Stockdale (1824) p. 23.

72. Personal correspondence (MS/LM 2002).

73. RIC Wheal Cock Cost Book 1822

74. CEC (1842) Evidence No. 21. p. 106.

75. WM Ninestones Cost Book 316/1.

76. CEC (1842) Evidence No. 86. p. 128.

77. Leifchild (1855) p. 282.

78. Lemon (1838) p. 63.

79. CEC (1842) Table 20.

80. Leifchild 1855 p. 227.

81. Kinnaird (1864) p. xxv.

82. CRO New Trelawny Cost Book STA 259/S.

83. WM Goonvean Cost Book 1988.233.

84. RCG 30th January and 27th February 1880.

85. W. Herbert Thomas in Barton (1989) p. 211.

86. Pryce (1778) p. 176.

87. CEC (1842) p. 32.

88. CEC (1842) p. 33.

89. Kinnaird (1964).

90. Mayne (1985) p. 52.

91. CEC (1842) p. 132.

92. CEC (1842) Evidence No. 50. p. 114 + Evidence No. 85. 128.

93. WB 3rd June 1878.

94. RCG 11th April 1874.

95. *Western Morning News* 21st September 1879.

97. RCG 11th April 1874.

98. RCG 30th April 1874.

99. MJ 26th October 1850 p. 586.

100. RCG 23rd September 1871.

101. RCG 6th January 1872.

102. RCG 8th June 1872.

103. WB 9th April 1877.

104. Harris (1974) p. 61.

105. RCG 30th January 1880 and 27th February 1880.

106. Honor (1869) p.37.

107. Kinnaird (1864) xxv.

108. Sara (1970) p. 43.

109. Furze (1936).

110. Kinnaird (1864) p. 439.

111. CEC (1842) p 129.

112. CEC (1842) p. 118.

113. Morrison (1980) p. 122.

114. CEC (1942) p. 67.
115. Morrison (1980) p. 318.
116. Kinnaird (1864) p. 122.
117. Honor (1869) p. 55.
118. WB 29th September 1887.
119. CEC (1842) p. 119.
120. Rowe (1993) p. 160

Chapter 3

1. Head, Sir F. Bond. *Quarterly Review* (1827) quoted in Earl (1994).
2. Doyle, J. and T. *Tamar Valley Traveller* (Cornish Safari Co. 1978) p. 21.
3. CEC (1842) Evidence No. 18. p. 105.
4. Barton (1971) p. 77.
5. Razzelle (1973) p. 28ff.
6. Spreadbury, I. D. (ed.) *Impressions of the Old Duchy; Book 1 Through Cornwall by Coach (1795)* (Kingston) p. 12.
7. CEC (1842) Evidence No. 6 and 7. p. 101.
8. Kinnaird (1864) xxv.
9. Paton (1984) p. 200.
10. WB 29th September 1887.
11. CEC (1842) Evidence No. 6 + 7. p. 101.
12. Honor (1869) p. 55.
13. Langworthy (2002) p. 2.
14. Kinnaird (1864) p. 122.
15. Kinnaird (1864) p. 439.
16. CEC (1842) p. 131.
17. CEC (1842) Evidence No. 6. p. 101.
18. WB 7th March 1968.
19. CEC (1842) p.119.
20. Simonin (1867) p. 438 and fig. 145.
21. Ballantyne (1897) p. 313.
22. Work aprons.
23. Mine captain.
24. *Cornishman* 5th January 1893 "Deep Down Dolcoath Mine".
25. *The Penny Magazine* No. 220 5th September 1835.
26. Sara (1970) p. 43.
27. Personal correspondence (JG/LM 2002).
28. Hocking (1875) p. 95.
29. Brooke 1967
30. Schwartz (2000) p. 75.
31. R. T. Paige, *The Tamar At Work* Dartington Trust 1982
32. *Old Cornwall; The Cornish Coif* (1973) p. 140-3.
33. Esquiros (1865) p. 65.
34. S. Winifred Painter, *Old St. Ives - the Reminiscences of William Painter* (Lanham 1927).
35. Tangye (1988) p. 54.
36. CEC (1842) Evidence No. 46. p. 111.
37. Giglet = young girl; personal correspondence (JG/LM 2002).
38. Sara (1970) p. 195.
39. WB 31st May 1844.
40. Tremelling (1841)

41. Personal correspondence JG/LM 2002.
42. Leifchild (1855) p. 164.
43. *Cornubian* 7th January 1887
44. Darlington (1878) p. 84.
45. Pepper (1862) p. 270.
46. 5th March (St. Piran being the patron saint of tinners).
47. Supposedly the day on which St. Piran first smelted tin.
48. WB 31st May 1844.

Chapter 4

1. Jenkin (1974) p. 20.
2. Lewis (1997) p. 155.
3. Darlington (1878) p. 161.
4. Watson (1843) p. 16.
5. Chamber's Repository; *The Mines and Miners of Cornwall* (March 1853), also from Honor (1869) p 37.
6. WB 28th March 1862.
7. Darlington (1878) p. 78.
8. Buckley (1990) p. 75.
9. CEC (1842) Evidence No. 89. p. 128.
10. CEC (1842) Evidence No. 86. p. 129.
11. CEC (1842) Evidence No. 112. p. 140.
12. CEC (1842) Evidence No. 19 + 20. p. 105.
13. CEC (1842) Table 17.
14. MJ 26th October 1850 p. 506.
15. De La Beche (1839) p. 594.
16. CEC (1842) p. 53.
17. Henderson (1858) p. 18.
18. Pryce (1778) p. 234.
19. Jenkin (1978) 2 p. 9.
20. MJ 15th February 1879.
21. CEC (1842) Evidence No. 6. p.101.
22. CEC (1842) Evidence No. 47. p.111.
23. CEC 1842 Table 18.
24. Darlington (1878) p. 80.
25. Henderson (1858) p. 17.
26. J. H. Collins. *Observations on the West of England Mining Region* (1912) p. 268 and Taylor, J. "Notice of Some Improvements in Dressing Ores" *Quarterly Mining Review* Vol. II (1831) p. 82-7.
27. Darlington (1978) p. 84.
28. CEC (1842) Evidence No. 21. p. 106
29. CEC (1842) Evidence No. 33. p. 108
30. Henderson (1858) p. 20.
31. CEC (1842) p. 55.
32. Pryce (1778) p. 136.
33. WB 25th April 1817.
34. Darlington (1878) p. 156.
35. MJ 16th January 1858 p. 36.
36. CRO Dolcoath Cost Book TEM/62.
37. CEC (1842) Evidence No. 50. p. 114.

38. Watson (1843) p. 16.
39. Jenkin (1948) p. 22.
40. CEC (1842) p. 57.
41. Brooke (1967).

Chapter 5

1. Brooke (1978) p. 21.
2. Pryce (1778) p. 21.
3. Burt (1969) p. 74.
4. Personal correspondence (PT/LM 2001).
5. Barton (1989) p. 182.
6. Noall (1982) p. 35.
7. Pryce (1778) p. 136.
8. Cunnack 1775 p. 22.
9. Barton (1989).
10. Barton (1989) p. 84.
11. Collins, *Rambles Beyond Railways* (1861) in *Messenger* (2001) p. 32.
12. Personal correspondence (FH/LM 2001).
13. Brooke (1967).
14. Pepper (1862) p. 238.
15. Payton (1984) p. 200.
16. *Cornishman* 5th January 1893.
17. Barton (1989) p. 211.
18. CEC (1842) Evidence No. 103 + 104 (p. 137 + 138).
19. Personal correspondence (FH/LM 2001).
20. CMRC Mining accidents (2002).
21. CEC (1842) Table 17.
22. Watson (1843) p. 17.
23. Henderson (1858) p. 8.
24. Henderson (1858) p. 10.
25. CEC (1842) p. 55.
26. Henderson (1858) p. 11
27. Salmon (1860) p. 24.
28. Henwood (1857) p. 157.
29. Henderson (1858) p. 12
30. *1861 Census Carnmellis* 1570/11/19/26.
31. *1861 Census Uny Lelant* 1587/6/1/76.
32. Tangye (1988) p. 53.
33. Salmon (1860) p. 23.
34. Fergusson (1873) p. 129.
35. Pryce (1778) p. 136.
36. Salmon (1860) p. 215.
37. Barton (1989) p. 183.
38. Barton (1968) p. 56.
39. R.C.G. 12th August 1881.
40. Sara (1970) p. 43.
41. Tangye (1988) p. 53.
42. *1861 Census Marazion* 1591/1/2/4.
43. Barton (1989) p. 242.
44. CFHS 106 Dec 2002 p. 14

45. CRO DDX 161; Minutes of the Cornish Tin Mining Advisory Committee.
46. Hamilton Jenkin (1948) p. 111.
47. RIC: Calenick Receipt Book 1704.
48. RIC: Calenick Smelting Works Petty Cash Book 1704-7.
49. *1891 Census Lugdvan* 1853/8/18/86.
50. Henwood (1857) p. 157.
51. Barton (1989) p. 138.
52. MJ 16th October 1875.
53. Barton (1989) p. 169.
54. Barton (1989) p. 175.
55. RCG 2nd April 1895.
56. Barton (1989) p. 230.
57. Troon Women's Institute (1952) p. 12.

Chapter 6

1. Fitton (1814) quoted Barton, R. (1966) p. 42.
2. WM Ninestones Cost Book 1988.367.
3. WM Goonvean 1988. 237.
4. Coon, Joseph M. *The China Clay Industry* Royal. Corn. Polytech. Soc. Vol. V1 (1927) p. 56.
5. BPP (1857) 62.87.ll p. 484-581.
6. Esquiros (1865) p. 43.
7. WB 23rd January 1868.
8. Personal correspondence (A J/LM 2003)
9. WB 23rd January 1868.
10. White (1861) p. 187.
11. Stoker (1852) p. 78
12. Barton, R. (1966) p. 95.
13. Thurlow (1996) p. 24.
14. Stoker (1852) p. 79.
15. Personal correspondence (JT/LM 2002).
16. Ann. Phil. 111 (1814) p. 181.
17. Collins (1878) p. 26.
18. Personal correspondence (JT/LM 2002).
19. *1881 Census* 2013/2.
20. Personal correspondence (JT/LM 2002).
21. *1891 Census St. Austell* 1822 1/2/4.
22. Barton, R. (1966) p. 88.
23. Barton, R. (1966) p. 98.
24. Barton, R. (1966) p. 103.
25. Great Exhibition (1851) Catalogue Vol. 1 p. 133.
26. Taber, Joan. *Stone and Quarrymen of the West Country* www.freepages.genealogy.rootsweb.com-stonemen.
27. WM 2002.5c: *Pochin's China Clay* (Pochin) p. 8
28. Chope (1967) p. 97.
29. Majendie (1818) p. 32-37.
30. Britton (1801) p. 331.
31. Paris (1818) p. 168.
32. Warner (1808) p. 224.
33. Barton (1966) p. 48.

34. Paris (1818) p. 200.
35. Collins (1878) p. 26.
36. Personal correspondence (JT/LM 2002).
37. *China Clay Trade Review* Vol. 1. (June 1919) p. 11.

Chapter 7

1. Murchison (1854) p. 118.
2. G. Henwood, *Four Lectures on Mining* (1855).
3. Corin (1997) p. 10.
4. MJ 28th August 1858 p. 562.
5. Boase (1819) p. 383.
6. Hunt (1878) p. 1004.
7. Hunt in *Ure's Dictionary* (1878) p. 1004.
8. CRO Minute Book of Penhalls and Blue Hills Mine 1879, *Stannary Court Records.*
9. Langsworthy (2000) p. 9.
10. Inch (1990) p. 9.
11. *1891 Census Truro* 1829/16/4/185.
12. CEC (1842) Evidence No. 75. p. 124.
13. Personal correspondence (PC/LM 2002).
14. PRO E101 260/22.
15. PRO E101 260/26.
16. PRO E101 260/30.
17. PRO E101 260/10.
18. CEC (1842) Tables 13, 14 & 15.
19. Bartlett (1994) p. 121.
20. CEC (1842) Evidence No. 84. p. 127.
21. Pryce (1778) p. 234.
22. CEC (1842) *Report by Joseph Fletcher for the Lead Mines of Lanark and Dumfries* p. 8.
23. Hunt (1970) p. 92.
24. CEC (1842) Table 17.
25. CEC (1842) *Report by Joseph Fletcher for the Lead Mines of Lanark and Dumfries* p. 4.
26. Hunt (1884).
27. Burt (1969) p. 70.
28. Hamilton Jenkin (1974) p. 46.
29. *1861 Census Perranzabuloe* 1556/19 to 1556/22.
30. CRO New Trelawny Cost Book STA 269/S).
31. *1861 Census Kea* 1563/15/12/3 and 1563/18/4/6.
32. Burt et al (1987).
33. Burt (1969) p. 73.
34. Spargo (1865) 2. p. 19.
35. *1861 Census St. Agnes* 1556/24.
36. Toll (1958) p. 17.
37. Booker (1974).
38. Richardson (1992).
39. Burt (1984) p 18-40.
40. *1841 Census* 249.
41. *1851 Census* 1884.
42. Massey, Roger. *Slimeford Tamar History* No. 12 (Winter 2002) p. 10-11
43. Toll (1958) p. 17.
44. Patrick (1990) p. 40.

45. Hearder (1841) p. 55.
46. Toll (1958) p. 17.
47. Messenger (1994) p. 116.
48. Personal correspondence (VFJ/LM 2002).
49. V. Flint-Johnson, CFHS Jour. 106 (2002) p.14.
50. *1861 Census St. Columb Major* 1544/3/7/54.
51. *1891 Census St. Brannel* 1825/3/4/24
53. Borlase (1758) p. 94.
54. Turner (1864) p. 14.
55. Thomas Clifton, *Handbook for travellers in Devon and Cornwall* (1850).
56. Jenkin (1888) p. 31.
57. Turner (1864) p. 14.
58. De La Beche (1839) p. 502.
59. Turner (1864) p. 11.
60. Mayers (2000) p. 41-66.
61. *1841 Census St. Teath* 152/14/45 + 152/14/37.
62. CEC (1842) Table 28.
63. *1851 Census St. Teath* 1898.

Chapter 8

1. Bottrell (1870) p.70.
2. WB 28th March 1862.
3. WB 31st October 1889.
4. Pryor (1973) p. 50.
5. Noall (1982) p. 6.
6. Henwood (1857) p. 30.
7. Henwood (1857) p. 32.
8. Henwood (1857) p. 84.
9. Leifchild (1855) p. 52.
10. *1861 Census St. Just* 1597/10/3/64.
11. *1861 Census St. Just* 1597/10/24/74.
12. Henwood (1857) p. 10.
13. Henwood (1857) p. 22.
14. Williams (1862).
15. *Cornish Telegraph* 7th July 1880.
16. RCG 27th January 1872.
17. Jenkin (1948) p. 194.
18. CRO Diaries of William Pease DDX 715/4.
19. WB 4th March 1864.
20. Jenkin (1974) p. 29.
21. *Cornish Telegraph* 7th July 1880.
22. RCG 27th January 1872.
23. Hamilton Jenkin (1974) p. 29.
24. WB 2nd September 1859.
25. WB 29th October 1891.
26. Henwood (1857) p. 17.
27. WB 12th February 1858.
28. CRO Broadsheet DXX 106/21.
29. CRO Poldice Cost Book DDX 475/4.
30. CRO New Trelawny Cost Book STA 269/S.

31. Noall (1982) p. 7.
32. *1861 Census Camborne* 1583/5/4/127.
33. *1861 Census Camborne* 1583/3/4/65.
34. *1861 Census Phillack* 1585/10/13/97.
35. *1851 Census Calstock.*
36. CRO Wheal Basset and Grylls Cost Book DDX 363/7.
37. CRO Wheal Agar Cost Book TL 96.
38. RIC Rosewarne Herland Cost Book.
39. CRO Wheal Trerew Cost Book STA 27/S.
40. RIC Goole Pellas Cost Book Mining V10.
41. RCG 11th April 1874.
42. Corin (1997) p. 22.

Chapter 9

1. *1841 Census St. Agnes* 15/232/13.
2. *1851 Census St. Agnes* 1909/562.
3. Jenkin (1951) p. 161.
4. CEC (1842) p. 80.
5. CEC (1842) p. 81.
6. Tyacke (1866).
7. Tremellin (1841).
8. Kinnaird (1864).
9. CEC (1842) Table 25.
10. CEC (1842) p. 82.
11. WB 10th August 1855.
12. Lanyon (1836) p. 45.
13. CEC (1842) p. 83.
14. Reiding, (1881) p. 812.
15. Moyle (1839) p. 57.
16. CEC (1842) p. 68.
17. CEC (1842) Evidence No. 89. p. 129.
18. CEC (1842) Evidence N0. 103. p. 137.
19. CEC (1842) p. 53.
20. Kinnaird (1864) xxv.
21. CEC (1842) p. 55.
22. CEC (1842) p. 54.
23. CEC (1842) Evidence No. 21. p. 105.
24. CEC (1842) Evidence No. 33. p. 106.
25. CEC (1842) Evidence No. 47. p. 111.
26. CEC (1842) Evidence No. 86. p. 130.
27. CEC (1842) p. 57.
28. Harris (1972) p. 74 note 13.
29. CEC (1842) Evidence No. 89. p. 108.
30. Moyle (1839) p. 57.
31. CEC (1842) Evidence No. 28. p. 107.
32. CEC (1842) p. 72.
33. Pepper (1862) p. 270.
34. MJ (1858) p. 36.
35. Chope (1967) p. 124.
36. Sara (1970) p. 43.

37. Brooke (1967).
38. CEC (1842) p. 99.
39. CEC (1842) p. 67.
40. CEC (1842) p. 86.
41. CEC (1842) p. 68.
42. Burt (1984) p.80.
43. CEC (1842) Evidence No. 46. p. 111.
44. CEC (1842) p. 96.
45. CEC (1842) Evidence No. 75. p. 125.
46. MJ 15th February 1879.
47. Barton (1968) p. 56.
48. Ballantyne (1897) p. 197.
49. Personal correspondence (PL/LM 2003).
50. CEC (1842) Evidence No. 61. p. 117.
51. CEC (1842) Evidence No. 75. p. 124.
52. Kinnaird (1864) p. 11.
53. CEC (1842) p. 57.
54. Baring Gould (1899) p. 110.
55. Dickens, Charles. *The Uncommercial Traveller* (1869) Chap. XXXII.
56. INHOEP Letter (4th Dec. 1999) p. 1.
57. Burt (1984) p. 191.
58. CEC (1842) *Report by Joseph Fletcher for Lanark and Dumfries* p. 13.
59. Harrison (1989) p. 185.
60. Harrison (1989) p. 184.
61. Thomas M. Legge, Kenneth W. Goadby. *Lead Poisoning and Lead Absorption Symptoms* (Arnold 1912) p. 36.
62. Burt (1984) p. 80.
63. MJ 2nd April 1904.
64. MJ 25th April 1903.
65. CEC (1842) Table 21.
66. *1861 Census Kea* 1563/14/3/24.
67. CEC (1842) Evidence No. 56. p. 116.
68. CEC (1842) p. 70.
69. Burt (1984) p. 80.
70. Reiding (1881) p. 809.
71. CEC (1842) Table 3.
72. WB 30th July 1841.
73. Personal correspondence (JT/LM 2002).
74. Paige, R. T. *The Tamar Valley at Work* (Dartington Amenity Trust 1982).
75. Tremellin (1841) p. 7.
76. CRO Bodmin Quarter Sessions QS1/12/300.
77. Cornubian 12th June 1868.
78. Cornubian 4th June 1897.
79. CEC (1842) p. 39.
80. Payton (1984) p. 2000.
81. WB 19th Jan 1949.
82. CRO Broadsheet DDX 106/10.
83. Vivian (1990) p. 10.
84. *Cornishman* 12th October 1893.
85. CEC (1842) p. 60.
86. CEC (1842) Table 9.

87. CMHRS: *Women's Mining Accidents.*
88. *Cornish Telegraph* 24th May 1888.
89. WB 16th May 1823.
90. CRO William Rashleigh Letters (24th December 1842) DDR/5335/30.
91. WB 24th Jan 1845.
92. MJ 1st Feb 1845.
93. WB 28th February 1862.
94. Vivian (1990) p. 10.
95. *Cornish Telegraph* 24th May 1888.
96. *Cornish Telegraph* 5th January 1872.
97. RCG 8th August 1874 p. 4.
98. WB 13th November 1812.
99. MJ 28th August 1858.
100. WB 19th January 1949.
101. Vivian (1993) p. 20.
102. CRO Broadsheet DDX 106/21.
103. WB 12th February 1858.
104. MJ 20th February 1858 p. 128.
105. Williams, J. E. *The Derbyshire Miners* (Allen and Unwin, 1962) p. 458.
106. Williams, J. E. *The Derbyshire Miners* (Allen and Unwin, 1962) p. 459.
107. Symons, M. V. *Coal Mining in the Llanelli Area Vol. 1: 16th century to 1829* (Llanelli Borough Council 1979) p. 339.
108. CEC (1842) p. 88.

Chapter 10

1. Schwartz (1999) p.14.
2. Hocking (1886) p. 94, 99.
3. CEC (1842) p. 84.
4. CEC (1842) p. 35.
5. RCG 12th December 1867.
6. Rowe (1993) p. 319.
7. RCG 18th April 1867.
8. RCG 12th December 1867.
9. RCG 28th November 1867.
10. WB 23rd January 1868.
11. WB 3rd March 1879.
12. WB 12th January 1880.
13. *1891 Census Helston* 1840/1/1/77.
14. *1891 Census Falmouth* 1835/1/1/129.
15. *1891 Census Bodmin* 1815/4/6/152-155.
16. *1891 Census Illogan* 1849/18/2/108
17. Prochaska, F. K. *Women and Philanthropy in Nineteenth Century England* (Clarendon, 1980) p. 88.
18. MJ 23rd March 1878.
19. WB 24th February 1879.
20. Personal correspondence (JSA/LM 2002).
21. www.lanner.fsnet.co.uk/Home.htm.
22. *Cornishman* 22nd August 1879.
23. WB 19th March 1896.
24. Deacon (1998) p. 96.

25. Private correspondences (IJ/LM 2002).

26. Factsheets, Llynwernog Silver Mine.

27. Personal correspondence (PC/LM 2001).

28. WB 6th October 1865.

29. WB 2nd November 1866.

30. WB 31st August 1866.

31. WB 5th October 1871.

32. WB 19th September 1872.

33. WB 15th June 1871.

34. *1881 Census Skipton* 4309/9.

35. *1871 Census Camborne* 11/100.

36. *1881 Census Skipton* 4309/11.

37. Auhl and Marfleet (ed.). *Australia's Earliest Mining Era: South Australia 1841-1851, Paintings by S. T. Gill* (Axiom 1988) p. 26.

38. Barton (1968) p.73.

39. Lay, Patricia, *One and All, The Cornish in New South Wales* (Heritage 2000 (1998)) Table 2.5.

40. Payton (1984) p. 12-14.

41. WB 19th June 1863.

42. WB 30th March 1866.

43. Personal correspondence (RJ/LM2001).

44. *1851 Census Calstock* 2a/264.

45. Personal correspondence (JE/LM 2002).

46. Rodman (1972) p. 103.

47. Rowe (1974) p. 99.

48. Personal correspondence (JW/LM 2001).

49. *The South Australian* 22nd January 1847.

50. Sanjani (1997) p. 29.

51. Hopkins (1994) p. 189.

52. Silvia Pettem, Go West Young Man, *Cornish World* (April 2000) p. 13.

53. Boldrewood (1893) p.35.

54. Pryor (1973) p. 65.

55. Personal correspondence (LM/LM 2002).

56. Personal correspondence (JL/LM 2002).

57. Personal correspondence (HT/LM 2002).

58. Personal correspondence (AC/LM 2002).

59. Personal correspondence (RB/LM 2001).

60. Personal correspondence (GB/LM 2002).

61. Ell, Sarah. *Pioneer Women of New Zealand* (Bush 1992) pp. 179-184.

62. Jack (1910) p. 108.

63. Hopkins (1994) p. 188.

Chapter 11

1. WB 2.9.1859.

2. CEC (1842) p. 113.

3. WB 14th December 1849.

4. R. Barton (1972) p. 8.

5. MJ 1858 p. 36.

6. CEC (1842) p. 83.

7. CEC (1842) Evidence No. 56. p. 116.

8. CEC (1842) Evidence No. 96. p. 133.

9, Schwartz (1999).

10. Schwartz (2000).

11. Burke (1986).

12. MJ 1858 p. 36.

13. Barton (1968) p. 56.

14. *Chamber's Repository* (March 1853) p. 37.

15. Leifchild (1855) p. 164.

16. CEC (1842) p. 86.

17. WB 12th September 1895.

18. Leifchild (1855) p. 165.

19. Buller (1983) p. 55.

20. Wheal Darkness quoted Burke (1986) p. 187.

21. Lanyon (1838) p. 39.

22. Schwartz (2000) p.77.

23. Hearder (1841) p. 55.

24. *The Ladies Journal* (1872).

25. Ballantyne (1897) p.65.

26. James p.242.

27. Buddle.

28. Spall.

29. Toss.

30. Jig.

31. Surface captain?

32. WB 5th February 1819.

33. Tangye (1988) p. 53.

34. CEC (1842) Evidence No. 36. p. 109.

35. CEC (1842) p. 84.

36. Lewis (1997) p. 91.

37 Gray, Todd. *Cornwall, Travellers Tales* (Mint Press, 2000) p. 94

38. Baring Gould, Sabine. *Book of Devon* p. 22

39. Tremellin (1841).

40. Razelle (1973) p. 33.

41. *Cornishman* 5th Jan 1893 "Deep Down Dolcoath Mine".

42. Hocking (1886) p. 13.

43. Hocking (1886) p. 49.

44. Personal correspondence (JT/LM 2002).

45. Personal correspondence (AS/LM 2003)

46. CRO Borlase MSS.

47. Hocking, Silas. *Tales of a Tin Mine* (Horace Marshall 1898) p.23-4.

48. CEC (1842) p. 61.

49. CEC (1842) Evidence No. 6. p. 101.

50. CEC (1842) Evidence No. 104. p. 138.

51. This does not mean 'to begin', but 'to hand in one's notice'.

52. *Cornishman* 22nd August 1879.

53. Reiding (1881) p. 808.

54. Tangye (1988) p. 53.

55. *Cornubian* 25th August 1899.

56. *Prospectus of a School of Mines in Cornwall* 1825 quoted Burt (1977) p. 69

57. Rideing (1881) p. 812.

58. Tremellin (1841) p. 12.

59. *1861 Census Bodmin* 1536/4/4/112.
60. *1861 Census Wendron* 1569/9/16/93.
61. *1861 Census Gwennap* 1576/3/4/26.
62. *1861 Census Camborne* 1583/1/26/15.
63. *1861 Census Camborne* 1583/4/32/99.
64. *1861 Census Gwennap* 1576/1/6/6.
65. Hamilton Jenkin (1948) p. 237-8.
66. Collins, J. H. *Observations on the West of England Mining Region* (Truro, 1912) p. 268.
67. MJ 26th October 1850.
68. RCG 23rd September 1871.
69. RCG 6th January 1872.
70. RCG 8th June 1872.
71. WB 9th April 1877
72. WB 10th August 1882.
73. WM Goonvean Cost Book 1988.233.
74. CEC (1842) p. 57.
75. CEC (1842) Table 17.
76. Kinnaird (1864) p. 80.
77. Brooke (1967).
78. *Cornish Magazine* (1886) p. 125.
79. Leifchild 1855 p. 228.

Chapter 12

1. CRO Brooke Index DDX745/40, Brooke (1978) p. 13.
2. Cunnack (1845) p. 15.
3. MJ 24th December 1842 p. 415.
4. Treleaven Letters quoted Brooke (1980) p. 31.
5. WB 18th May 1844.
6. WB 30th August 1844.
7. CRO Porth Towan Lease DDSHM/1375.
8. RCG 9th July 1870.
9. WB 12th May 1843
10. WB 18th May 1844.
11. WB *Cornish Magazine* (1886) p. 125.
12. Tangye (1988) p. 50.
13. *Cornubian* 31st May 1895 p.4.
14. Mitchell p. 169.
15. Best, R. S, *Life and Good Works of J. P. Edwards* (Dyllansow Truran, 1981) p. 32.
16. WB 2nd November 1869.
17. Barton, R. (1966) p. 86.
18. Barton, R. (1966) p. 90.
19. WM Carclaze Cost Book 1838-52, 1989.1712.
20. Barton, R. (1966) p. 98.
21. *1861 Census St. Austell* 1547/2/1/12.
22. Personal correspondence (JT/LM 2002).
23. Tremellin (1841) p. 7.
24. Tremellin (1841) p. 9.
25. Tremellin (1841) p. 12.
26. Tremellin (1841) p. 13-14.
27. Tremellin (1841) p. 15.

28. CRO Bodmin Quarter Sessions QS1/12/300.
29. Tremellin (1841) p. 41.
30. *1841 Census Kea* 147/9/1/31.
31. CEC (1842) p. 128. Evidence No. 86.
32. Stephen, F. J. *The Perranzabuloe Mining District*, Royal Cornwall Polytech. Soc. Vol. 57 (1889).
33. Mayers (2000).
34. Private correspondence (EC/LM 2001).
35. Reiding (1881) p. 808.
36. Reiding (1881) p. 809.
37. *Western Echo* 19th May 1928.
38. *Cornishman* 26th July 1883.
39. Hamilton Jenkin (1978) St. Ives p. 38.
40. CRO Chellow Collection DDCH 27/10.
41. *St. Ives Times* 4th May 1934.
42. *St. Ives Times* 23rd August 1985.
43. Personal correspondence (JS/LM2002).
44. www. Nijelo.webcentral.com.au/CANSW/gilcent/gil_linktable.htm
45. Personal correspondence (JT/LM2002).
46. Personal correspondence: P L/LM J2003)
47. *Cornishman* 6th April 1967.
48. Brooke (1967).
49. Work apron.
50. WB 7th March 1968.

REFERENCES

Agricola, Georgius. *De Re Metallica* (1556) H. & L. Hoover (Ed.) (Dover, 1950)

Atkinson, Frank. *Industrial Archaeology; Top Ten Sites in North East England* (Ward, 1971)

Bagenal, Timothy B. "Mortality Rate Estimates of Gunnerside Lead Miners from the Census" *British Mining* No. 59 (Memoirs 1997) pp.79-88

Ballantyne, R. M. *Deep Down* (Ward Lock, 1897)

Barham, Charles. *The Employment of Children and Young People in the Mines of Cornwall and Devonshire, and on the State, Condition and Treatment of such Children and Young Persons 1842* Winstanley, Ian (Ed.) (Pics Publishing, 1999)

Baring Gould, Sabine. *A Book of Cornwall* (1899)

Bartlett, Stephen. *The Mines and Mining Men of Menheniot,* (Twelveheads Press, 1994)

Barton, D. B. *A History of Copper Mining in Cornwall and Devon* (Truro Bookshop, 1961)

Barton, D. B. *Essays in Cornish Mining History Vol. 1* (Bradford Barton, 1968)

Barton, D. B. *The Mines and Mine Railways of East Cornwall and West Devon* (Bradford Barton, 1971)

Barton, D. B. *A History of Tin Mining and Smelting in Cornwall* (Cornwall Books, 1989)

Barton, Rita M. *Life in Cornwall: At the End of the Nineteenth Century* (Bradford Barton, 1974)

Barton, Rita M. *Life in Cornwall: In the Early Nineteenth Century* (Bradford Barton, 1970)

Barton, Rita M. *Life in Cornwall: In the Late Nineteenth Century* (Bradford Barton, 1972)

Barton, Rita M. *Life in Cornwall: In the Mid Nineteenth Century* (Bradford Barton, 1971)

Barton, Rita. M. *The Cornish China Clay Industry* (Bradford Barton, 1966)

Beare, Thomas. *The Bailiff of Blackmoor,* (1586) J. A. Buckley (Ed.) (Penhellick, 1994)

Beche, H. T. de la. *Geological Report on Cornwall, Devon and Somerset* (Longmanns, 1839)

Berry, Claude. *Cornwall* (Hale, 1951)

Boase, Henry. "On the Tin Ore of Botallack and Levant" *Trans. Royal Soc. Cornwall* Vol. 2 (1819) p. 383

Boldrewood, Rolf. *A Miners Right* (Macmillan, 1893)

Booker, Frank. *Industrial Archaeology of the Tamar* (David & Charles, 1874)

Borlase, William. *Natural History of Cornwall* (1758)

Bottrell, W. *Traditions and Hearthside Stories of West Cornwall* (1870) Reprint Newcastle (1973)

Britton, John and **Brayley, Edward Wedlake.** *The Beauties of England and Wales Vol. II Cornwall* (1801)

Brown, J. '"Women Workers at Shropshire Mines" *British Mining* No. 39 (1989) p 89-96

Brooke, Justin. Transcript of Interview with Mrs. Minnie Andrews (1967)

Brooke, Justin. "Stannary Tales" *British Mining* No. 8 (1978) p. 20

Brooke, Justin. *Stannary Tales* (Twelveheads, 1980)

Brooke, Justin. *The Tin Streams of Wendron* (Twelveheads, 1994)

Buckley, J. A. *A History of South Crofty Mine* (Dyllansow Truran, 1990)

Buckley, J. A. *Cornish Mining At Surface* (Tor Mark, 1990)

Buckley, J. A. *The Cornish Mining Industry: A Brief History* (Tor Mark, 1988)

Buller, Rev. John. *A Statistical Account of the Parish of St. Just in Penwith (1842)* Fascimile (Dyllansow Truran, 1983)

Burke, Gill. "The Decline of the Independent Bal Maiden: The Impact of Change in the Cornish Mining Industry" in John, Angela V. (Ed.) *Unequal Opportunities: Women's Employment in England 1800-1918* (Blackwell, 1986)

Burt, Roger. (Ed.) *Cornish Mining; Essays on the Organisation of Cornish Mines and the Cornish Mining Economy* (David & Charles, 1969)

Burt, Roger. *John Taylor, Mining Entrepreneur 1779-1863* (Moorland, 1977)

Burt, Roger. *The British Lead Mining Industry* (Dyllansow Truran, 1984)

Burt, Roger and Wilkie, Ian. "Manganese Mining in the South West of England" *Jour. Trevithick Soc.* No. 11 (1984) p 18-40

Carpenter, Frank. "China Clay Workers" *Old Cornwall* Vol. XI No. 5 (1993) p. 211

Carter, Jilly. *Cornish Reflections* (Bossiney Books, 1988)

Chamber's (Ed.) "The Mines and Miners of Cornwall" *Chamber's Repository* March 1853

Claughton, Peter. "Silver-Lead, A Restricted Resource" *Peak District Mines Hist. Soc. Bull.* Vol. 12 No.3 (1994) p. 54

Clough, Robert. "Lead Miners Tools" *Northern Cavern and Mines Res. Soc. Trans.* (1960-1) p. 28-39

Collins, J. H. *The Hensbarrow Granite District (1878)* facsimile (Cornish Hillside, 1992)

Corin, John. *Levant, a Champion Cornish Mine* (Trevithick Society, 1997)

Cunnack, Richard John. *The Cunnack Manuscript Brooke, (1845ff)* Justin (Ed.) (Trevithick Soc., 1993)

Darlington, John. "On the Dressing of Ores" *Ure's Dictionary of Arts, Manufactures, and Mines (1878)*, transcript (Dragonwheel Books, 2002)

Deacon, Bernard. "A Forgotten Stream" *Cornish Studies* No. 6 (Exeter, 1998) p. 96ff

Deacon, Bernard. "Heroic Individualists" *Cornish Studies* No. 14, Exeter (1986)

Earl, Bryan. *Cornish Mining* (Cornish Hillside Publications, 1994)

Earl, Bryan. *The Cornish Arsenic Industry* (Penhellic, (1996)

Ercker, Lazarus. *Fleta Minor*, trans. Sir John Pettus (1683)

Esquiros, Alphonse. *Cornwall and Its Coasts* (Chapman & Hall, 1865)

Ford, Trevor and Willies, Lynn. "Mining before Powder" *Peak District Mines Hist. Soc. Bull.* Vol. 12 No.3 (1994)

Ferguson, Henry T. "Mechanical Appliances for Dressing Tin and Copper Ore" *Proc. Inst. Mech. Eng.* 1873 p. 119

Fiennes, Celia. *The Journeys of Celia Fiennes* ed. Christopher Morris (Cresset Press 1949)

Furze, Sidney. "Tin Dressing" *Roy. Cornwall. Polytech. Soc. Rep.* 1936, p. 21ff

Gerrard, Sandy. *The Early British Tin Industry* (Tempus, 2000)

Goodridge, J. C. "Devon Great Consols; A Study of Victorian Mining Enterprise" *Trans. Devon. Assoc.* No. 96 (1964)

Gray, Todd. *Cornwall, Travellers Tales* (Mint Press, 2000) p. 94

Guthrie, A. *Cornwall in the Age of Steam* (Tabb House, 1994)

Hamilton Jenkin, A. K. *Mines and Miners of Cornwall Part 1; St. Ives* (Forge, 1978)

Hamilton Jenkin, A. K. *Mines and Miners of Cornwall Part 2; St. Agnes and Perranporth,* (Forge, 1978)

Hamilton Jenkin, A. K. *Mines and Miners of Cornwall Part 3; Around Redruth* (Forge,

1979)

Hamilton Jenkin, A. K. *Mines of Devon* (David & Charles, 1974)

Hamilton Jenkin, A. K. *News from Cornwall* (Westway, 1951)

Hamilton Jenkin, A. K. *The Cornish Miner* (Allen & Unwin, 1948)

Harris, T. R. *Dolcoath: Queen of Cornish Mines* (Trevithick Society, 1974)

Harrison, Barbara. "Some of Them Gets Lead Poisoned': Occupational Lead Exposure in Women, 1880-1914", *Social History of Medicine* Vol. 2 (1989) pp 171-195

Head, Sir F. Bond. *Quarterly Mining Review* (1827)

Henwood, George. "Cornwall's Mines and Miners", transcript of articles in *Mining Journal* 1857-8, Burt, Roger (Ed.) (Bradford Barton, 1972)

J. H. (**Mine Engine Driver**). *Reminiscences of Old Times, 1871-1908*, transcript Groombridge, M. J. (CRO DDX 152/11, 1955)

Henwood, George. "The Bal Maiden" *Mining Journal* Jan 1858 Vol. 16 p. 36

Henwood, W. J. "On the Manipulation to which the Ores of Tin and Copper are Subjected in the Central District of Cornwall" *Geol. Soc. Of Cornwall* Vol. 4 (1826) pp. 145-165

Henwood, W. J. *Metalliferous Deposits of Cornwall and Devon* (London, 1843)

Hearder, G. P. *Hearder's Guide to the Tamar* (Hearder, 1841)

Hocking, Salome. *Norah Lang, the Mine Girl* (Crombie, 1886)

Honor, Charles Garton. *Fish, Tin, Copper* (Lister, 1869)

Hooson, W. *The Miners Dictionary 1747* transcript (IMM, 1979)

Hopkins, Ruth. *Cousin Jack, Man for the Times* (Hopkins, 1994)

Hudson, Kenneth. *The History of English China Clays* (David & Charles, 1959)

Hunt, Robert. *British Mining* (Lockwood, 1884)

Hunt, Robert. *A Historical Sketch of British Mining 1887* (EP Publishing 1999)

Inch, A. R. "Bal Maidens" *Cornish Family History Soc. Jour.* No. 56 (June 1990) p. 9

Jack, Ellen E. *Twenty Seven Years in the Far West; the Fate of a Fairy* (Donahue, 1910)

James, C. C. *History of Gwennap*, (Private Publication)

Jenkin, John. *Delabole Slate Quarry; a Sketch by a Workman on the Quarry* (Launceston, 1888)

Job, Barry. "Women Workers at British Collieries and the Mines Inspectorate" *British Mining* 59 (NMRS 1997)

Joseph, Peter. *Mining Accidents in the St. Just District 1831-1914* (Trevithick Soc., 1999)

Kalmeter, Henry. *The Kalmeter Journal* Justin Brooke (Ed.) (Twelveheads Press, 2001)

Langsworthy, David. *The Bal-Maidens and Children on the Dressing Floors of Levant Mine* (Private Publication, 2002)

Lanyon, Richard. "On Various Diseases of Miners, their Causes and the Best Practical Means of Remedying Them" , *Royal Cornwall Polytechnic Soc.* Vol. 1 (1838) pp. 35-53

Lanyon, Richard. "Statistics of Camborne" *Royal Cornwall Polytechnic Soc.* Vol. 9 (1841), p. 99-119

Lay, Patricia. *One and All - The Cornish in New South Wales* (Heritage 2000 Plus, 2000)

Leifchild, J. R. S. *Cornwall, Its Mines and Miners* (Longmans, 1855)

Lemon, Sir Charles. "The Statistics of the Copper Mines of Cornwall", in Burt, R. (Ed.) *Cornish Mining; Essays on the Organisation of Cornish Mines and the Cornish Mining Economy*, (David and Charles, 1969)

Lewis, G. R. *The Stannaries* (Bradford Barton, 1965)

Lewis, Jim. *A Richly Yielding Piece of Ground, The Story of Fowey Consols* (Cornish Hillside Publications, 1997)

Lowry, Henry Dawson. *Wheal Darkness* (Hutchinson, 1927)

Majendie, A. "A Sketch of the Geology of the Lizard" Trans. *Roy. Geol. Soc. Cornwall* Vol. 1 (1818) p. 32.

Mattingly, Joanna, Buckley, Allen and Hall, John. "A Tin Miner and a Bal Maiden

– Further Research on the St. Neot Windows" *Royal Institution of Cornwall Jour.* (2001) pp. 96-100

Mayers, Lynne. "The Women Slate-Packers of Port Gaverne" *Cornwall Fam. Hist. Soc. Jour.* No. 105 (Sept. 2002) p. 16-17

Mayers, Lynne. *Miners, Midwives and Mathematicians* (Private Publication 2000)

Mayne, J. A. D. and **Williams, J. A.** *Coins and Tokens of Cornwall* (Constantine, 1985)

Meyerstein, E. W. "A Key to Cornish Mining" *The Mining Journal,* (1907)

Messenger, Michael. *Caradon and Looe: The Canal, Railways and Mines* (Twelveheads, 2001)

Michell, F. B. "Ore Dressing in Cornwall" *Jour. Trevithick Soc.* No. 6 (1978) p25-52

Mitchell, Frank. *Annals of a Cornish Town, Redruth.*

Morrison, T. A. *Cornwall's Central Mines: The Northern District 1810-1895* (Hodge, 1980)

Morrison, T. A. *Cornwall's Central Mines: The Southern District 1810-1895* (Hodge, 1983)

Moyle, Samuel. "On the Ventilation of Mines" *Royal Institution of Cornwall Jour.* (Oct 1839) p. 57

Murchison, J. H. *British Mines* (Mann, 1854)

Muspratt, Sheridan (Ed.). *Chemistry, Theoretical, Practical and Analytical, as Applied to the Arts and Manufactures* (Mackenzie, 1886)

Noall, Cyril. *Botallack* (Dyllansow Truran, 1972)

Noall, Cyril. *The St. Ives Mining District Vol. 1* (Dyllansow Truran, 1982)

Noall, Cyril. *The St. Ives Mining District Vol. 2* (Dyllansow Truran, 1993)

Noall, Cyril. *The St. Just Mining District* (Bradford Barton, 1973)

Norwood, Stephany. *Balmaidens: a Study of Victorian Female Workers in the West Country,* B. Ed (Hons.)Thesis, Wolverhampton Polytechnic (1991)

Paris, J. A. "Observations on the Geological Structure of Cornwall" *Trans. Geol. Soc. Cornwall* Vol. 1 (1818) pp. 168-200

Paton, Philip J. *The Cornish Miner in Australia* (Dyllansow Truran, 1984)

Pepper, John Henry. *The Playbook of Metals* (Routeledge, Warne & Routledge, 1862)

Pococke, Dr. Richard. "Travels through England 1750" in Chope, R. Pearse *Early Tours in Devon and Cornwall* (David & Charles, 1967)

Pryce, W. *Minerologia Cornubensis, (1778)* Barton, D. B. (Ed.) (Bradford Barton 1972)

Pryor, Oswald. *Australia's Little Cornwall* (Rigby, 1973)

Raistrick, Arthur. "Ore Dressing in the 18th and Early 19th Centuries" *Mine and Quarry Eng.* (1939) p. 161-166

Razelle, P. E. and **Wainright, R. W.** *The Victorian Working Class: selections from letters to the Morning Chronicle 1849-50* (Frank Cass, 1973)

Reiding, William H. "In Cornwall with an Umbrella" *Harper's New Monthly Magazine* No. 378 (November 1881) Vol. 63 pp. 801-822

Rodman, Paul (Ed.). *A Victorian Gentlewoman in the Far West* (Huntingdon, 1972)

Rowe, John. *Cornwall in the Age of the Industrial Revolution* (Cornish Hillside Publications, 1993)

Rowe, John. *The Hard-Rock Men: Cornish Immigrants and the North American Mining Frontier* (Barnes & Noble, 1974)

Ruhrmund, Frank. *About St. Just in Penwith* (Bossiney, 1979)

Salmon, H. C. *Mines of the Sixties* transcript Hall, G. W. (Ed.) (Griffin, 2000)

Sara, Muriel. *Cornwall Remembered* (Hayle, Muriel Sara, 1970)

Schwartz, Sharron P. "In Defence of Customary Rights" *Cornish Studies* No. 7 (Exeter, 1999) pp. 9-31

Schwartz, Sharron P. "No Place for a Woman: Gender at Work in Cornwall's Metalliferous

Mining Industry" *Cornish Studies* No. 8 (Exeter, 2000) pp. 68-96

Schwartz, Sharron P. and **Parker, Roger.** *Tin Mines and Miners of Lanner* (Halsgrove, 2001)

Simonin, L. *Mines and Miners or Underground Life*, translated by Bristow W. H. (1868)

Spargo, Thomas. *Mines of Cornwall and Devon* (1865)

Stanier, Peter. *Mines of Cornwall and Devon* (Twelveheads, 1998)

Stoker, H. M. "An Essay on the China Stone and China Clays of Cornwall" *Royal Corn. Polytech. Soc.* (1852) p. 77

Tangye, Richard. *Redruth and Its People* (1988)

Taylor, Charles D. "Tin Stream Works at Restronguet Creek" *Proc. Mech. Eng.* (1873) p. 155

Taylor, Rev. Isaac. *The Mine* (Harris, 1829)

Taylor, John. "On the Economy of the Mines of Cornwall and Devon", *Trans. Geol. Soc.* 12 (1814) pp. 309-327

Thomas, R. *A Survey of the Mining District from Chacewater to Camborne* (London, 1819)

Thurlow, Charles. *China Clay* (Tor Mark, 1996)

Todd, A. C. and **Laws, Peter.** *Industrial Archaeology of Cornwall* (David & Charles, 1972)

Todd, Arthur Cecil. *The Cornish Miner in America* (Bradford Barton, 1967)

Todd, Arthur Cecil. *The Search for Silver, Cornish Miners in Mexico 1824-1947* (Lodenek, 1977)

Toll, R. W. "Arsenic in West Devon and East Cornwall" *Mining Mag.* (1953) p. 84

Toll, R. W. "Manganese in West Devon" *Mining Mag.* (1958) p. 17-19

Toll, R. W. "The Arsenic Industry in the Tavistock District of Devon" *Sands, Clays and Minerals* (Apr 1938) p. 224

Tredinick, R. *A Review of Cornish and Devon Mining Enterprise, 1850-56* (1857)

Tregallas, I. T. *Peeps into the Haunts and Homes of the Rural Population of Cornwall.* (Truro, 1879)

Tremellin, Patty. *Patty Tremellin: The Life of a Cornish Mine Girl written by Herself* (Wright and Albright, 1841)

Turner, John T. F. *A Familiar Description of the Old Delabole Slate Quarries* (Stonehouse, 1864)

Ure. *Dictionary of Arts, Manufactures and Mining* (1856) and (1878)

Varcoe, Philip. *China Clay: The Early Years* (Francis Antony, 1978)

Vivian, John. *Tales of Cornish Miners* (Tor Mark, 1993)

Warner, Rev. Richard. *A Tour through Cornwall in the Autumn of 1808* (Bath,1809)

Watkins, G. and **Young, S. E.** *Poldark Mining Ltd.: A Guide to the Mine and Machinery Collection*

Watson, Joseph Yelloly. *A Compendium of British Mining with Statistical Notices of the Principal Mines in Cornwall* (London, 1843)

Whetter, James. *Cornwall in the 17th Century - an economic history of Kernow* (Lodeneck Press, 1974)

White, Walter. *A Londoner's Walk to the Lands End and a trip to the Scilly Isles* (Chapman & Hall, 1861)

Williams, J. *Cornwall and Devon Mining Directory 1862* (Kent, 1862)

Williams, Merfyn. *The Slate Industry* (Shire, 1991)

Willies, Lynn. *Lead and Lead Mining* (Shire, 1982)

Woodrow, A. "A History of the Conlig and Whitespots Lead Mines" *British Mining* No. 7 (1978) pp. 1-3

Zanjani, Sally. *A Mine of Her Own - Women Prospectors in the American West 1850-1950*

(Nebraska Univ. Press, 1997)

Select Committee on the Rating of Mines, BPP 1857 62.87-91

Epitome of Evidence to Lord Kinnaird's Commission Appointed to Inquire into the Condition of All Mines in Great Britain to which the Provisions of the Act 23 and 24 Vict. C. 151 do not apply with Reference to the Heath and Safety of Such Persons Employed in Such Mines, BPP 1864 70.192-207

How a Lead Mine Worked at Surface, Mid Wales Mining Museum (1981)

A History of Mining in Mid Wales, Mid Wales Mining Museum (1981)

"The Work done by Women in the British Isles; the Balmaiden." *The Ladies Journal of the Court, Fashion and Society* Vol. 2 No. 29 (1872)

"Notes of a Journey to the Mines of Cornwall and Wales", *The Penny Magazine* No. 220 (5th September 1835)

HM Government Report for the Committee appointed to enquire into the state of the Copper Mines and Copper Trade of his Kingdom (London, 1799)

The South Australian, 22nd January 1847

Troon Scrap-Book: Women and Girls on the Mines and 'Streams' (Bal Maidens), Troon Women's Institute (1952) p. 12

MINES, QUARRIES, AND CLAY PITS, MENTIONED IN TEXT

[Print in bold type indicates an illustration]

INDEX

[Print in bold type indicates that the topic is illustrated]

D

E

F